ROM

Communicating with the Museum Visitor

Guidelines for Planning

ROM

Communicating with the Museum Visitor

Guidelines for Planning

PREPARED BY
THE COMMUNICATIONS DESIGN TEAM
OF
THE ROYAL ONTARIO MUSEUM

TORONTO / CANADA

APRIL, 1976

© COPYRIGHT 1976; THE ROYAL ONTARIO MUSEUM
SECOND PRINTING; OCTOBER 1976
THIRD PRINTING; JULY 1979
ISBN 0-88854-193-7
COVER DESIGN; MEDIA CENTRE, UNIVERSITY OF TORONTO

PREFACE

In the Fall of 1974, the Royal Ontario Museum (ROM) embarked on a comprehensive planning process intended to define its goals, chart its future, identify needs for physical facilities, and arrange for the provision of those needs. I was retained as Project Director, charged with the development and coordination of this integrated planning process. After a painstaking period of identifying and analyzing issues, with the vigorous participation of the ROM staff, I submitted a report titled Guidelines for Planning which contained a wide range of recommended policies regarding nearly all aspects of the Museum's activities. A Committee of the Board of Trustees received opinions from ROM staff, from Board members, and from the public at large through the medium of an extensive public opinion survey. In due course, this Committee produced the ROM Statement of Intent (see Appendix A) which, having been approved by the Board, now stands as the official policy of the Royal Ontario Museum on a wide range of matters relating to the future of the Museum, its avenues of service to the citizens of Ontario, and its role in the world museum community.

It was early recognized that the overall planning process would have three separate, though highly interdependent streams:

1 - institutional planning and internal organization

2 - physical needs analysis, programming, and design

3 - exhibit and display conceptualization and design

With the publication of the ROM Statement of Intent, it was clear that the Museum recognized the paramount importance of the quality and effectiveness of its exhibits and galleries in attaining its objectives; and that the highest order of planning and design skills in streams 1 and 2 would be rendered pointless if not matched in stream 3. Further, I suggested that the extremely complex and sophisticated process of conceptualizing and designing museum exhibits is

commonly neither well done nor coordinated throughout
the museum world, and that there is no researched and
recognized methodology for doing it well. There are,
of course, outstanding exceptions to the general
mediocrity, but these often appear to be more inspired
accidents than excellence achieved through the careful
application of knowledge and technique. Since the ROM
plans an extensive program of new construction and gallery renovation, there has to be something more reliable than inspired accident to assure success.

I therefore recommended the establishment of an integrated team of people from within the Museum and outside of it, representing recognized knowledge in the
following areas:

- learning processes and communications theory
- human factors design, and group and individual
  response patterns
- integrated display design
- curatorial functions and perspectives
- audio-visual techniques
- graphics theory and design
- object technology: preparation, conservation,
  security
- effectiveness evaluation techniques
- architectural and engineering implications
- task management techniques

After careful consideration and enquiry, I suggested
a group of persons whom I felt would provide this
diverse expertise and who would, I hoped, act as a
real team by interacting and reinforcing, and by
assuming group responsibility for the success of the
whole process. My recommendations were accepted, and
so the ROM Communications Design Team (CDT) came into
being.

The basic ground rules for the CDT were spelled out
in a Commission paper which was distributed at the
first meeting on September 17th, 1975. This paper is
included as Appendix B of this report, and summarizes
a number of important matters such as:

- a summary of the policy of the ROM, as outlined in the Statement of Intent, regarding Galleries and Displays, Theme, and Orientation

- the importance of the visitor communication program

- the need for the Communications Design Team

- the Terms of Reference of the CDT

- the members of the CDT, and their particular areas of special knowledge

- the overall work program

The work program was detailed on a scheduling chart, or Logic Diagram, and consisted of the following major initial steps:

a) carry out an extensive literature search to establish an information base on all of the relevant areas of knowledge

b) visit a selected range of museums, as time and cost permitted, to obtain further information and opinions

c) have the members of the CDT prepare Background Papers on the following topics:

    - Museum-wide Considerations
    - The Existing Buildings: Opportunities and Constraints
    - Outreach and Education
    - Learning and Communications
    - Human Response Patterns and Human Factors Engineering
    - The Curator's Role in the Interpretation Process
    - Graphics, Colour, and Visual Impact
    - Audio-Visual Media Techniques
    - Spatial Considerations and Display Elements
    - Display Process
    - Lighting
    - Maintenance and Security
    - Conservation

d) integrate and synthesize all of the foregoing into a Guidelines document adequate to serve as a basic reference work and common denominator for all those involved in the conceptualization,

design, preparation, operation, maintenance and
evaluation of exhibits: not as a last-word handbook,
but as a catalogue of information which would act as
a catalyst for an on-going process of refinement, and
aid each participant in understanding the problems of
the others.

This, then, is the purpose of the present volume. The
literature search has been completed; the visits have
been made to other museums (and we have been greatly
encouraged by comments about the value and uniqueness
of our undertaking); the Background Papers have been
submitted, reviewed, revised, and printed (and largely
incorporated in this volume, either in the text or
appendices); and this report is the result of the
exacting work of boiling all this down into a work of
practical, everyday usefulness.

This tool, however, would be of little use without an
organizational structure which allows effective coordination of all the people involved in the creation
of exhibits. The lack of such effective coordination
at present has been noted by many ROM staff members,
and is the most common problem observed at the other
museums which have been visited by CDT members. The
new organizational structure at the ROM provides
the means of overcoming this problem, with the creation of an Exhibits department encompassing nearly all
of the non-curatorial skills required for the creation
of new or upgraded displays, under the general
administration of an Assistant Director - Education
and Communication, whose responsibilities include not
only coordination of the creation of exhibits, but
also the entire educational effort of the ROM and the
evaluation of the effectiveness of this effort. Thus,
the basic informational and organizational tools have
been provided.

At the time of writing, the overall planning process
at the ROM has had to be suspended because of uncer-
tainty about government funding commitment. When
accepting the recommendation to suspend, the Board of
Trustees authorized the completion of this report
because of its potential on-going value to the ROM.

As Chairman of the ROM Communications Design Team, I
extend my warmest thanks to all the members of the
Team who participated with such enthusiasm and

friendliness in the face of fairly relentless pressure.
The high level of knowledge displayed by the members
was expected; the fact that the meetings were actually
fun was a bonus, and a pretty significant one.

In particular, I would like to thank Henry Sears, one
of the members of the CDT, who was primarily responsible
for the final writing and production of this document.
He was assisted by his staff and in particular, by Betty
Kaser with the writing and by Jennifer Wong with tne
production of the report.

I am sorry that, as of this date, we are prevented from
proceeding with our planned next steps of evaluating
the present exhibits at the ROM, establishing priorities for change, and monitoring the implementation of
new concepts. Perhaps we will still be able to do
these things. If not, I still hope that this volume,
and its supporting documents, will be of enduring value
to the Royal Ontario Museum, and perhaps to others in
the museum world as well.

David H. Scott
April, 1976

ACKNOWLEDGEMENTS

This document is a product of the efforts of a large
number of people. All of the members of the
Communications Design Team (CDT) made substantial contributions to these guidelines, reading and absorbing
large quantities of information, debating a broad range
of issues, and writing a series of background papers.
The team's Chairman is David H. Scott. Members from
the Royal Ontario Museum are: James E. Cruise (Director),
John Anthony (Design and Display), David Barr (Entomo-
logy and Invertebrate Zoology), W. Hewitt Bayley
(Museology), Bernard Leech (Conservation), Ivan Lindsay
(Preparators), Riley Moynes (Education), David Pepper
(Art), Jon Vollmer (Textiles) and David Young (Extension).
Other members of the team are: David S. Abbey (Evalua-
tion Research Ltd.), Paul Ellard (Ellard-Willson Ltd.),
Robert Halsall (Robert Halsall and Associates Ltd.),
Gene Kinoshita (Moffat, Moffat and Kinoshita/Architects),
Andrew Lipchak (Ministry of Culture and Recreation),
Edward Llwellyn-Thomas (Faculty of Medicine, University
of Toronto), Kent Rawson (Moffat, Moffat and Kinoshita/
Architects), Henry Sears (Urban Design Consultants),
Robert Tamblyn (Engineering Interface Ltd.), Terry Valdo
(Media Consultant), and Robert Wiele (Robert Wiele
Associates).

The support of Dr. J.E. Cruise, the Director of the ROM
is particularly appreciated. In addition, the
Government of Ontario, through the Ministry of Culture
and Recreation, assisted not only through representation
on the CDT, but through funding support as part of their
contribution to the overall planning costs.

In addition thanks are due to people at other institutions who provided assistance. Members of the CDT made
two sets of visits to selected museums to interview
directors, educators, designers, curators and other
museum staff. The first series of visits focused on
the discussion of major issues. A subsequent set of
visits was undertaken to obtain comments and reactions
to the background papers which had been prepared in the
interim. The insights offered by these various practi-
tioners proved invaluable in supplying the overview

needed to integrate the background papers into one document. Their realistic approach to the opportunities and problems encountered in developing exhibits was equally important in helping to produce a pragmatic document. The following is a list of those institutions visited and the people interviewed during those visits.

American Institutes for Research, Washington, D.C.:

  Harris H. Shettel, Director, Learning Environment
       Research Group

American Museum of Natural History, New York, N.Y.:

  Malcolm Arth, Director of Education Department
  Fred Bookhardt, Jr., Designer
  George Gardner, Head of Exhibition and Graphics
       Department
  Robert Matthai, Director, Special Project
  Dr. Nicholson, Director

Chicago Historical Society Museum, Chicago, Ill.:

  Harold K. Skramstad, Director

Field Museum of Natural History, Chicago, Ill.:

  William Berger, Curator and Chairman of the Master
       Plan Committee
  Alice Carnes, Head of Education Department
  Robert Inger, Assistant Director of Science and
       Education
  William Pasek, Head of Exhibits

Milwaukee Public Museum, Milwaukee, Wis.:

  Edward Green, Director of Exhibits
  James Kelly, Designer
  Edith Quade, Head of Education
  Kenneth Starr, Director

Museum of the City of New York, New York, N.Y.:

  R. Barraghawath, Senior Curator

Metropolitan Museum of Art, New York, N.Y.:

  Louise Condit, Head of Education Department
  Stuart Silver, Design Director
  Melanie Snedcof, Public Education Division

Smithsonian Institution, Washington, D.C.:

Eugene Bohlen, Programmer, Exhibits Office, National Museum of Natural History (NMNH)
Jane Glazer, Training Program Manager, Office of Museum Programs (OMP)
Harry Hart, Chief of Department of Exhibits, NMNH
Margaret Klapthor, Curator, NMNH
Robert A. Lakota, Research Psychologist, Psychological Studies Program, OMP
Benjamin Lawless, Assistant Director of Design and Production Department, National Museum of History and Technology
Edward P. Lawson, Chairman of Department of Education, Hirshhorn Museum
James A. Mahoney, Chief Designer, Office of Exhibits Central
Robert Organ, Head of the Conservation-Analytical Laboratory
Frank A. Taylor, Research Associate

In addition, one consultant, Don Crowdis, now residing in Nova Scotia, was of particular assistance in helping to identify museums to visit, people to see, and in ensuring that the work was sufficiently comprehensive.

Terry R. Valdo, the Coordinator of the CDT, provided the link between the Project Director, the other staff at the ROM, the members of the CDT and the support staff. His energy, patience and sense of humour ensured that schedules were met, papers delivered and comments provided.

Staff support to the CDT was provided by Urban Design Consultants. The final writing of the Guidelines report was a joint effort of Henry Sears and Betty Kaser. The literature search was directed by Jennifer Wong with the assistance of Gail Burgess; David Jackson assisted with background documentation; graphics design was handled by John Russell; sketches were completed by Doug McConnell, based upon photographs taken by Terry Valdo; and the final editing was done by Anne McWhir. The typing was supervised by Susan Lankin, with the assistance of Marilyn Ballard.

TABLE OF CONTENTS

INTRODUCTION

As outlined in the Preface, this document was commissioned by the Royal Ontario Museum (ROM) to assist in the development of a comprehensive exhibit program. Although they were prepared for the ROM, the guidelines were written without reference to any set of existing exhibits or specific institutional constraints. They therefore should be applicable to other museums, and it is hoped, will be generally useful to people interested in planning exhibits.

The ROM is a major museum with a large, varied and important collection, housed in an older building in the central downtown area of Toronto, Canada. The ROM's main building (excluding the attached Planetarium and the nearby Sigmund Samuel Building) consists of approximately 300,000 square feet of which about half is devoted to public galleries. Construction of the oldest section of the building commenced in 1910; a major addition was undertaken in 1932; the Planetarium was added 1970 and a cafeteria the following year. The museum has about twenty curatorial departments whose collections embrace the natural sciences, art, and archaeology. There is also a full range of support departments providing the skills necessary to service a major museum.

As noted in the Preface, thirteen background papers focusing on different aspects of the general subject were prepared by the members of the Communications Design Team (CDT). The information and insights developed in these papers (well over 600 pages) were subsequently distilled, condensed and synthesized to produce this document. Except where substantial parts of background papers are included as appendices, specific credits to individual authors are not given in the text. The complete background papers are published separately as a companion document.

The guidelines are intended as an information resource for those involved in the day-to-day decisions of designing exhibits, as well as for those who establish exhibition policies and provide the framework for

gallery design. The information is organized around
issues, outlining possible options, with the intention
of assisting individuals to make educated judgments in
their own fields, and to understand the implications
of decisions made by those in other disciplines. It
should be emphasized that the document is not a set of
rules nor a handbook for design.

The guidelines are organized into three sections: the
first deals with issues of consequence to the museum
as a whole; the second section deals with specific
issues relating to the design of an individual gallery
or exhibit. Since the effective application of information requires a process - a method of working - both
of these sections also include an indication of the
administrative procedures necessary to achieve it. The
value of an orderly and logical method of dealing with
complex matters involving large numbers of people,
highly specialized and technical knowledge, and costly
and time-consuming techniques cannot be over-emphasized.

The third section consists of the reference list and a
series of appendices which provide complementary detailed information on a number of selected topics.

SECTION I · MUSEUM

PART A· MUSEUM-WIDE CONSIDERATIONS

INTRODUCTION

This Part of the report deals with museum-wide
issues which should be examined in the development of
an overall strategy for communicating witn the public.
Effective communication requires more than a well-
designed exhibit: the total museum environment, from
its general image, through its educational approach,
to the amenities provided for the visitor, will affect
his/her response to the exhibits. An overall approach
not only establishes the setting in which communication can take place, but creates an atmosphere which
can either enhance or detract from the quality of the
visitor's experience in the museum.

A museum can sparkle, kindle excitement, and be an
uplifting experience, or it can be tawdry and depressing in spite of the glory of its collections. A
museum environment is not neutral; its quality and
atmosphere directly affect those who visit it, and at
best is the result of the combined skills and cooperation of all those who work in a museum. The process
whereby the resources of the museum are marshalled
to achieve effective communication is discussed in
Part B of this Section.

This discussion of issues is intended to explore
problems rather than to present solutions. However,
it does not pretend to be unbiased; it presumes some
basic attitudes. It is assumed, for example, that
museums are sensitive to demands for increased
accountability and are interested in providing a useful public service. Moreover, it is taken for grant-
ed that museums wish to attract and communicate with
visitors by making the museum experience both pleasant and interesting.

IMAGE AND ROLE

All characteristics of a museum - both as an institution and as a physical space - condition its public image. To some extent, a museum's image is reflected in its visitors. The image projected by a museum should not result merely from chance, but should be consciously determined, consistent with the museum's role and directions.

Image and the visitor

Most people have some image of a museum even before they have visited one, and this image can determine whether they ever visit a museum at all. After the first visit, it is likely that the museum-goer will have formulated a general impression or image which will help to determine whether or not he/she will visit again.

Image and the museum

Such images tend to be personal, and they are therefore difficult to define clearly or to assess in terms of impact. However, there are a number of aspects of a museum's image which should be considered if a museum wishes to encourage the public to visit (and ultimately to join, to be a volunteer, to bring the family, etc.). The image of a museum is expressed in a variety of ways - through the nature of exhibits and public spaces, through the location and character of the building itself, as well as through public statements.

Image and role

The degree of emphasis accorded to a public role and its expression in a community context, will have a significant impact on the image a museum projects. Until the twentieth century, museums were mainly centres for academic research and depositories devoted to collecting and conserving objects. Today most museums are publicly supported to varying degrees, and like all such institutions are being asked to demonstrate more directly the benefits which accrue from their activities. Concern about this aspect of museums is often expressed in terms of their educational potential.

"A natural history museum has three principal activities. These are the assembling and care of collections, education, and research, and it is suggested that, if

a museum is to be well balanced, then all should be regarded as of equal importance."1

"Museums, as public institutions devoted to the pre-servation of specimens, the study of collections, and the dispensing of information pertaining to their col-lections and studies, have the responsibility to the public and to themselves to increase by whatever means possible their rate of dispensation of information."2

Image and change

In order for a museum to provide an educational experience, it must be able to attract visitors. However, because the museum is often seen as static and unchanging, many visitors feel that if it has been seen once, there is no need to see it again. In fact, many museum visitors go to the museum as casual visitors only twice in a lifetime - once as a child with parents and once as a parent with children. Questions that are frequently raised in this respect include:

+ How static or dynamic an image should a museum have?

+ To what extent should a museum update its exhibi-tions as new discoveries are made or as new explanations are needed?

+ To what extent should new objects be added to galleries as they are acquired?

+ To what extent should a museum strive to be rele-vant to today's issues?

The approaches taken on these issues are fundamental to the image which will be projected by a museum. For these are not simple questions, nor are there obvious answers to them. The implications resulting from their consideration can lead to significant institutional changes. The acceptance of a new role and the determination to convey a new image require skills not always available within a museum and not always even recognized as important ones. Creative management skills and adaptable administrative structures are required where museums opt for major changes of role and image.

Some museums have attempted to come to grips with these issues. For example, a number of museums take the attitude that change is an important means of attracting and entertaining visitors. The

Metropolitan Museum of Art in New York has a very active program of temporary exhibitions, and staff at the museum express the view that no exhibition should be considered permanent.[3]

However, many examples can be cited which demonstrate that most museums have not dealt to any great extent with these concerns. One view expressed in this regard is that museums convey knowledge as if it were completely unchangeable. In most museums there is little evidence of ongoing research, and few indications that present knowledge is not perfect.

Another commonly raised issue concerning relevancy and change in museums, expressed by some anthropologists, is that without contemporary views of cultures to complement the static historical images commonly presented in museums, processes of change are not acknowledged and the visitors can be misled. In other words, the issue is whether a static image can in itself affect the accuracy of information being presented.

Image and who visits the museum

To some extent the image of a museum is reflected in who the visitor is. Most museums do not have accurate information on their visitors. Only 30% of American museums surveyed by the National Research Centre of the Arts were able to provide actual attendance figures.[4] This survey estimated annual museum attendance in the USA at over 300 million visits, but indicated that the characteristics of these visitors were not clearly established (p. 131). The Yankelovich survey of visitors to the Metropolitan Museum of Art, conducted in 1973, described the audience as *"distinguished by its youthfulness, high degree of education and affluence."*[5] A study of visitors at the Royal Ontario Museum conducted during 1958-1959 indicated that although the visitors were generally representative of a cross-section of the population of Metropolitan Toronto, they were more highly educated (three times as many university and college graduates) and had somewhat higher incomes.[6] Although there is not enough statistical information to draw any definite conclusions, there is considerable evidence that museums do attract a more educated public and that a visit to a museum is perceived as a "cultural" activity, not a casual one.

One study in Germany was directed to determining the characteristics of the museum non-visitor.7 Preliminary findings indicated that cultural institutions are acceptable to the degree that visitors feel comfortable. According to this study many people believe that they need special preparation in order to visit the museum, and that it is otherwise accessible and *"intelligible to only certain segments of the population."*

Although not specifically concerned with the non-visitor, similar results were obtained in a Canadian study of public attitudes towards museums.8 Non-goers (identified as people who had not visited a museum during the year preceding the study) were distinguished from the goers (those who had visited a museum during the previous year) *"by their prime concern in being made to feel more welcome and more at home within the museum"* (p. 223). This study found museum "goers" to consist of two distinct groups, *"a large majority who are very infrequent visitors, averaging less than one visit per year, and a small core group who visit frequently and account for a highly disproportionate number of visits"* (p. 105). (For general museums, 7% of the visitors accounted for 41% of the visits.)

Museums today are generally concerned about increasing the number of visitors.9 Various methods are being used by museums to increase and expand their visitorship. For example, many museums actively encourage visits by school groups, not only providing an educational service, but nurturing a future audience; outreach programs have been developed by many museums in order to expand their influence beyond the museum walls; some museums have effectively employed the media to transmit a new image to a broader population. The Royal Ontario Museum has developed displays within an adjacent subway station to attract and inform the public.

Image and new roles

In summary, it is obvious that many museums are in the process of evolving new roles with respect to communicating with the public. The public image of museums is, however, frequently at variance with these new roles. If new roles are to be effective, the "image" the museum projects should clearly change to reflect these roles more directly. The museum exhibit environment can form an integral part of a new image. *"Like society at large, museums and other institutions of material culture are transformed by their own exhibition environments. These play a fundamental role in changing, defining, and redefining basic purposes and policies."*[10]

THEME

---

*The advantages of using a museum-wide theme as a basis for
subject organization are countered by the difficulties in
choosing one that is comprehensive but not over-generalized.
Various approaches to this problem are suggested.*

The notion of theme appears to have emerged in relation
to the desire to communicate more effectively with the
public, and to be part of the growing concern of
museums to provide exhibits that contribute to the education of their visitors. Simply displaying objects (as
in the "attic" approach) is no longer considered by most
museums to be an adequate means of helping visitors to
appreciate their full significance. Concern with providing links between objects and between objects and
concepts has resulted in attempts to provide thematic
threads.

*Themes in
galleries*

At the scale of the individual exhibit or gallery, a
variety of methods for developing a story-line or
theme is now commonly used. For example, themes are
often made explicit through the use of didactic
materials, through sequential ordering of material, or
through the means of presentation as in the case of a
diorama or habitat setting where a context is provided
for the objects on view. Themes are also developed
separately from the actual exhibit, through guides and
teachers who present the available material coherently
to groups of visitors.

*Themes for
museums*

At the scale of the museum, most general museums are
still organized on the basis of traditional subject
areas. A few museums, however, have attempted to come
to grips with a more integrated approach to the presentation of knowledge. To a large extent this approach
is reflected in the definition and adoption of a
thematic concept which provides a cohesive and comprehensible basis for communicating with the public. In
Chicago, for example, in the development of an exhibit
master plan at the Field Museum, the following approach
was taken:

"To understand the rationale for the selection of

*subjects for exhibits, one might look at a traditional
definition of 'natural history', subdivided according
to various disciplines and their subject matter. Then
one can work out an exhibit plan that crosses these
boundaries. This was the direction taken by the
Exhibits Planning Committee."*11

After a lengthy discussion, the Exhibits Planning
Committee decided on the establishment of three general
themes for the museum: *"diversity, history and
functions."* It was felt that these themes *"would give
coherence to both anthropological and paleontological
exhibits."*

In the development of a long-range plan for exhibits
renewal at the National Museum of Natural History in
Washington, the following approach was decided upon:

*"Most of our current exhibits are oriented toward
particular disciplines and do not adequately reflect
either the modern practice of natural history or the
interests or needs of the public. Integration of the
important concepts and principles of natural history
is needed to present a clearer and more comprehensive
picture of natural history to the public. This
approach will cut across disciplinary lines and will
integrate the large-scale processes of the natural
and cultural world. Our goal is to represent the new
awareness of the integrative processes of geology,
evolution, adaptation, and ecology. Future exhibits
will concentrate on such topics as the mechanisms of
organic evolution, cultural adaptation to differing
environments, diversity of life, the evolution of the
earth, origin of western civilization and evolution
of man."*12

The Royal Ontario Museum has proposed that a theme be
illustrated in a major orientation exhibit:

*"A theme shall be adopted to illustrate that the main
purpose of the Museum is to bring the past into the
present and future; to emphasize the interaction and
interdependence of man and all things in nature; to
provide a cohesive and integrating thread throughout
the Museum and to demonstrate what the Museum is all
about and what it seeks to do. The expression of the
theme shall be subtle and shall avoid stridency, or
dominance over content, design or display. The theme
shall be specifically illustrated in a major exhibition located and organized to serve as an introduction*

*and orientation to all of the Museum's displays.
All other displays and exhibitions shall contain,
implicitly or explicitly, some recognizable relationship or reference back to the theme and the theme
exhibit, although this need not be specifically explained to the public at every point."*[13]

The attraction of a comprehensive theme, in particular
a "content" theme, is that it provides a visible and
comprehensive means of unifying the entire subject
matter of the museum in order that this can be communicated to the public. The difficulty lies in evolving
a theme which is agreeable to all concerned and which
is not so abstract or generalized as to be difficult
to implement, or meaningless in the implementation.
One approach suggested for general museums is the
adoption of a comprehensive theme, with a series of
sub-themes, emphasizing a museum's particular and
unique strengths.[14] Not only would such a theme be
more comprehensible to the public, but it would also
express the unique character of a particular institution and communicate this to the casual visitor. The
use of such an approach at the Royal Ontario Museum,
which has an outstanding Chinese collection, would be
reflected in an indication of this strength in its
thematic statements.

A more commonly proposed approach is the organization
of galleries in such a way that galleries displaying
related subject matter are clustered together. In
this clustering method, themes for related subject
areas can be developed somewhat more easily than can
a general theme applicable to an entire museum.

An alternative approach to theme involves the use of
a process theme rather than a content theme, impart-
ing a sense of unity to public presentations through
the way in which artifacts are presented rather than
through the organization of what is presented. This
could be achieved through the use of a specific style
of graphics, a consistent use of a-v techniques for
presentation of artifacts, or the consistent presentation of objects in contexts (e.g. habitats). Although such an approach to theme lacks the conceptual
unity of a content theme, it can be achieved with
greater ease and can provide greater freedom of content in individual galleries. On the other hand,
consistency in a communications approach can also be
a limitation on the method of presentation.

EDUCATION AND LEARNING

The importance of tours and other educational programs, together with an expanded approach to education and the need for evaluation of the educational effectiveness of exhibits are discussed.

*Education and
the museum*

The museum is not a conventional educational institution; there is no obligation for the museum visitor to learn. Yet because the museum can present the actual object, it has an opportunity to provide a unique educational experience without necessarily employing traditional educational methods.

While acknowledging a responsibility to "educate", museums are not very clear on what their educational role is or should be. Many different views on education are implicit in the design of exhibits, and indeed in some instances it is questioned if the purpose of an exhibit is to educate at all. Some selected views regarding this issue are noted below:

"To me a museum as such, a building containing collections, and with exhibits which are open to the public, is a centre for exposure rather than for education."[15]

"... a museum can be defined as an institution aiming at education through entertainment."[16]

"I believe the museum's role in education can be better served by lectures, kinescopes and films than by passive exhibits."[17]

"Does education require making the process of museum-going a coldly critical, intellectual, learning experience? ... is there not, here, a kind of education through esthetics which teaches in a way that critical suspension of judgment can never teach?"[18]

"A museum doesn't give logical education, a museum doesn't teach well - people teach themselves. But the museum does have the responsibility to help people to teach themselves."[19]
(Underlining added)

While these views have significance for individual museums, there is little to be gained from debating them in this document. Many people go to a museum to learn, whether through exposure to objects, through aesthetic appreciation, through enjoyment, or as a result of direct teaching devices. (A discussion of some of the various types of learning and their application within museums can be found in Appendix D.)

The concern here is not with which educational role is most appropriate for museums - for this is a problem for each individual museum - but with how any museum can provide an environment in which the visitor can learn if he/she so chooses.

The approach which follows (adapted from a paper by Robert Lakota which is presented in full as Appendix C) is compatible with any general educational policy, and with any set of specific techniques, and it interprets the word "education" in the widest possible sense.

LEARNING SUPPORT FOR THE VISITOR

Learning and the visitor

This approach is concerned with establishing a climate for learning by providing better access to information. All of the educational approaches used by museums - didactic or non-didactic exhibits, conceptual exhibits, audio-visual oriented exhibits, etc. - can be employed within the context of this approach. Specific teaching methods such as programmed learning, discovery learning, etc., can be similarly employed.

Fundamental to the learning support approach is the view that offering visitors free choices based on their interests and inclinations is essential to the character of most museums.

"The general approach to be presented is one of assisting visitor understanding through a clear representation of exhibit subject matter and organization. Providing this conceptual frame of reference supports the learning skills visitors have already developed and helps assure that they will make better visit decisions toward meeting their own objectives."[20]

This will, of course, be of direct benefit to the casual visitor. The visitor who is a member of an organized group taking a conducted tour is assisted more formally through the direction of the teacher or guide, but such visitors can also benefit from this "self-help" approach.

Lakota outlines the basis for the learning support
approach as follows:

*"Most visitors enter the museum with a variety of learn-
ing skills, and can, under the proper conditions, apply
those skills effectively in gaining information from exhibits. Unfortunately, many museums contain barriers to
visitor learning in the form of insufficient information
on the purpose, content and organization of the exhibits.
If there is an organizational plan for an exhibit,
whether it is chronological, conceptual or any other
taxonomic scheme, the basis for that organization should
be communicated directly to the visitor at the outset.*

*"Keeping this information from visitors forces them to
conceptualize and organize the exhibits themselves, a
time consuming process that only few visitors attempt
successfully. By holding on to the romantic notion that
everything must be discovered by visitors to have any
'real' impact, we are not only assuring that fewer visitors will profit from their visit, but are also avoiding the necessity of being specific about our intentions.*

*"Certainly any exhibit contains information, objects,
and relationships to be discovered by visitors. However, to assure that more visitors will make those
discoveries and understand what it is they discovered,
tell visitors as clearly as possible:*

1. *What the exhibit is about.*

2. *What it has to do with them.*

3. *How it is organized, and*

4. *What they can expect to learn from it.*

*"Then, restate these points at the appropriate locations
within the exhibit and provide an active review at the
end."*[21] (Underlining added)

Lakota acknowledges the familiar argument that learning
through the examination of objects requires different
skills than learning through words. This argument is
often used to support the idea that objects should not
be encumbered with words (didactic material) but should
be allowed to speak for themselves. However, as Lakota
points out:

*"... we need not assume that visitors have suddenly lost
their facility for language when entering a museum. Nor
is it necessary to remove the emphasis from the collection as a major source of information. Instead, learning support techniques take advantage of existing*

learning abilities as a means of developing perceptual
skills by helping visitors effectively direct their
observations, as well as by providing a basis for
understanding what they see."[22] (Underlining added)

EVALUATION OF EDUCATIONAL EFFECTIVENESS

The scope of evaluation

If the museum is taken seriously as a learning environment, the evaluation of its effectiveness in this
role must be considered. Evaluation as it is dealt
with in this report extends beyond the evaluation of
existing exhibits or specific teaching objectives.
It includes testing as part of the design and development process (see Section II-B, p. 198) - a continuous
activity starting from the earliest design stage and
continuing until a gallery is completed. This approach
is particularly valuable as specific educational objectives can be set and then tested even before a gallery is opened.

The need for evaluation

This is not to suggest that the evaluation of completed
exhibits is not important. Indeed, as pointed out by
Shettel, one of the current failings of museums is the
lack of any kind of evaluation.

"The notion that museums are at least in part educa-
tional institutions and that they should assess the
effectiveness of their didactic programs and exhibits
is not one that is widely shared by the museum profes-
sion. The general reluctance to embrace evaluation
may be a defensible position if a museum had as its
only mission the collection and cataloging of objects
of worth. However, as soon as these objects are
placed on display, there is then at least a presumed
intention to communicate some kind of message to an
audience."[33]

A responsible attitude towards evaluation

While a rigorous approach to evaluation is desirable,
a responsible <u>attitude</u> can be of even greater value.
Evaluation can occur on a variety of levels, ranging
from a highly structured experiment to an informal
assessment of results. However, without a commitment
to change as a result of evaluation, such efforts are
meaningless. At the very least a responsible attitude
towards exhibit design implies asking questions about
the educational impact of exhibits. It simply makes
good sense to be clear about what an exhibit is intended to convey to the visitor. It is not difficult to

observe how visitors respond to an exhibit, and to in-
quire about what they have learned from it. Such observations can provide very useful feedback.

*Evaluation and
the statement
of exhibit
objectives*

A major requirement of evaluation is the clear statement of objectives at the outset. The requirements of
providing learning support for the visitor (as previously outlined), will help ensure that objectives are incorporated into the design of exhibits. Telling a
visitor *"what the exhibit is about, what it has to do
with him, how it is organized and what he can expect
to learn from it ..."*[24] not only helps the visitor to
"see" better, it also provides a useful discipline to
those involved in exhibit design.

*Literature on
evaluation*

There is a considerable amount of literature on the
subject of educational effectiveness of exhibits. It
ranges from methods of evaluation to the results of
specific studies. A comprehensive listing is contained in a recent publication of the Office of Museum
Programs at the Smithsonian Institution ("Studies of
Visitor Behavior in Museums and Exhibitions: An
Annotated Bibliography of Sources Primarily in the
English Language," by Pamela Elliott and Ross J.
Loomis). Familiarity with this literature can obviously be of use in designing and in undertaking structured evaluations, as well as in providing useful insights into less formal assessments.

EDUCATIONAL PROGRAMS

Guided tours

In addition to providing an environment in which learning can take place, many museums offer a variety of
specific educational programs, the most common of which
is the guided tour. Obviously the educational impact
of a tour will depend to a large extent on the skill
of the teacher or docent. While a discussion of teacher or docent training programs and teaching techniques
is beyond the scope of this study, it is clear that
these are crucial for education through guided tours.
It should be emphasized, however, that teaching within
a museum is not the same as teaching in the classroom.
Some museum educators maintain that the most important
quality for a docent is enthusiasm, and that the en-
thusiastic docent can easily be trained to help the
visitor to learn. Significantly, the visitor who has
been motivated by a docent is more likely to return to

visit the museum on his/her own.

Guided tours for school classes

According to a study by Melton, guided tours are the most effective way of seeing a museum for fifth graders and younger children.[25] This same study found that children in the sixth grade and beyond responded better to self-guiding materials. These results are also consistent with results of developmental and perception research, which show that for persons up to age twelve, information is received more readily if it is presented orally. After age twelve, on the other hand, visual information is processed more effectively.[26]

Advance preparation for school class tours

For school classes, classroom preparation for a tour of the museum contributes greatly to learning.[27] Moreover, it has been found that such preparation is most effective when it takes place as soon as possible before the trip. Melton's study corroborated these results and found in addition that preparation which simulates the exhibit itself is most effective (e.g. photographs of the exhibit), especially if accompanied by a test.[28]

Materials to provide advance preparation for students in the classroom can be prepared in conjunction with the design of an exhibit. This procedure was successfully incorporated with an exhibition on Impressionist paintings at the Metropolitan Museum of Art in New York. Kits were prepared for teachers, including such materials as: a print plaque, a selection of slides of the paintings together with information on them, a poster, biographies, a reading list, and ditto masters for suggested lessons. Self-guiding materials prepared for older students can also be used by the casual visitor.

Discovery rooms

Discovery rooms have been developed at some museums (such as the National Museum of Natural History) as educational devices. These usually include a number of artifacts which can be handled and examined carefully. The attending personnel act as resources rather than as instructors. This enables children to explore and become familiar with a wide range of objects at their own pace and in a relaxed atmosphere.

Museum clubs and other educational programs

Other educational programs include museum clubs for both adults and children. Special Saturday morning activities have been developed by some museums (such as the ROM) to attract children independently of school

programs. Some museums encourage sketching of artifacts to enhance learning and enjoyment.

In addition, outreach programs are used by many museums,
not only to prepare students for visits to museums, but
to bring the museum into the schools and remote communities. Special kits or travelling exhibits are often
used for this purpose. One of the by-products of gallery development can be mock-ups (see Section II-B,
p. 198) which are eminently suited to this type of program.

AN EXPANDED APPROACH TO EDUCATION

*Education as an
integrating
device*

Educational programs like the foregoing are usually
offered by education departments in museums. While
these programs are a very valuable contribution to
the educational role of a museum, a much more comprehensive approach to education is possible. Virtually
every activity of the museum can be considered educational. Those activities which directly affect a
museum's educational potential range from collecting
the artifacts, to displaying them, to arranging guided tours of a particular selection. For example, an
educator at the Metropolitan Museum of Art indicated
that in her view, one of the most significant educational activities of a museum is collecting: *"If a
curator is excited about the artifacts he collects,
there should be some way of conveying that excitment
to the public."*[29] A recently opened exhibition at
this museum presented the highlights of the last ten
years of collecting by each of the curatorial departments in the museum. The exhibit - "Patterns of
Collecting" - not only presented fine examples of artifacts, but also described how they were obtained, their
significance, and in many cases the reasons for their
acquisition. This illustrates one of the possibilities
for a broader approach to education in museums.

But more than this, a museum's approach to education
involves the whole environment created through the
combined efforts of all museum staff. Educational considerations can and should pervade all aspects of the
public components of a museum. Educational aims should
affect the design of galleries (from the nature of the
textual material to the circulation patterns); they
should influence the organization of subject material

within the museum as well as the nature and the extent of orientation material; they should influence
the character of facilities and amenities. Education
in this broader sense is the kind of communication
that museums can aspire to.

ARRIVAL AND ORIENTATION

Making visitors feel both physically and psychologically comfortable is a key to the enjoyment of a museum. Discussion centres on the contribution of appropriate staff attitudes, orienting devices and techniques, both at entrance points and throughout the museum.

ARRIVAL

Arrival and the building

The first step in good orientation is a pleasant arrival. In a study concerning the attitudes of the Canadian public towards museums, it was found that the occasional (casual) visitor, in particular, needs to be made to feel welcome.[30] Moreover, it has been noted that the casual visitor is, in fact, not so casual, but has made a purposeful and premeditated trip to the museum. *"Many casual visitors have made a pilgrimage. They've made a conscious decision ... They've come across the street, across the town or across the country in order to see the institution."*[31] For such visitors, a welcoming attitude will obviously be greatly important.

The location, scale and style of the museum building and its environment make an impression on the visitor even before he/she enters its door. Many older museum buildings, for example, are attractive and distinctive and present a pleasant image. But on the other hand, some traditional architectural conventions may seem to express a formal, unwelcoming atmosphere.

"The architectural conventions used in the design of museums still communicate the earlier concern of the safekeeping of the museum's contents and often overshadow even the most elementary signs of welcome. Massive stone facades with minimal fenestration and small bronze plaques giving the name of the museum and the hours of operation are two frequently used conventions. Huge stone lions with bared teeth might be used as decoration, and it would require imagination to think that such beasts were put there to make visitors feel welcome."[32]

It is useful to bear in mind that the permanence of such facades often outlasts changes in attitudes within an institution. However, thoughtful additions such as the large colourful banners used at the Metropolitan Museum of Art in New York can help soften such a forbidding image.

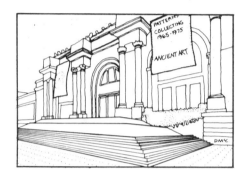

Banners soften the facade of the Metropolitan Museum of Art.

Greeting

Once beyond the entry door, *"a humane introduction by someone who is already familiar with it is the best way to come to know that the museum is an exciting place."*[33] This is the view of a number of museum educators. A member of the educational staff at the Field Museum indicated that, in her opinion, a prerequisite for learning is that the visitors have a "good" experience. *"They should be greeted by someone other than a guard."*[34] At the Metropolitan Museum of Art in New York, education staff handle an information desk which is clearly and centrally located. These staff reach out to visitors and attempt to discover their interests, in order to direct them to those parts of the museum they will find most meaningful.

It is important to remember that information people, guards, and, in some instances, the director, are the most visible people in a museum: their attitudes and morale can have a significant impact on the visitor's experience. This is particularly true for the handicapped, whose most basic physical requirements are often not adequately met.

Arrival and lighting

An important physical aspect of arrival is the lighting of the entrance foyer. This area must be treated as a *"conditioning area in which the visitor's eyes are permitted to adjust from the high levels of daylight*

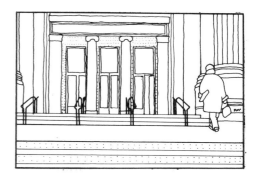

Entrance

The information desk

The Great Hall

Visitors are pleasantly received at the Metropolitan Museum of Art. As they enter through the main doors, the first sight is a large prominent information desk. This is set in a large, somewhat formal hall made comfortable by the welcoming attitudes of museum staff, fresh flowers, and an overall sparkling visual quality.

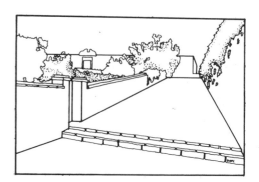

Approach to the museum

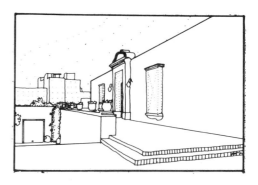

Entrance to the museum

The entry courtyard

Arrival is equally important for a small museum. At the Rafael Larco Herrera Museum in Lima, Peru, visitors are prepared for their arrival at the museum. They enter through a gate at the street, walk up a gently sloping ramp, turn to the left, enter the main doorway and arrive at the entry courtyard. This care-fully considered sequence has oriented the visitor upon arrival.

*to the necessarily low levels required for conserva-
tion.*"[35]   Proper lighting of the entrance areas must
ensure that visitors are not plunged into darkness and
gloom upon their arrival (see Section II-A, p. 147).

Museum educators emphasize the need for special facilities for the arrival of groups. A separate entrance,
including a parking area for buses, has been found to
be most effective and convenient. At the Metropolitan
Museum of Art in New York separate entrances are provided for both junior and secondary school classes, in
addition to the entrance for the casual visitor.
Although two such entrances will obviously not be
required for most museums, a separate entrance for
student groups will not only ensure an orderly arrival
for students, but will also prevent their interfering
with the arrival of the casual visitor.

ORIENTATION

Museum literature, both experimental and intuitive,
emphasizes the need for museum orientation. Not only
is there a psychological need to know where one is and
where one is going, but an orientation system can also
assist the visitor in making the best use of his/her
limited time.

Most museums use one or more of the basic orienting
devices - maps and floorplans, directories, information
staff, signs. Although in most instances it is not
known how effective these devices are for the visitor,
some museums have attempted to assess the methods they
use. Some insights from these studies and other literature concerning orientation are discussed below under
the two basic types of orientation - physical and conceptual.

*The need for a
comprehensive
system*

Physical Orientation: Where a series of devices for
physical orientation is used, it should obviously
be designed as one comprehensive system. In a study
by Winkel it is stressed that "*the availability of a
comprehensive orientation system is absolutely essential if the museum is to ensure that visitors compre-
hend and appreciate its goals and purposes. The
absence of an integrated approach may very well lead
to inefficient strategies for viewing the exhibit halls
with a resultant increase in frustration, boredom and*

fatigue."[36]   The same study also points out that the design of an efficient and integrated locational system demands clarification of the roles played by different devices in guiding the visitor through the museum.

Maps and signs   A comparison of the effectiveness of maps and signs in assisting visitors to find their way through a museum showed that both maps and signs were helpful, and that visitors tended to use each device for different reasons.   Maps were used to obtain an overall image of the area presented, but it appeared that visitors generally did not recall map details.   Rather they depended upon signs to supply specific directions.   The study concluded that "*an integrated orientation system could usefully employ both maps and signs since these in combination reduced different indicators of disorientation*" (p. vii).

Graphics of maps and signs   If maps and signs are to be effective in helping the visitor, it is essential that they are appropriately designed and located.   Accurate floor plan maps should contain the names of halls in their clearest and shortest form.   Any symbols incorporated in signs or maps (e.g. to indicate washrooms, telephones, restaurants) are useless, unless the public is familiar with them. (See Appendix E for commonly accepted symbols.)   In order to select the most suitable design format for both maps and signs, alternative schemes should be carefully tested prior to their introduction in any institution.[37]

A prominent sign near the information desk, Museum of History and Technology, Smithsonian Institution, simply and clearly indicates to the visitor what can be found and where.

Type and location of maps and signs   With respect to the array and location of orientational aids in a museum, Lakota has made the following suggestions:

*"Effective orientation systems provide as many
directional cues as possible. Such a system may
include large floor plan maps at entrances ... Maps
could be reduced to eight by ten size and used as
visitor handouts. Maps similar to, though perhaps
smaller than those at the entrances, could appear at
each of the major choice points within the museum.
Corresponding signs at these choice points should only
include halls on that floor ... Signs including halls
not on that floor should be placed at stairways and
elevators."*[38]

*Directories,
information
desk and floor
plans*

Winkel's study also assessed the relative effectiveness of information people, maps, signs and directories
in the Smithsonian Institution's Museum of History and
Technology.[39] Special maps and signs were developed
for the study to supplement existing directories, and
additional information people were provided at the
entry to halls to supplement those regularly at the
information desk. Results showed that at the museum
entrance, the information desk was used more than the
directories, but that visitors tended to use the experimental floor plan maps more than either of these. The
information people stationed at the entrance of a wing
were asked not about the exhibits but about more general problems, such as where to find the cafeteria or
another Smithsonian building. Winkel concluded that
*"the questions asked of information people are differ-
ent from those which lead to the use of maps and therefore the former should be seen as complementary to the
latter"* (p. ix).

*Colour coding
and numbering*

Lakota suggests that directional cues can be provided
by colour coding halls and using specific colours as
backgrounds for exhibit title signs at entrances.[40]
But since there will be variation in the abilities of
visitors to discern colour, this should never be the
only component of a physical orientation system. The
same study suggests that directional cues can be provided by numbering halls sequentially on the basis of
floor and wing. Lakota notes that *"most visitors are
likely to have had considerable experience locating
apartments and offices in fairly complex buildings"*
(p. 88), and such a system would allow the visitor to
employ these skills.

Landmarks

Pointing out another possible approach to orientation,
José Bernardo discusses the work of Lynch on city

landmarks, and indicates that large museums, like cities, also have a series of landmarks.

"They have landmarks in their collections and landmarks in their spaces. There should be no reason why we could not integrate them into one organic unit, where the collection of landmarks become guiding centres which coincide with the points of spatial interest around which a museum building is organized."[41]

If a museum has an architectural feature such as a multi-storey interior court, this can become a land-mark and orientation point. *"Because he returns to it again and again, on different levels and from different directions, the void amidst repletion becomes a redund-ant experience, helping the visitor to feel at ease in his surroundings."*[42]

The large two-storey central court at the Field Museum assists in orienting visitors as they continually return to the courtyard, entering or exiting from the surrounding halls.

Conceptual Orientation: In addition to the need for physical orientation, there is a need for conceptual orientation. The visitor needs to know what there is to see as well as how to get to a hall or exhibit of his/her choice. Most museums have at least floorplans with the subject names of halls indicated, and staff at a central information desk to answer general ques-tions about content. But some additional methods which have been proposed or which are actually used in some museums will be of interest in developing a con-ceptual orientation system.

Conceptual orientation through theme and grouping of halls

One of the attractions of a general museum theme with individual halls related to that theme is that this can provide a basis for helping the visitor to under-stand the nature of a museum's collection, and to perceive the highlights of a collection and/or

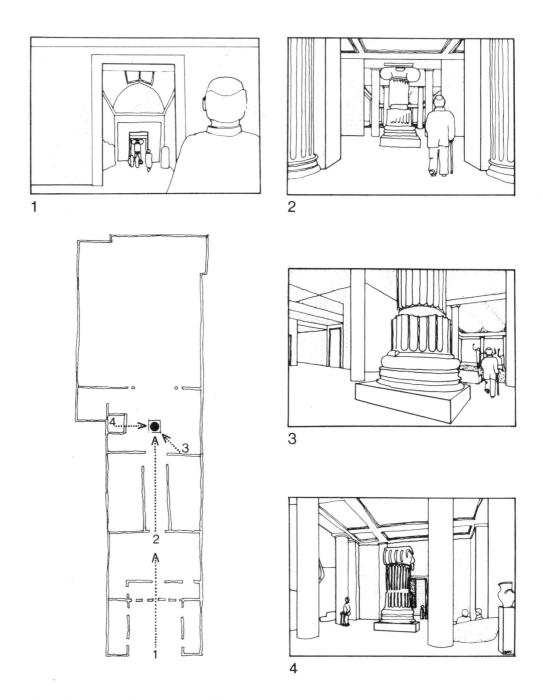

A column at the Metropolitan Museum of Art serves as a landmark guiding the visitor from the Great Hall to the area containing elevators, the restaurant and public washrooms.

relationships among collections. In museums with large
and comprehensive collections, the technique of grouping together halls of similar content is sometimes
used. These methods can assist the visitor by indicating connections, and by thus providing a basis for
conceptual orientation.

Defining and conveying relationships and concepts to
the visitor at this scale is, however, a complex matter.
It is an area which can benefit from additional research and experience to determine the most effective
methods.

*"The whole problem of the relationships which exist
among exhibit areas from the visitors' perspective is
a very rich source for further exploration. It is not
necessary to argue either that exhibits should be
arranged according to visitor perceptions or to the
perceptions of the museum staff. By knowing how people
perceive these relationships it is possible to develop
an educational program which not only challenges the
visitor but is sensitive to the types of associations
which people commonly make."* [43]

*Conceptual
orientation and
tours*

A common method of assisting the visitor to develop
conceptual relationships is that of self-guiding tours.
Simple identification and sequencing devices, like
brochures indicating typical tours, can be made available as handouts. These can constitute a tour route
for the entire building, guiding the visitor to exhibits with conceptually related content. In some museums,
tours are developed with audio-cassettes narrated by
the director or curator.

*Orientation
centres*

Many museums are currently discussing the usefulness
of orientation centres, although few have actually
provided them as yet. These are discussed both as
general orientation devices, and as specialized orientation centres for groups of galleries. While there is
a consensus of opinion that orientation is valuable
within individual galleries, the provision of an orientation "centre" or exhibit for the whole museum is a
matter of some debate. The obvious attraction of a
central display in assisting the visitor to find his/
her way around the museum is countered by the possibility of the display becoming a "mini-museum", and detracting in the long run from the museum itself. The
visitor has limited time to spend at the museum, and
not too much of that visit should be spent in becoming

"oriented". One commentary on orientation centres suggests that such a centre should be not an exhibit but simply a source of information on galleries and museum activities.[44] For example, a proposal for an orientation centre at the Hirshhorn Museum at the Smithsonian suggested using a film, rather than an exhibit with a sample or replica of the collection, to demonstrate to the visitor how to view modern art.[45] Similarly, a highly successful orientation centre at the Mexican National Museum of Anthropology in Mexico City consists of a presentation of the history of Mesoamerica. This provides a basis for understanding the collections, rather than a "preview" of the collections.

Orientation and a learning support approach

Lakota discusses conceptual orientation from the point of view of his learning support approach to education (see preceding chapter, EDUCATION AND LEARNING, p. 18). Some implications of this approach may provide the basis of a conceptual orientation system. Lakota suggests a series of components, such as: the provision of enough descriptive information at the entrance to each hall to enable the visitor to make informed choices; the provision of rational organizational plans (whether chronological, conceptual or other taxonomic schemes) to assist the visitor in understanding what confronts him/her; and the use of familiar terms rather than obscure or technical ones (dinosaur gallery rather than vertibrate paleontology gallery).[46] Lakota recommends that such an approach to orientation be integrated with a physical orientation system. In effect, both physical and conceptual orientation to a museum and its exhibits can be viewed as support systems for the visitor's learning activities. Lakota notes that this basic support would provide visitors with information *"as to the content, location and objectives of the exhibits within the building, and displays within exhibits."*

An orientation system and the museum building

It is clear that orientation is best regarded as a "system" which provides assistance to the visitor where he/she requires it. This suggests a variety of devices (maps, signs, etc.) and information at a series of locations (such as the entrance to a cluster of galleries, the entrance to a specific gallery, etc.). It is also noteworthy that there is great demand for orienting information among visitors themselves. *"It appears that visitors have an insatiable demand for orienting information ... Apparently some visitors simply feel more secure if they have redundancy in the informational system.*"[48] This need must, however, be weighed against the alternative of overdesigning an orientation system. The extensiveness of a "system" obviously also relates to the size and comprehensibility of the museum building itself. A unique orientation network must be established for each building, reflecting both the idiosyncrasies of that building, and the way in which the museum is organized.

Orientation and groups

In evolving a system of orientation, it must be remembered that a group has different requirements from the individual visitor. Groups are oriented throughout their visit by a tour guide. Initial orientation for a group can be most effectively handled in a special reception area, so as not to intrude upon the casual visitor. In some museums, special facilities such as theatres and "children's museums" are established to meet the needs of particular groups. The group also presents a special opportunity to sell the idea of the museum and to encourage individuals to return on their own.

Orientation and the casual visitor

For most visitors, a trip through the museum is independent of group arrangements. A deliberate effort must be made to ensure that casual visitors are warmly greeted and assisted to find their own way through the museum. A good orientation system is important not only in helping visitors to be comfortable, but, as mentioned earlier, in assisting the visitor to learn.

PACING

The concept of pacing is proposed as a means of reducing both physical and mental fatigue for the museum visitor. Specific issues related to pacing include: the creation of diversity and contrast throughout the museum; the effect of crowds and circulation; and the provision of appropriate resting places and other amenities.

Pacing and museum fatigue

Museums usually consist of a series of halls or galleries. It is useful to think of the way in which a visitor moves through these galleries in terms of pacing; that is, in terms of the visitor's ability to deal comfortably with a succession of experiences. This ability will be affected by a multiplicity of simultaneous sensations. Museum fatigue is known to result from such factors as object satiation, disorientation, lack of contrast, as well as physical discomfort (e.g. excessive heat, exhaustion, noise).

Methods of pacing

The pacing of a particular visitor depends, of course, on whether he/she is a member of an organized tour, alone, or accompanied by a family or by peers. One main function of a docent is to pace tours. But there are also a variety of ways in which a museum can assist the casual visitor to pace himself/herself. In large museums most visitors will make choices as to what they want to look at, pacing their visits according to their own interests and the choices provided by the museum. The provision of an effective orientation system (as described in the preceding chapter) will provide direction to the visitor at the outset and help to avoid disorientation throughout his/her stay. For those visitors who wish further assistance, a museum can provide itineraries. These can be pre-packaged, based on related topics and/or extent of visit. Information people can be particularly useful in assisting visitors to develop individual itineraries based on their interests and abilities.

Presumably some visitors will select their own itineraries in advance, either guided by available material or else following their own interests and schedules. Others will wander through the museum in a relatively

unpremeditated fashion, starting at the first gallery
and following where it leads them. Most visitors will
likely be somewhere between the two, making some pre-
selection and some spontaneous choice as they are
attracted or repelled by first glances into a gallery
or exhibition hall, and only limited by the circulation
system of the museum.

In order to absorb what is perceived, the visitor must
be able to regulate the type and intensity of his/her
experience. Contrasts and changes in the museum
environment will assist in maintaining the visitor's
interest. After a visually stimulating gallery, for
example, a visitor may wish to see something more
tranquil, or perhaps only another gallery which is
identifiably different from the one just visited.

Museums in general have not been designed to enable the
visitor to pace himself/herself easily. Quite commonly,
orientation information is inadequate; there is a frustrating obligation to wander through one gallery to get
to another; there is a tendency to mind-blurring uniformity of display technique; and the contemporary
reliefs such as restaurants are often treated as after-
thoughts, or non-essential extras.

*A good example
of pacing*

One of the few examples of a museum that works well
from the point of view of pacing is the Mexican National
Museum of Anthropology, which has a set of galleries
around a spacious courtyard. This layout permits the
visitor to select as many or as few galleries as desired from an easily perceived organizational basis
(galleries organized by regions), with contrasting
fresh air visits in between or a relaxing break at the
pleasant centrally located eating facilties. This is
obviously difficult to emulate in cooler climates and
within existing structures. However, consideration of
the similar needs of visitors everywhere will provide
some useful clues to the appropriate organization of
any museum.

The following discussions of diversity, circulation,
and amenities will provide some specific insights into
what can be done to assist the visitor in pacing at the
scale of a museum.

DIVERSITY

Pacing and diversity

One of the most significant ways a museum can help the visitor to pace himself/herself is through providing a variety of experiences. Diversity can be accomplished at the scale of the museum in a number of ways: through treating the galleries as a collection of individual experiences; through emphasizing the unique features of a building; and through providing contrasts between galleries and the public non-gallery spaces.

Melton has shown that a major factor in museum fatigue is object satiation (similarity of paintings or furniture as regards style, period, subject matter, etc.).[49] He points out that the resulting decrease in interest can be controlled to some extent by arranging exhibits to provide the greatest possible diversity. In the same way it can be assumed that "gallery satiation", resulting from insufficient contrast between adjacent galleries, can have a similar impact upon the viewer.

Diversity and gallery design

Galleries are the most obvious means of creating diversity. The nature of a collection, particularly in larger museums, has inherent in it the opportunity (almost obligation) to present a variety of displays. It is perhaps self-evident to state that each gallery should be appropriate in style and character to the artifacts presented within it. A gallery housing a Greek temple will be different from one showing Roman coins. Failure to create diversity can result in a museum that quickly tires the visitor. Any single approach to gallery design, no matter how meritorious, can be tedious if used consistently and without relief. Many older museums develop some diversity as galleries are upgraded or replaced, contrasting, therefore, with the older galleries nearby. Diversity is accomplished in these cases not consciously, but as a by-product of change.

Diversity can encompass most of the major consideration in the design of a gallery - the general atmosphere, the educational approach, the methods of display, the use of media, and the use of lighting techniques. For example, visual diversity can be achieved through the use of lighting to create contrasts among galleries: a gallery with a low level of ambient lighting and dramatic highlighting is very different from a gallery which is uniformly lit to an average level. Spatial contrasts are another means of making possible a variety of sensations for the visitor. Variations in ceiling height can be particularly effective in creating different atmospheres, and a variety of materials and colours on ceilings, walls and floors will further extend visual alternatives.

It should be cautioned that diversity and contrast can be abused. The overall integrity of a museum should not be jeopardized by a carnival atmosphere or visual chaos. Dramatic effects and constant contrasts can be as boring as uniform blandness. In fact, excessive diversity can overstimulate the senses and lead to fatigue and apathy. The conscious ultilization of diversity requires the same care and consideration as the delineation of a single "style".

Diversity and architectural features

In addition to variations among galleries, museums can exploit the unique features of the buildings themselves. Some buildings, or features within buildings, can be artifacts in themselves. For example, the Art and Industry Building of the Smithsonian, built in 1876, is being restored into a fine monument as interesting as the artifacts it contains. Few buildings are of this special quality, but many museums contain features which can be emphasized as visual contrasts and landmarks. Many existing buildings have major spaces such as domes or multi-storey areas, which can provide welcome contrasts to the gallery and corridor areas. These can often serve as orientation devices as well as points of interest for the visitor on his/her trip through the museum.

These are obviously only a few illustrations of the ways of creating a diverse experience for the visitor. Some other opportunities could include the use of outside views in contrast to artificially lit galleries; the use of formal public spaces in contrast to more casual gallery areas; the use of sound (e.g. fountains) and movement in selected locations. All of these are important aspects of diversity.

CIRCULATION

Circulation and pacing

To enable the visitor to pace himself/herself according to his/her own interests and needs, the circulation system of a museum should allow him/her to arrive at

the desired galleries as directly as possible, and/or
to select along the route those galleries he/she
chooses to see. Since there is seldom a complete
corridor system and galleries are usually corridors as
well, where possible they should be arranged so that a
visitor is not obliged to proceed or return through
galleries he/she is not interested in.

Circulation and
choice

In many instances it will not be possible or perhaps
even desirable to provide direct access to all galleries without going through another gallery. Circulation
systems can be used deliberately to focus attention on
certain collections. For example, a popular gallery
might be located so as to attract people through less
popular parts of a museum. At the Metropolitan Museum
of Art, it has been found that many visitors see the
Chinese Collection because they have to go through that
gallery to get to the special exhibit area. On the
other hand, a decision might be made to locate a popular gallery near the main circulation paths to avoid
disrupting quieter areas nearby. In any case, care
should be taken to provide as many choices as possible
for the visitor. Where cul-de-sacs are necessary or
desirable, it should be made clear to the visitor what
his/her circulation path will be. Lengthy cul-de-sacs
requiring a great deal of repetitious viewing should
be avoided.

Circulation and
right-hand
preference

It has been observed and documented that most visitors
turn to the right when entering an exhibit hall (although it has also been noted that this tendency is
now declining since there are increasing numbers of
left-handed people). Since it is likely that the same
behaviour will occur at the scale of the museum, general circulation patterns should be designed with this
in mind. If there is a preferred sequence of galleries, there is some advantage if it flows to the right,
resulting in a smoother crowd flow through the museum
as a whole.

Circulation and
orientation

As noted earlier, circulation and orientation are obviously interdependent, and the two sets of considerations must be persued simultaneously from the viewpoint of a visitor moving through the museum. Confusion arising from poorly-thought-out circulation systems
creates a significant amount of stress for the visitor.
Orientation assistance is required in situations where
the existing circulation system is confused and

disorderly. Some museums, such as the National Museum of History and Technology in Washington, D.C., have realized their shortcomings in this respect and have undertaken to provide such orientation assistance for their visitors.

Circulation and traffic flow

Traffic flow is another aspect of circulation which must be considered, in order to ensure that the visitor can proceed with ease and at his/her own rate through the museum. The density of visitors in a given space at a given time can alter the effectiveness of communication with the public. Bernardo points out that noise, heat and crowding are factors which contribute to museum fatigue.[50] He also notes that *"the actual capacity of a museum to handle people efficiently is a function not of the area or volume of the museum building, but of the width of its corridors and aisles"* (p. 107). This relationship between the density of crowds and widths of corridors and exits has long been recognized by building codes, which often spell out in detail how wide a passageway should be for building use and occupancy. Circulation routes must obviously be designed in accordance with the anticipated pressures created by the number of visitors. If large numbers of visitors are expected (e.g. 100,000 per day at the National Museum of History and Technology, Smithsonian Institution in Washington) circulation patterns should be designed to include a relatively straightforward and direct alternative route so that those who want simply to "get through" can do so.

In one study the effect of large numbers of people moving through a museum is described in terms analogous to the movement of water in a river.[51] A constriction in the circulation (e.g. a central display island) was found to result in an accelerated rate of flow around it. This suggests that visitor "flow" should be treated with great care, and that the visitor's pattern of movement should be determined by what the visitor wants to see rather than by the pressures of crowd flow. In contrast to the results of this study, other experience would suggest that island displays can be used to attract the visitor. To some extent the way visitors react to island displays depends on the volume of crowd flow and the way in which visitors are moving through the museum or gallery at that particular location; these are determined by the availability of alternative routes, the intrinsic nature of the artifacts in the display, etc.

Circulation and groups

Most museums, large and small, have to deal with the special circulation problems of guided tour groups. Museum educators frequently mention the need for corridors of adequate width, so that groups and casual visitors do not have to interfere with one another. The Historical Society Museum in Chicago, which has large numbers of school classes visiting daily, has a traffic coordinator who keeps track of where various groups are within the museum at any one time.

Line-ups

A particular problem arises for museums when special temporary exhibitions of great popularity take place. The location of special exhibit halls should take into consideration the possibility of a large increase in the number of visitors. It has been suggested that the psychological aspects of crowding can be diminished when lines are run around corners so that people don't have to see how long a line is. Also it has been noted that if people are told how long they have to wait, waiting in line is more acceptable.[52] This will also give people a basis for choosing whether they want to wait or not; the length of the line will probably be reduced, since not all people will decide to join it. At the Metropolitan Museum of Art in New York, brochures pertaining to special exhibitions are often made available to visitors in line-ups and the opportunity is also taken to display pertinent posters and/or didactic materials on walls adjacent to the line-up.

Another method of treating line-ups, shown to be effective at recreational centres such as Disneyland, is to break *"the usual single line into many short lines by an arrangement of railings that neatly and without a word needing to be spoken, divide the patrons into small groups who are then kept moving through a sort of maze until they reach their destination ... People simply feel better if the line they are in is short and if it is constantly moving."*[53] A museum should be aware that visitors may be less receptive to an exhibit if gaining access is a frustrating experience. Every effort should therefore be made to minimize such possibilities.

Circulation for elderly and handicapped

Physical arrangements of the museum should also recognize the special needs of the elderly and handicapped, including *"a minimum of stairs, or the installation of*

elevators, ramps and doorways to accommodate wheelchairs, and frequent and accessible seating areas."[54]
A wheelchair floor plan could be marked by bits of
tape (inconspicuous to others) on the floor.[55]

Circulation and hall location

In designing a circulation system or deciding upon the
location for a new hall, several known aspects of visitor behaviour should be considered. In a study
examining three aspects of hall performance - attraction,
holding power and effectiveness[56] - it was found that
location was an important factor with respect to all
three.[57] Visitors were found to be attracted to halls
that were conveniently located. Conversely, halls that
were located away from a well-defined path were less
likely to be visited, unless they were intrinsically
interesting (Hope Diamond effect*).

The same study also found that the halls located so as
to be among the first visited had a high level of
visitor interaction with the exhibits (less fatigue).
This supports the results of earlier research which
indicated that visitors tend to spend a disproportionate
amount of their time in the first few halls they visit.[58]
It would also appear that galleries located on the
second and higher floors will be visited with less
frequency than those galleries on the ground floor.
A gallery's location should not be underestimated, for
it will help to determine the extent to which the gallery will be visited and the attention it will receive.

AMENITIES

Pacing and amenities

The amenities of a museum - those facilities which
cater to the well-being of the visitor - can be
considered an integral part of pacing. It is not possible to separate the visitor as serious viewer from
the visitor as pleasure-seeker. This is not to suggest
that a museum attempt to become an entertainer (which
it is unlikely to do well in any case) but that the
museum should treat visitors with the respect due to
guests, catering to their comfort and providing them
with pleasant facilities. Visitors at ease with their
environment both physically and psychologically are
more likely to constitute a receptive audience.

Museum restaurants

The provision and maintenance of washrooms and coat-
checking facilities are the obvious requirements. A

---

*This name has been given to the effect of a particularly inter-
esting artifact such as the Hope Diamond which attracts visitors
no matter how remotely it is located.

restaurant or cafeteria can be a major amenity, for
large numbers of visitors treat the cafeteria or
restaurant as a place to relax and to enjoy a contrasting experience during their stay at a museum. A
restaurant should be pleasant and should serve good
food; it should not be the typical tawdry basement
corner. One museum staff member commented, *"I wish we
had a cafeteria that looked out on a great view from
some height instead of peering up out of a basement."*[59]
Another commented that, *"it is stupid to offend people
at that level."*[60] Some suggest that a restaurant can
be an attraction in its own right, drawing visitors
into a museum, and providing the opportunity to extend
a meal into a broader experience.

Museum shops Another important amenity is the museum shop. Almost
all museums have them, but often they are hidden in
obscure locations or jammed into left-over spaces in
an insensitive and haphazard fashion. Many visitors
enjoy browsing and relaxing in the familiar shop
environment, especially if such shops are well located,
attractive and adequately stocked. It is an excellent
place to make available the kinds of publications which
will extend the museum experience beyond its walls.

*Pacing and
rest areas* From the viewpoint of pacing perhaps the most crucial
and complex set of amenities is the system of rest
areas (transition areas, or seating areas) which can
serve the visitor in a number of ways: encouraging
relaxation, changing the pace of activities, enabling
"seeing out," providing the visitor with a suitable
place and time for reflection or just for getting his/
her bearings. They can provide a warm, casual oasis,
in contrast to buildings which have historically
tended to be monumental in scale and formal in style.
Such areas can take a variety of forms: a seating area
off the main corridors (e.g. Field Museum), a major
feature of the museum (the restaurant at the Metropolitan), or spaces acting as transitions between
galleries.

A carefully considered system of rest "nodes" can be
integrated with an orientation system. For example,
rest areas can be extensions of clusters of galleries,
acting both as rest areas and transition/orientation
areas. They might include pamphlets and books, either
for sale or for use within the area, quiet but topical
music, and a person who can answer the hundred most

common questions about the set of galleries about to be introduced.

A skylighted restaurant area with a central reflecting pool and fountains is an added feature of the Metropolitan Museum of Art.

A spacious rest area including a pleasant view, is incorporated into the second-storey walkway surrounding the central court at the Field Museum.

Pacing as a comprehensive approach

Three aspects of pacing which are of consequence at the scale of a museum have been discussed - diversity, circulation, and amenities. This concept is explored further in Section II-A, p. 115, in a chapter on PACING WITHIN A GALLERY. Obviously the visitor's experience will not be separated into such neat compartments. A visit is a layering of all experiences and an approach to pacing must combine the experience of individual galleries and of the museum as a whole.

SECURITY

Security problems are identified; precautionary measures are proposed. It is emphasized that visitors can be affected negatively by obvious security measures and that appropriate gallery design can include unobtrusive deterrents.

Security issues

The major security issues which have been identified by museums are theft, damage, and fire. Theft is considered a real but limited danger, because, first of all, the total ransacking of a museum is an extremely rare occurrence, and secondly, because stolen objects are usually recovered in virtually the same undamaged form.[61] Fire is an ever-present major risk. It can result not only in the complete destruction of objects, but also in personal injury to visitors and museum personnel. The third security consideration, the prevention of damage (both wilful and accidental), although less dramatic than other security issues, is often the major concern of museum personnel involved in security.

Adequate museum security should include measures for the protection of the building, its contents, its staff and its visitors. Such comprehensive security requires the integration of a variety of measures into a general system or approach. But a complete examination of the issues involved in the delineation of such a system is beyond the scope of this report. Security measures are discussed here only insofar as they impinge upon the visitor and affect the design and arrangement of galleries. Operational measures effected on a museum-wide scale are considered, as well as specific measures applied in galleries, including both design considerations and the selection of mechanical and electronic devices.

OPERATIONAL CONSIDERATIONS

Security and checkrooms

Precautionary measures can be taken at the time the visitor enters or leaves the museum. Chapman has indicated, for instance, that *"a well run checkroom*

*is an efficient security factor and it is also a
courtesy to the public.*"[62]   All visitors can be
required to check not only their coats, but any appur-
tenances which might be used to conceal or damage
objects (e.g. parcels, umbrellas). Some museums have
instituted a bag and briefcase search as the visitor
leaves; however this measure can create resentment and
hostility among visitors.* In order to reduce damage
at the Hirshhorn Museum (part of the Smithsonian) in
Washington, carriages are not permitted in the gallery
but backpacks are provided for infants. In this instance, a courtesy service serves as a preventative
measure.

*Security and
orientation*

Some museums make use of the time devoted to orientation of groups to inform visitors about appropriate
behaviour in museums. This is particularly important
for children, who cannot always be expected to realize
that there are necessary limitations on their behaviour in a museum setting (e.g. touching sculpture).

Security guards

The major operational security force in most museums
is the museum guard. It is important to be aware that
a guard is also often the museum staff member who has
the greatest contact with the visitor, and who is most
often asked for information. In all instances of contact with the public the need for a courteous approach
must be emphasized. This is taken very seriously at
the Winterthur Decorative Arts Museum where the guard
training program is considered to be 65% public relations and 35% security procedures.[63] The extent to
which guards should be guides is, however, a debatable
question and will vary from institution to institution.
The visitor expects the guard to be familiar with at
least the location of galleries and various amenities.

The high visibility of guards in military type uniforms is considered in itself a deterrent to unsuitable behaviour. On the other hand, it is argued that
uniforms are oppressive to the innocent majority of
visitors, and therefore, contribute to an unpleasant
image. A Smithsonian study has found that there are
advantages in having both uniformed and non-uniformed
security personnel.

*Visitors to public institutions are receptive to searches in
direct relationship to their assessment of the seriousness of
the hazard, e.g. in airports.

PREVENTATIVE DESIGN CONSIDERATIONS

Security and signs

In addition to guards, signs (e.g. Please Do Not Touch) are probably the most commonly used security device in museums. Of course they must be designed and located in such a way as to be clearly visible and comprehensible. Signs that are worded so as to gain cooperation are more likely to be successful in most instances, as well as less offensive to visitors, than abruptly prohibitive signs. The signs used at the Hirshhorn Museum at the Smithsonian are excellent examples of good graphics and positive wording.

A sign at the Hirshhorn Museum, Smithsonian Institution, is informative without being offensive.

IN THE MUSEUM...
PLEASE...MUSE, CONVERSE, SMOKE, STUDY, STROLL, TOUCH, ENJOY, LITTER RELAX, EAT, LOOK, LEARN...

Signs will not always be an adequate deterrent in themselves, but their effectiveness can be considerable if they are thoughtfully conceived.

Security and spatial arrangement

The physical arrangement of a series of galleries can also be an important and subtle security device. Plans for connecting exits and entrances to galleries should consider the need for surveillance by guards. This can produce *"an incompatibility between the desirable location of doors which gives the best circulation for display, and an arrangement which enables a guard to see many rooms at one time"*;[64] but compromises may have to be made if watchful scrutiny is deemed necessary. For example, some galleries can be divided by low partitions rather than by full height walls.

Spatial arrangements within individual galleries must also be considered from this point of view. A gallery layout ideally suited to enhancing the visitor's appreciation of the artifacts may be at odds with the need for providing adequate surveillance to ensure the safety of those artifacts. For example, alcoves which establish intimate and manageable perceptual environments can, at the same time, conceal the actions of those few visitors who might tamper with the display.

The extent to which surveillance will be a factor in the design of a particular spatial arrangement will depend on the value of the collection, its vulnerability to vandalism or theft, the type of display techniques employed, and the security methods in use at the museum. The number of guards (or guides) available to circulate through the galleries is almost inversely related to the need for visual supervision. A scarcity of guards at an institution might in itself dictate the desirability of a more open spatial environment.

Security and display cases

The size, fragility and value of many artifacts will necessitate the enclosure and protection provided by display cases. The design and construction of cases must not only provide for access and maximum visibility but must also satisfy the requirements of both security and fire prevention. It has been suggested that one method of protecting objects against both fire and theft or damage is to employ only incombustible or fire-proof materials.[65] However, this is difficult, since glass, a major element of all cases, is not a useful fire barrier. Certain materials, such as tempered glass, although expensive, offer increased resistance to vandalism as well as to accidental breakage. While it is necessary to lock most display cases and to limit access to keys, in the event of fire this constraint on access can inhibit removal of the artifacts. This is particularly true in museums where display cases have been constructed over a long period of time, resulting in different locks and a large number of keys. To reduce this problem, priority should be given to updating and rationalizing case lock-and-key systems in museums.

Innovative security measures

Although traditional preventative measures will always have an important place in museums, consideration should be given to innovative techniques of discouraging damage and theft. One such method is the provision of a "sacrificial object." For example, Bernardo has described an exhibit of antique cars where no

boundaries between cars and the public were erected.
Visitors were told they could climb inside one particular car, but were requested not to touch the other
cars. *"The 'sacrificial car' proved to be enough to
discourage vandalism to the other units, even though
the audience was a young summer audience in a beach
surrounding."*[66] At the Milwaukee Public Museum, where
a stuffed elephant was being damaged by the hands of
an over-eager audience, the problem was eliminated by
installing a prominently mounted elephant-hide silhou-
ette of the animal with a "touch me" sign.[67]

Wherever possible, advantage should be taken of the
potential of subtle combinations of display elements
and the placement of objects to create psychological
barriers rather than actual ones. Careful manipula-
tion of gallery design can provide an environment
which enhances the viewers' perception and enjoyment
of the objects while diminishing the possibilities
for damage to the artifacts. For example, the use of
railings (which also serve as comfortable supports for
elbow-resting), or gravelled areas, can act as subtle
but effective methods of maintaining distances between
the object and the visitor.

*A raised box filled with gravel
provides both an effective
barrier and a flexible display
element, Whitney Museum, New
York City.*

Ropes are frequently used to provide a barrier, the
effect of which is generally more psychological then
physical. Similarly, objects which are subject to
damage (e.g. statues or totems) can be placed on
plinths rather than on the floor, so that they cannot
be kicked, either accidentally or wilfully.

MECHANICAL AND ELECTRONIC DEVICES

In conjunction with other security measures, a museum-
wide electronic system can present a psychological
deterrent: *"Even an intrepid band of art thieves,
knowing a museum is protected by an alert electronic
system, will almost certainly avoid it."*[68]

*Selection of
mechanical and
electronic
devices*

As pointed out by Michaels, the choice of a device
will depend upon *"the type, size, characteristics, and
value of the object to be protected, the environmental
conditions in the space, the presence or absence of
museum personnel in the area, the type and number of
persons expected to use the area as well as the hours
involved."*[69] The selection of appropriate mechanical/
electronic devices is also related to such factors as
capital cost and ease of maintenance. Devices can be
costly and their acquisition should be approached with
caution. As in all security matters involving valuable artifacts, the curatorial department should be
involved in the consideration of devices to be employed. The responsibility for the operation of these
devices should remain within the museum, in order to
ensure that they are constantly operational.

The installation of security equipment should be an
integral part of the planning of new galleries. Fire
extinguishers take up wall space and can unintention-
ally become prominent display features. Alarm systems, if accommodated during the design stage can be
made invisible. At the Milwaukee Public Museum open
dioramas are protected by alarm systems buried in the
flooring at the edge of the public walkway. On the
other hand, a valuable jewel collection being installed at the American Museum of Natural History in New
York includes a very visible electrically operated
gate which is intended to act as a deterrent as well
as a protective device.

There is a great variety of security equipment, detection devices and alarm systems. Some of these are
noted below:[70]

+ Devices commonly used for protection against fire
  include carbon dioxide or dry chemical extinguishers, automatic smoke and heat detection systems in
  conjunction with special sprinkler systems and
  alarm systems.

+ Walkie-talkies and other portable communications devices are used to supplement non-portable devices such as telephones and intercom systems.

+ The presence of intruders in a building or in specific closed spaces (e.g. cases) can be detected and signalled by a number of electrical, electro-mechanical and optical techniques. These devices include sound detectors, ultrasonic detectors (movement in an area covered by the emission of ultrasonic waves causes disturbances in the wave pattern), impact and vibration detectors, wired carpets which respond to pressure, contact circuit alarms (activated by breaks in or closing of the circuit), and wired or self-contained trap boxes which can be fitted on or over objects and which emit a loud alarm when the object or the device is tampered with.

+ Passageways or open areas can be protected by visible or invisible light barriers. The beams of light are picked up by a photo-electric cell; any interference between the light source and the cell causes an alarm to be set off.

+ Special protection to certain objects can be provided by pressurizing or depressurizing air-tight showcases. Manometers detect any sudden change in pressure (as when the glass is broken) and an alarm is activated.

It has been pointed out innumerable times by those in the museum profession and by those concerned with museum communication that most security arrangements obtrude themselves between the observer and the object, preventing the visitor from "fully experiencing" the object. Consideration should always be given to alternatives which are less likely to create barriers.

PART B· PROCESS

INTRODUCTION

Part A of this section dealt with museum-wide issues
to be considered in developing general museum policies
for communication with the public. This section is
concerned with the process whereby such museum-wide
issues are considered, goals and objectives are
established, and a strategy is developed which can
direct the activities of the museum towards the
accomplishment of its goals.

Most institutions will already have some process or
set of procedures for the design or renovation of
galleries and exhibits. However, many institutions
are in the midst of reconsidering their approaches
in this area, and are undertaking an exploration of
the most effective ways of communicating with the
public. This is the case with the Royal Ontario
Museum, which has established a team to undertake this
exploration and which has now produced this document.

Together with new approaches, new processes are required. All the knowledge in the world about communications, education, design and curatorial expertise
is essentially useless unless a museum establishes
an appropriate process for the effective application
of such knowledge. Such a process must be comprehensive, extending from the conceptualization of
new approaches through to the evaluation of effectiveness. This report deals with process at two scales:
the museum and the gallery (see Section II-B, p. 55
for gallery process). Obviously this division is an
artificial one, because the two are part of the same
general process and must be integrated with one another. For example, as museums explore and clarify
their museum-wide educational roles, the application
of specific learning principles could become a
fundamental criterion for exhibit design at the

scale of the gallery.

One value of such a process is that it facilitates dealing simultaneously with a series of complex interrelated problems. The development of galleries involves large numbers of people - designers, curators (frequently from more than one department), educators, conservators, preparators, electricians, carpenters, security and maintenance people. The effective deployment of all these people in the work of a series of galleries requires careful management and organization.

Another rather obvious reason for an effective process is economic efficiency, for the cost of producing exhibits is a major museum expenditure. For example, the American Museum of Natural History in New York indicated that the cost of producing exhibits amounts to 20% of the total annual museum budget. The cost of exhibits alone is a major proportion of the budget in any museum actually involved in a program of new or renovated galleries. This proportion devoted to communication with the public is much greater with the addition of education, outreach and other components of a communications strategy.

In order for a process to take place, decision-making bodies will obviously be necessary to consider the issues, develop policies, and coordinate the resulting activities. The precise nature of the administrative structure will vary from institution to institution. However, it is likely that new structures will be required as new policies are developed. In a small museum one person might assume the major responsibility while in larger museums a committee or a department might be more appropriate.

Since each individual institution has its unique internal structures, both formal and informal, there is little value in specifically defining a vehicle for undertaking the direction of a display process. Similarly, a precise definition of the scope of work required would have only limited applicability. However, in general terms, a process can be described for specific application according to the needs of each institution.

Finally, the fact that large museums are used as examples in the following section in no way discounts the need for careful development of communication goals, strategies and implementation procedures at even the smallest museum. Indeed, there is a sense in which these matters are even more important where resources are limited; and smallness presents its own unique opportunities for excellence.

The following chart illustrates the major components of such a process and their inter-relationships.

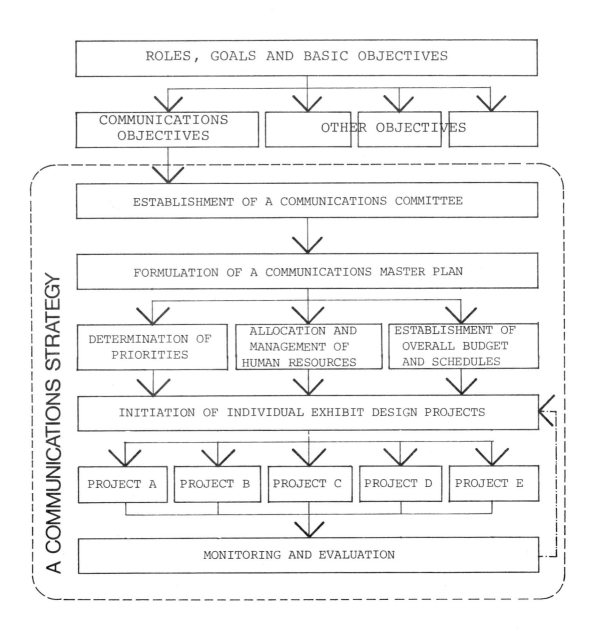

ROLES, GOALS AND BASIC OBJECTIVES

Discussion centres on the importance of defining general museum policies to ensure that an approach to communicating with the public has the necessary institutional commitment and resource base from which to develop.

It is useful to begin the consideration of a museum-wide process for communicating with the public, by examining the major institutional policies which should give direction to these activities and provide a focus for them. A policy for communicating with the public cannot be effective in isolation, but should form an integral part of the overall role and goals of a museum. A strategy for communication must have institutional support in order to compete for the financial and human resources of a museum. Without the support of the entire museum, a strategy for communication could be in conflict with other aspirations of a museum.

Basic policies of the Royal Ontario Museum

The role of the museum in contemporary society is a topic of concern to many institutions today. At the Royal Ontario Museum such consideration has resulted in the establishment of a series of basic policies expressed as follows:

"The Goal of the Museum shall be the furtherance of man's understanding of himself, his society, and the natural world of which he is a part.

"The Basic Objectives of purposes of the Museum in and toward the achievement of its Goal shall be:

a) the collection and preservation of natural specimens, artifacts, documents, books and other relevant materials to document the story of the universe and of all living things, including man and his brief span among them.

b) the employment of scholars as curators responsible for the care and systematic growth of the collections, and for the study and interpretation of the significance of those collections and the subjects represented by them.

c) participation in man's search for knowledge through the support of scholarly research, field work and publication by the staff in order that the holdings in the Museum's collections, and their significance, may be known to all men.

d) the interpretation of that knowledge through gallery exhibits, writing, teaching, lecturing, operation of a planetarium and other media of communication which will open to all people a deeper understanding of man and the universe in which he lives." 71

Thus a goal or "role" (the terms "roles," "goals" and "objectives" are used in various contexts by individual museums) and a series of basic objectives have been defined and adopted by the Royal Ontario Museum at the highest administrative level, the Board of Trustees. One of the four basic objectives directly concerns communication with the public. In this case, then, the institutional commitment to communication is clearly part of and consistent with the overall goal of the museum.

CHECKLIST OF ISSUES

Issues concerning roles, goals and basic objectives

The nature of debate on the role of a particular museum in its community is a product of many factors - the location, the size and importance of the institution, its age and prestige, the degree to which it has changed through the years, the quality of its collections, the nature of its funding, and the quality of its leadership. The concern here is with those aspects of the role of a museum which relate to communication with the public, and the following are some of the kinds of questions that should be considered in establishing goals or basic objectives in this area:

+ *How do the aspirations of the museum with respect to communicating with the public relate to its other functions such as research, and the collection, documentation and preservation of artifacts?*

+ *What responsibility does the museum have to make its collections and knowledge available to the public?*

+ *Does the museum wish to increase the number, range or type of visitors it attracts? Does it wish its current visitors to return more frequently?*

+   *Is the museum so organized that its overall communi-cations activities are the responsibility of an identifiable group and an individual who heads the group?*

+   *What proportion of human and financial resources are to be allocated to the communications function?*

DEVELOPING A STRATEGY

The major steps in developing an approach to communicating with the public are outlined. Following these steps ensures that exhibit development and renewal can occur in an orderly and coordinated fashion. Issues discussed include the establishment of a group responsible for evolving a communications master plan, the considerations such a plan should be based on, the determination of priorities, human resources, overall budgets, schedules, the initiation of individual projects and the monitoring and evaluation of activities.

A communications strategy

Once the role, goal and basic objectives of the museum have been established and the policy with respect to communicating with the public established, then a communications strategy can be formulated and implemented. The term strategy is used here in the broadest sense and is intended to embrace all of the activities of the museum with respect to communicating with the public. It includes the determination of who within the museum will be responsible for communication activities; the establishment of a communications master plan which defines the approach which will govern those activities; and the initiation, scheduling and evaluation of all such activities.

A COMMUNICATIONS COMMITTEE

A committee to develop a communications strategy

In order for specific objectives to be formulated and a strategy or master plan to be properly evolved, some authority (for convenience we will refer to it as a "committee") is needed to undertake these tasks. This committee could be large or small, formal or informal; it might consist solely of museum staff, or a combination of staff and outside consultants. However, in order to be effective and responsive it should have representation from all the major interests of the museum, including curators, designers, educators, artists, security and maintenance people, and those responsible for conservation and preservation.

At the Royal Ontario Museum, the recent administrative reorganization has placed the activities of such a group under the supervision of the Assistant Director of Education and Communication. A special group, the "Communications Design Team," has been established to undertake a consideration of exhibit policy, and this report represents the first stage of that consideration.

Leadership and strategy

A fundamental requirement for successful team work is good leadership. An effective leader must understand the processes of planning, problem-solving, decision-making and group dynamics. He must be clear about the group's aspirations, know how to implement plans, and understand methods of evaluation. A good leader will ensure that roles are clearly defined, will create opportunities for meaningful and effective participation by all those involved, and will schedule all activities to permit adequate consideration of issues before decisions are made.

The product of any process will only be as precise and applicable as the insights of those who formulated it. Methods for ensuring that relevant views are not only heard but also utilized at the appropriate time could include the soliciting of staff opinion, and the establishment of problem-solving and feedback mechanisms. Leaders who understand process and are sensitive to the broad context are absolutely essential, but so is the flash of genius or inspiration which the process is designed to encourage and exploit to the fullest. Process without inspiration is sterile: inspiration without process is impotent.

CHECKLIST OF ISSUES

Issues concerning a committee to develop a communications strategy

The following are some questions to be considered in regard to the group to be established within a museum to deal with a communications strategy.

+ *What will be the make-up of the committee? What representation is required from various museum departments? What proportion of each member's time is to be allocated to this function?*

+ *What authority does the committee have to recommend or set policies, authorize or institute projects, to delegate responsibility for performing tasks, to monitor all authorized activities? To whom does the committee report?*

+ *Who is most appropriate for the role of leader (chairman) and what authority will he/she have?*

+ *What resources must be made available to the committee? staff? consultants? budget? time?*

DEVELOPING A COMMUNICATIONS MASTER PLAN

A communications master plan

The first major step in developing a communications strategy is the delineation of a basic approach to communicating with the public, referred to here as a communications master plan. A communications master plan must be based on specific sub-objectives which flow from the basic policies of the museum as outlined in the previous chapter, ROLES, GOALS AND BASIC OBJECTIVES. For example, it may be decided that a comprehensive theme is to be adopted to provide a better means for communicating with the public. This and other such sub-objectives will provide the basis for determining what will fit where and why.

A communications master plan must consider both conceptual and physical opportunities and constraints. It should be based upon decisions which result from the consideration of the kinds of issues discussed in Part A of this section, for example, the relationship of the museum to the public, the educational approach to be adopted, the role of theme, and the importance of general circulation patterns. This will require an extensive base of information concerning existing exhibits and collections, the museum's architectural layout, the visitors, relevant outside studies and experiences, and evolving museum policies.

Conceptual aspects of a communications master plan

The conceptual aspects of a plan should include the establishment of an educational approach and a method of communicating that approach to the visiting public. In developing such an approach a major consideration is to provide a system of organization of galleries and collections which will be easily understood by the visitor. This is true whether the system involves a spatial reorganization relating to major interdisciplinary concepts (as at the Field), whether a clustering of related topics is evolved, or whether a strong theme is used and reflected in each of the galleries.

*Physical
aspects of a
communications
master plan*

Obviously, the conceptual aspects cannot be developed into a communications master plan in isolation from the physical setting. An existing building is a major determinant of the possible range of spatial arrangements. Each institution must understand the strengths and weaknesses of its own building. For example, the architectural configuration of a building can have an important impact on the location of the various components of a museum. Lobbies, entrance-ways, and highly visible galleries are prime locations for orientation areas and introductory exhibits; remote and inaccessible halls can be utilized to present information of rather esoteric interest; high-ceilinged galleries can house large objects such as airplanes or dinosaur skeletons.

Any communications master plan must give consideration to major traffic arteries. As noted in Part A of this section, p. 44, galleries which constitute major arteries, or galleries located just off major traffic routes, will probably be visited with the greatest frequency. This was considered by the National Museum of Natural History, in the development of an exhibit master plan - the museum's four main axial halls are to be concept and process-oriented, integrating the broad concepts of natural history. This plan is related to a major objective of the museum: "*to represent the new awareness of the integrative processes of geology, evolution, adaptation, and ecology.*"[72]

An understanding of the character of a building can also assist in developing a plan based upon its inherent strengths, and dealing as effectively as possible with its inherent weaknesses. In this regard, some buildings are obviously more workable than others. The Director of the British Museum has made the following comment with respect to future planning and the museum: "*At the British Museum the intrinsic distinction of the architecture will rightly dominate our future thinking.*"[73]

A communications master plan which matches a conceptual base with the characteristics of a building provides the point of reference for decisions relating to all of the activities to be undertaken. It also provides the basis for other aspects of strategy which flow from it - the determination of priorities, the allocation of human resources, scheduling and budgeting.

CHECKLIST OF ISSUES

Issues concerning the development of a communications master plan

The following are typical questions or issues to be considered in establishing a master plan for communications with the visitor. The consideration of these must be within the context of those general policies adopted by the institution (roles, goals and basic objectives). For example, if it is a policy of the institution to adopt a more aggressive educational role, then the development of an approach should include the consideration of questions which can help define this role more precisely. The following questions are not exhaustive but represent the kinds of issues which must be considered in evolving a useful master plan.

+ *To what extent should the museum teach? entertain? provide learning support? What is to be the major thrust of the educational approach? Should it be uniform or varied? How much emphasis is to be placed upon guided tours, and to what extent should this be reflected in gallery design? How didactic should displays be? To what extent will audio-visual techniques be employed?*

+ *Would the goals and objectives of the museum be furthered by the adoption of a comprehensive theme for the museum? Should there be a series of sub-themes within a major theme, or a series of related themes if no overall theme is adopted? How should the theme affect the presentation within individual galleries (e.g. form of storyline)? Should the theme affect the spatial distribution of galleries?*

+ *Is the image that the museum projects the one it wishes to project? Is it congruent with the role the museum has adopted? How static or dynamic should the image be? To what extent should the museum update its exhibitions as new discoveries are made or as new explanations are needed? To what extent should new objects be added to galleries as they are acquired? To what extent should the museum participate in community affairs? Should the museum advocate positions it considers important or relevant? (e.g. ecology), or should it avoid taking a stand?*

+ *Who are the museum's visitors? How frequently do they attend? Who are the non-visitors? Which of these does the museum wish to attract?*

+ *What is the first impression of the visitor when he arrives at the museum? How is the visitor greeted? Are there adequate reception facilities for the individual visitor? the group? the school class? Are there adequate facilities for tour buses (e.g. lay-by, parking, etc.)? What orientation assistance is provided to the casual visitor and the group, both upon arrival and throughout the museum?*

+ *How effective are the existing exhibits/galleries in meeting the objectives of the museum with respect to communication? Is there a need for a re-organization of the spatial distribution of galleries (i.e. by subject matter)? If so, what are the criteria for that redistribution? What emphasis should be given to permanent exhibits? temporary exhibits? travelling exhibits?*

+ *Is there a need for a theme gallery? an orientation gallery? discovery rooms or special self-study areas? introductory subject halls for a series of related galleries? areas to accommodate special activities such as art shows, concerts, etc.?*

+ *Are there architectural features of the museum which should be employed in the development of the physical plan (e.g. interior courts, major stairways)?*

DETERMINATION OF PRIORITIES

Once the communications master plan, including the spatial distribution of exhibits within a museum, is established (or reaffirmed), then the major priorities for action must be determined. This is crucial because a plan is of little value without a logical sequence for implementation. It is also critical because immediate priorities become the visible actions of a museum; a concept is revealed not through the long-range plan, but through relatively short-term actions.

Establishment of realistic priorities

To achieve precise priorities for exhibit development, the communications master plan must first establish a general profile for each space for which major changes are contemplated. This would include an indication of the scope of the subject matter (e.g. whether interdisciplinary or not), the size of the space, and the extent of required change (replacement, major renovations, face-lifting). These considerations can then lead to a determination of where to begin, and the order in which to create new galleries. Other considerations which enter into the determination of realistic priorities include scheduling implications, who is needed to contribute to each project (how many curators, designers, in-house fabricators, etc.), the degree of disruption that each change will involve, and the costs.

Illustrative criteria for setting priorities

Some illustrative criteria for setting priorities (based on the experiences of the Field Museum and the National Museum of Natural History) follow:

+ If there is a new direction proposed, then galleries or spaces which will contribute most to the new direction of the museum should be given high priority on the work list.

+ The least satisfactory exhibits (unpopular, inadequate persentation of collection, obsolete in light of new discoveries, etc.) should be given a high priority for renewal.

+ The most satisfactory galleries (good presentation, popular) should either be left alone or altered only to maximize their impact.

The above criteria are not in any particular order, nor are they by any means the only means of establishing priorities.

Priorities and disruption

It must be emphasized that a major renewal of exhibits can be disruptive over a long period of time. Priorities should be established so as to ensure that the museum continues to serve as an attractive and interesting place to visit throughout such a program. For example, all the popular galleries should not be redone at the same time.

CHECKLIST OF ISSUES

Issues to consider in the determination of priorities

+ *What short-term actions should be considered to enhance the overall image of the museum while long-term planning is still in process? What physical building changes, if any, should be considered in order to improve the overall impact of the building with respect to the visitor (e.g. air conditioning, lighting, etc.)?*

+ *Which galleries should be renewed, replaced, or upgraded? What are the criteria for making these judgments?*

+ *If a major gallery is closed for an extended period of time should highlights from its collection be displayed in a temporary exhibit?*

+ *Are there specific problems with traffic flow throughout the building that should be solved before implementing the master plan?*

+ *What are the constraints or priorities as a result of funds and human resources?*

ALLOCATION AND MANAGEMENT OF HUMAN RESOURCES

A project team

Several aspects of human resource planning are related to the implementation of a communications master plan. A major gallery will often require a special team to implement it (see Section II-B, p. 171). In addition to establishing a good working process, the museum committee establishing each project team must consider the need to establish teams which have key people with all of the requisite skills, compatibility among the principal participants, and a leader with appropriate managerial and leadership qualities.

Selecting members of the project team

The first consideration is the selection of <u>key people</u> (such as designers, curators, and educators) for each major project. This must start from an understanding that a museum is a multi-faceted institution and that the development of new galleries is only one of its functions. The design and implementation of a gallery can be a very intensive activity, demanding a high degree of commitment on the part of all major participants. This is particularly relevant to team members selected from curatorial departments who are usually heavily involved in their regular duties. If the time burden of their function on a project team is not acknowledged and accounted for, their ability to function effectively on the team can be impaired. For some curators, involvement in the development of a gallery can be particularly stressful, as it may be a once-in-a-lifetime activity.

Scheduling of human resources

In addition to selection and involvement of key personnel, there must be careful management of all the

personnel necessary to develop a gallery. These
include tradesman such as carpenters, plumbers and
electricians and others with special skills unlikely
to be available from outside the museum (preparators
and conservators). One aspect of the management of
these particular skills is careful allocation, to
ensure that <u>unique talents are available for specialized tasks when they are required</u>. Any program that
ignores this will fail to produce quality on schedule
even if all other factors have been carefully planned.
One dramatic example of inadequate planning in this
respect was demonstrated at a museum where a specialist on sabbatical was hired to supervise the design
and installation of a display related to his area of
specialization. As there were not enough preparators
scheduled to assist him, the gallery remained incomplete
upon his departure. The result of this was considerable delay in opening the gallery.

A broader aspect of this type of planning is the careful balancing of museum staff with the scale of exhibit
program undertaken. This was acknowledged in the
National Museum of Natural History's "Long-Range Plan,"
which states:

*"No more than three halls can be under development
without seriously straining the capacity of the curatorial resource, and especially the curator-staffed
Exhibits Committee. This constraint dictates that a
span of approximately twenty years time is necessary to
reshape the Museum's exhibits."*[74]

CHECKLIST OF ISSUES

*Issues to
consider in the
allocation and
management of
human resources*

+ *Who are the key people to be involved in each
  project? How are they selected? Who will lead the
  project team? Has sufficient time been allocated to
  ensure that all participants can perform their tasks
  adequately and without undue stress?*

+ *What additional special skills are required for
  each major activity (e.g. carpenters, artists,
  electricians, preparators, etc.)?*

+ *To what extent will outside assistance (consultants,
  contractors, etc.) be necessary? How will their
  work be integrated into the system of gallery
  development?*

ESTABLISHMENT OF OVERALL BUDGETS AND SCHEDULES

The need for flexibility in budgeting and scheduling

The length of time required to complete a major gallery can be considerable. It has been found to vary from a few months up to six years, depending upon the size of the gallery and the efficiency of the museum. Long-term planning can therefore involve a very long time span (e.g. twenty years at the National Museum of Natural History, thirty years at the Field Museum) and most major institutions find it necessary to establish both detailed plans for five or ten years and overall longer-term plans. With respect to budgeting and scheduling, which must deal with the short term as well as the long term, it is important that plans be both firm enough to provide direction to the multitude of activities involved in the development of a gallery, and at the same time, flexible enough to accommodate to changing circumstances.

Relating a series of simultaneous activities

Scheduling often involves relating a series of simultaneous activities. For example, it must include consideration of the impact of the work of new gallery development as well as the scheduling of the work itself. If a major gallery is being redone, where are the artifacts to be stored during the extensive period of renovation? How is circulation affected? What is the effect on nearby galleries?

Budgeting

Budgeting can be equally complex. For example, as noted previously, some skills required for gallery development are scarce and planning must be capable of juggling available people. If outside consultants or tradesmen are required to supplement the museum staff, this must be carefully budgeted as staff costs and costs for outsiders are frequently paid out of separate budgets. This can be further complicated by the demands of special exhibits with specific opening date requirements (e.g. special outside exhibits on tour such as the Chinese Exhibition) or galleries specially funded by outside sources.

Individual projects funded by outside sources, either government or private, often have to be done within specific schedules and to meet specific criteria, so that coordination with other activities may be difficult.

Management of budgets and schedules

Individual projects can be both lengthy and costly. A series of projects requires even more complex management to ensure that time and cost constraints are met. The management of these activities might be the function of the entire committee involved in the administration of the communications strategy or of a sub-group or individual delegated that specific responsibility. At the Metropolitan Museum of Art this activity is done with the assistance of operational supervisors who have little direct authority but who directly monitor projects and report on their progress. At a museum the size of the Royal Ontario Museum where perhaps two or three major projects might be carried on at one time, one project director could potentially undertake the direction and monitoring of all projects. At a larger museum or one involved in a greater number of projects at a specific time, several project directors might be required.

Flow charts

There are a variety of techniques that can be employed to assist those who are responsible for the scheduling and monitoring of a series of simultaneous activities. A very effective one is the visual portrayal in chart form of all major activity streams for a project, showing time required for major steps, interdependencies, and target dates. Such a chart can be extremely effective in communicating to a heterogeneous committee the whole picture of what is required, how it all interconnects, and whether it is on schedule. It brings together in one easily understood format information necessary to carry out each of the major management functions: plan, organize, motivate, communicate, control, evaluate.

CHECKLIST OF ISSUES

Issues to consider in developing overall schedules and budgets

+ *What major separate streams of activity are required for each project?*

+ *What are the major steps in each stream?*

+ *How long will each step take?*

+ *In what ways do the planning activities interact to form a logical sequence?*

+ *What review and approval steps must be built into the process?*

+ *Has adequate time and space been allocated for the removal, storage and reinstallation of all artifacts?*

+ *How much money is available for gallery development and other communication activities? How are allocations made for individual galleries and other activities within that budget?*

+ *How are the costs for individual projects controlled and how are variations from preliminary budgets accommodated?*

+ *Are funds allocated for evaluation and for adjustments which flow from evaluation?*

THE INITIATION OF INDIVIDUAL PROJECTS

Once a communications master plan is established, it is implemented through the initiation of individual projects in accordance with the priorities which have been set. Although the process of developing an individual project (for example a gallery or an exhibit) is often assigned to a special project team (see Section II-B, p. 171), the basic ground rules for that gallery must have been established by those responsible for the development of the communications strategy. This will ensure conformity of each new gallery to the overall strategy for gallery development. These ground rules should include:

+ the terms of reference, indicating the purpose of the project within the overall strategy (e.g. educational thrust)

+ a space allotment

+ the selection of key personnel and a commitment to adequate human resources

+ a preliminary budget and schedule.

THE MONITORING AND EVALUATING OF PROJECTS

Monitoring   A critical function of an overall strategy is monitoring, to ensure that each project proceeds with its development according to priorities and schedules. Although responsibility for each project may be delegated to a project team, it is imperative that a method of monitoring progress exists. This will ensure that unintended deviations from objectives do not occur, that budgets and schedules are adhered to, or variations agreed upon, and that long-term and overall implications of human resource allocation are not disrupted. An overall scheduling chart as previously discussed, plus individual charts for each separate project, are indispensable. So is a general coordinator to monitor the progress of implementation of the overall communications strategy, and of individual projects which form part of that strategy.

Evaluation   An additional critical function is the evaluation of the individual activities, to determine how effectively they fulfill the objectives of the museum. Effective evaluation is a complex matter (see Section II-B, p. 198) which is most useful if it is an ongoing part of the design process. Not only should it form an essential part of the process of designing a gallery, but it should also form a major activity of the museum committee responsible for the communications strategy. All the actions of the museum should be tested for their impact upon the visitor, and the results of such tests should immediately be reflected in other ongoing activities. For example, lessons learned in one gallery can immediately benefit the next. A communication strategy must also be responsive to the feedback generated by evaluation. A strategy should be viewed as a dynamic direction, not a static set of statements.

CHECKLIST OF ISSUES

Issues to consider in monitoring and evaluation

+ *Who is to assume responsibility for monitoring of ongoing activities?*

+ *What system of review and control is to be employed (e.g. scheduling chart)?*

+ *Who is to assume responsibility for the evaluation function?*

+ *How are criteria to be established, and effectiveness measured?*

+ *How will the work of outside consultants and contractors be assessed and controlled?*

PART C·THE COMMUNICATIONS MASTER PLAN

The process by which a museum develops and implements a communications strategy is described in some detail in Part B of this section of the report. This part is a brief description of the key component of such a strategy - the Communications Master Plan. The Communications Master Plan consists of a statement of the basic approach of a museum to communicating with the public. Since this is such a crucial aspect of a process, it is useful to describe its essential elements

As noted previously, the Communications Master Plan should flow from the basic policies of the institution; it should be an integral part of museum policy with respect to the roles, goals and basic objectives of the museum. The major elements of a Communications Master Plan, as set out below, should be assessed against overall museum policies to ensure that they complement and reinforce them, rather than compete or conflict with them.

ELEMENTS OF A COMMUNICATIONS MASTER PLAN

An Approach to Education: The first consideration of a Communications Master Plan concerns the establishment of an approach to education. This should become the basic guide to the nature of information to be conveyed and to the means of communicating it. It should include some direction for an educational approach within galleries; delineation of out-reach programs including school tours as well as non-school tours, travelling exhibits, etc.; the nature of pamphlets and other aids to visitors.

An Approach to Orientation: Another important consderation is an approach to orientation. This can include a wide range of museum activities extending from the graphics to be used in the museum to the use of an orientation gallery. It includes all the ways in which a museum assists visitors, throughout a visit, with various aspects of design information both in galleries and public areas.

An Approach to the Galleries: Perhaps the key consideration is the approach to display within galleries. This should incorporate both education and orientation approaches in the presentation of artifacts and supportive information. It should include the desirable spatial distribution of galleries within the museum based upon an understanding of how effectively existing galleries utilize space, how subject matter is to be organized, and the extent of temporary or special exhibition contemplated. It should include an approach to the presentation of didactic information, and an assessment of the extent of change required, based upon a review of the quality of existing galleries and their impact upon visitors.

An Approach to Public Areas: Another essential set of considerations is the proposed nature of the public non-gallery areas - lobbies, restaurants, bookshops, etc. This would be based upon concerns about image, arrival, and orientation, and pacing.

An Approach to Theme: The museum should consider whether a content theme or a related series of sub-themes is to be employed to assist in communication with the visitor; whether a theme gallery is to be included; and/or whether themes should be evolved for individual galleries.

An Approach to Graphics, Signage, and Other Communication Devices: This approach concerns all the major graphic aspects of the museum; signs, text panels, guide books and floor plan maps, pamphlets and handouts, as well as tape cassettes, or similar devices.

An Approach to Staff: The staff in contact with the public - the information people, guides, docents, and guards - are an important part of any Communications Plan. Their duties, attitudes, and appearance have a major impact upon the visitor.

SUMMARY

The Communications Master Plan is a series of
approaches, rather than a specific set of rigid objectives. It must also be unique to each institution and
its collections, priorities, etc. It is not an ideal-
ized theoretical document. It must be both general
enough to provide guidance without undue constraint,
and specific enough to be applicable in concrete terms
in the development of a strategy. It must be flexible
and dynamic, adjustable to changing realities; not a
static and rigid set of statements which will adorn a
shelf among other artifacts.

SECTION II · GALLERY

PART A · INDIVIDUAL GALLERY CONSIDERATIONS

INTRODUCTION

The development of a gallery or an exhibit within a museum is a unique design problem. The Director of the British Museum made the following comment on exhibit design:

"It presupposes a real understanding of the nature of the object shown, and a real conviction as to the qualities that distinguish it from other objects of the same kind. It is this that separates designing for . museums from other kinds of design."[75]

There are innumerable considerations and judgments which combine to determine how a gallery or exhibit should be designed. It is not a simple mechanical process, nor is it a magical outpouring of subjective creativity. The purpose of the guidelines is to present in a useful format the available information about what is largely a creative process. It is intended that this will enable museum personnel to make more informed decisions and to follow less stressful procedures. In the long run, of course, it is the talent and expertise of the individuals involved which make the exhibit either brilliant or banal.

The design of a gallery is usually beyond the competence of a single individual, and often requires the cooperation of several specialists working together. This has been aptly described by Sir John Pope-Hennessy.

"It would be much too simple to say that the designer's task is to supply a harmonious integrated setting, in which the curator can dispose of his objects. That may be the ideal, but in different human situations different solutions are required - and only when co-operation, total co-operation, between specialist and designer is achieved - as it was in those beautiful Greek and Roman galleries in the British Museum, on a world scale the

*only fully successful museum installation in this
country - will a completely gratifying end product be
produced."*[76]

To make such cooperation possible there is a need for a
set of procedures which carefully establishes the working relationships of participants. This section of the
report is divided into three parts. The first part is
an assembly of information and insights on a variety of
issues; the second part is a discussion of the process
through which such information can be applied; the third
is an indication of how to evaluate an existing gallery.

The development of a gallery requires the simultaneous
integration of a host of considerations. It is impossible to think in terms of the arrangement of artifacts
without thinking in terms of their lighting, of their
sequencing and arrangement, of the way in which they
might be mounted, and of the spatial constraints and
opportunities. Of necessity, these issues are discussed separately in the sections which follow. However,
each must be considered as part of a coordinated
approach to the design of a gallery.

It should be pointed out that conflicting issues will
inevitably arise in such a complex task as designing a
new gallery. Conflicts can be occasioned by any number
of factors, such as cost, availability of objects, and
time constraints. Decisions concerning these problems
will often take the form of "trade-offs" between the
conflicting elements, but it is crucial to make decisions on an informed basis so that reasonable trade-
offs result. By exercising maximum ingenuity, the
trade-off can be a positive solution to the problem
rather than a mere compromise.

TELLING THE STORY

The complex task of ensuring that a gallery is comprehensible to visitors demands careful consideration of exhibit content, methods of presenting the information, and the nature of the audience. This discussion deals with the importance of information accuracy and relevance and ways of organizing information to assist visitors to learn. It also elaborates on the use of display techniques and media approaches. The different elements affecting a gallery's general atmosphere are noted, as well as the significance of this in communication.

The content of galleries

Although there are galleries within museums which are based upon a concept which is independent of the collection, most galleries and exhibits basically present a collection or a part of a collection. In fact the one unique characteristic of a museum is that it presents original artifacts. It is this that separates it from other educational or cultural institutions: it is the artifact which offers unique and special learning opportunities. The starting point for any gallery (other than a purely conceptual gallery) is, therefore, the collection of artifacts that it will contain. A reasonable measure of the quality of a gallery is the extent to which that gallery enhances the artifacts and enables the visitor to perceive and appreciate them.

The approach taken to a specific gallery is a product of a set of conditions unique to that gallery. It will depend upon such factors as the basic policies of the museum with respect to exhibit design, the interests and personalities of those charged with undertaking the design and development, the nature of the collection to be displayed, the budget, and the time available to develop the gallery. Whatever these conditions are, there are some issues which should be considered in establishing an approach. These issues collectively relate to the means of "telling the story".

CONTENT AND THE VISITOR

*Content and
human interest*

Artifacts often have interesting and easily communi-
cable histories (e.g. a tapestry which took a workman
his entire lifetime to complete) and this kind of
information can often enhance communication with the
visitor. This type of approach is reflected in a current temporary exhibit at the Metropolitan Museum of
Art - "Patterns of Collecting: Selected Acquisitions
1965-1975" - where not only the artifacts but also
interesting highlights of the process of acquisition
are presented.

A similar highly successful example is a gallery at the
Field Museum in Chicago which incorporates information
on the activities of the museum (archeological explorations, etc.) and identifies the curators involved.
This very attractive "temporary" show has endured for
a decade, indicating public interest in the overall
activities of a museum, an interest which many museums
could exploit more fully.

*Content and
stereotypes*

Another issue frequently raised in museum literature is
the tendency, particularly in anthropological exhibitions, to present selections of objects which lead to
the perpetuation of stereotypes. For example:

*"All too frequently a museum visitor gets the erroneous
idea that the ceramics made in pre-Columbian times by
the Mayan, Mexican, or Peruvian Indians consisted
entirely of magnificent, multi-colored and elaborately
decorated ceremonial vessels ... and that the Indians
of North America spent their entire lives on horse-
back, wearing feather bonnets, wielding tomahawks and
pursuing white settlers or buffalo."*[77]

The caution raised by these remarks is clear. A museum
presentation has an air of authority and is generally
unchallenged by the public. The responsibility for
accuracy and relevance is therefore greater than in a
less authoritative setting.

*Content and
biases*

The likely interests of the visitor should also be considered in order to offset professional biases of the
curator or designer. This is not to suggest that only
popular exhibits should be developed or that curatorial
preference should be ignored, but that the major function of the display or exhibit is to communicate with
the public, and that every aspect of the visitor's

needs (physical, intellectual and emotional) should be
given consideration. The perspective generated by such
an appraisal can help produce a display which is likely
to communicate more successfully with the visitor.
This point is emphasized by the Director of the British
Museum in a comment on museum specialists: *"Their defect is that they know their own collections much too
well. They simply cannot see them from outside."*[78]
(Underlining added)

Exercising selectivity in objects and information to be
presented is an important part of defining a future
gallery. The criteria for selecting artifacts and
information to be presented in a gallery must be carefully evaluated in order to minimize unreasonable
biases. This can be achieved without necessity for
compromise of curatorial integrity.

COMPREHENSIBILITY AND LEARNING THEORY

*Content and
learning*

Approaching "story-line" from an instructional point
of view, Shettel has indicated that in order to learn,
a certain amount of information must be absorbed before
progressing to another set of information; and that
different people will go through this process at different rates. He therefore concludes that content must
be presented in relatively small increments, with the
size of the "step" determined by the difficulty of the
subject matter and the anticipated characteristics of
a heterogeneous audience.[79] Similarly, Lakota has suggested that information is most effectively presented
when concepts are built from the concrete to the
abstract.[80]

At the same time, there has been much discussion about
the danger of *"under-estimating the intelligence of the
viewer"* and *"gauging exhibits at too low an information
level,"* with suggestions that *"museologists need not be
afraid to attempt to present even more abstract concepts through their exhibits."*[81] It is important to
note that studies which arrive at such recommendations
have used mostly university-educated participants,
interested in learning and motivated to learn; the
results may not therefore be entirely relevant to all
"casual visitors", and equal caution should be taken
not to over-estimate the information level of the visitor.

It is obvious that information that is over the head of the audience runs the risk of being completely misinterpreted, or of being completely ignored. A pertinent example has been described by Robert Matthai who studies children in a museum setting. He observed that, in a display of a series of similar objects, younger children always assume that the larger objects are older than the smaller ones, in spite of any information which may have been given as to dates, etc.[82] In developing the means of presentation, the probable competence of the visitor must therefore be borne in mind in order to reduce the possibility of misinterpretation.

Content and organization

The work of education researchers in learning theory can also provide exhibit planners with an approach to organizing information in ways that make a gallery comprehensible and actively promote visitor learning. Lakota has reviewed much of this research in one of his studies.[83] He points out that the inspection activities of the learner (i.e. what is seen or examined, and the degree of concentration) control the nature and amount of learning and that it is possible for museums to assist visitors to learn by directing their inspection activities. From his review of the literature, Lakota documented the following recommendations:

"1. *Provide a conceptual framework for understanding the organization of the exhibit. If there is a non-apparent logical basis for the arrangement of the exhibit (historical, phylogenetic, geographical, sequential, etc.) tell it to the visitor, simply and clearly.*

   a. *If [the exhibit is] presented without an apparent logical structure, visitors will spend most of their time organizing the exhibit themselves (Meyers, 1973).*

   b. *If visitors are given knowledge of that organization, retention and recall of exhibit material will be increased (Meyers, 1973).*

   c. *This information is especially important for exhibits with low subject matter familiarity (Dyer, 1973) and high technical content (Tobias and Duchastel, 1972).*

"2. *Tell visitors the concepts or classes of things they are to learn (Anderson, 1970).*

> "3. *Encourage visitors as to the likelihood of their
>   learning something (Anderson, 1970; Shettel, et.
>   al., 1968).*
>
> "4. *Direct visitors to 'find' certain objects, classes
>   of objects, or their attributes (Anderson, 1970;
>   Powell, 1944; Bloomberg, 1929)."*[84]

Providing information on the structure of the material
and the concepts or classes of things to be learned
gives the learner a means of organizing the material.
In other words, such information defines cues which
direct the search and inspection activities of the
learner. This frame of reference aids the visitor to
process, or make sense of, the material presented.

*Content and
orientation*

Making a gallery comprehensible by providing the visitor with organizing information can be part of orientation procedures. Lakota has developed the provision
of orientation information into a comprehensive approach, a learning support system. The application of
this approach at the scale of the museum was discussed
in EDUCATION AND LEARNING, p. 18. For an individual
gallery the application of this approach involves providing learning support both at the entrance to a gallery and within it. Specific techniques which can be
used are discussed in "Good Exhibits on Purpose," a
paper by Lakota, which is presented in full as Appendix C.

*Content and
theme*

The use of a theme is another way of organizing the
content of a gallery to make it more comprehensible to
the visitor. A theme can prepare visitors and assist
them by reinforcing conceptual and emotional impres-
sions throughout a gallery. It has been noted that a
compelling and easily discernable focal point, located
near the gallery entrance and illustrating the theme,
can allow the visitor to assimilate information
quickly.[85] One study found that themes help the visitor to organize and summarize information presented in
a gallery, and that *"visitors found messages organized
into comprehensive stories or concepts tied together
by central themes to be more interesting than unrelated
facts and identification of objects."*[86] This conclusion is echoed in Shettel's study, which maintains that
an exhibit *"must appear to the viewer as having a theme
and a coherent unity, with all of its parts contributing
to that theme ... [When this is not the case] viewers
will sense the lack of 'direction' and will reflect it*

in a relative lack of interest and attention."[87]   Such research supports the contention that a theme has great potential for conveying a sense of unity to the visitor, although obviously the clarity of presentation of a theme will ultimately determine its usefulness.

TECHNIQUES OF DISPLAY

Content and display techniques

Ensuring that all display elements enhance the subject matter, is an essential consideration in conveying information to the visitor. The effectiveness of an exhibit is diminished if the visitor begins to feel puzzled or distracted by a jarring relationship of design to information. As Paul Fine has noted, the artifacts are the foundation upon which a presentation is based, and the way in which they are presented should emphasize intrinsic merits and stimulate the viewer to a better understanding of the content.

"The power of the museum exhibit as an educational tool, is that it can combine powerful visual experience with thought content. Even if the aim is to convey a general principle, it follows that the more vivid the totality of the concrete experience (visually, emotionally, esthetically), the more substance there will be to the abstract principle being taught."[88]

Specialization and display

Fine goes on to discuss the range of learning possibilities that can be explored with the use of appropriate display techniques and cautions that the specialist may not always be aware of these potentials.

"The specialist who has spent his life concentrating on one field, focusing on only one of the possible sets of meanings, may forget the presence and range of the wealth and variety of other potential meanings which are present in his context ... Or he may forget the richness of experience that gives interest to the whole context, in which case his display becomes as dry as dust." (p. 41)

The same limitations regarding specialization apply whether the specialist is a curator or a designer. It has been noted that the conventional role of a designer is to *"create a concrete visual experience which gives esthetic pleasure and which leads to emotional and motivational rewards, not to critical questioning."*[89] The validity of such a role is highly questionable in the light of current approaches to education in the design of exhibits. De Borhegyi has commented that natural history exhibits often suffer as a result of such contemporary display techniques as the use of less material in display cases highlighted by spotlighting, the use of bold and colourful backgrounds, and the replacement of long labels with short attention-getting captions. In his opinion, such methods often result in the design overwhelming the actual object, in the distortion of the meaning of the specimen and its relative importance within the culture represented, and in misleading simplification of label material.[90] These points appear to be supported in part by a study by Parsons which showed that a reduced density of artifacts - permitting "artful" display - seemed at variance with the visitors' reactions. People not only wanted *"to see more specimens, but apparently, they understood more, learned more, and enjoyed it more when there was more to see."*[91]

On the other hand, traditional densities of artifacts in displays also have limitations. Experiments have shown that visual monotony contributes directly to fatigue. In these experiments, participants who were exposed to *"designs of great similarity reported a sudden mysterious disappearance of distinctions in shape."*[92] Experiments on the limitations of human memory, conducted by psychologist George Miller, found that *"we could recall only seven independent items at a time."*[93] But he also indicated that these limitations could be circumvented by more effectively structuring messages.

The implication of such studies for gallery design and the density of artifacts is that rather than promoting the uniqueness of objects, in the sense of separate entities, an emphasis should be placed on relationships (although not necessarily on similarities). It is necessary to provide variety and maintain interest, and still to preserve a sense of unity. This requires following a narrow path with some care. While on the one hand monotony can induce physiological and psychological fatigue, too chaotic a presentation can overload and confuse the visitor.

A sense of unity   One way of achieving a sense of unity is through unity of style in the design of a gallery. At the same time this is considered to be one of the most important

aspects of gallery design.[94]   The selective use of
contrast and diversity is not contradictory to this
aim, but can be the means of achieving it. This process of attempting to create unity out of diversity is
an intangible creative striving for integrity of presentation. The final result, if successful, can induce
a receptive awareness in the visitor, or if unsuccess-
ful, can result in an unsettling negative response to
the gallery as a whole.

As the motives for developing displays become more
complex, the likelihood of any one individual being
capable of dealing with every aspect of the content
and design of a gallery becomes increasingly remote.
To ensure that design techniques reinforce the artifacts and the educational intent of an exhibit, the
need for collaboration among curator, designer and
educator is obvious.

*Content and
media*

Various media can be used to assist in telling the
story. (These are discussed in some detail in the
chapter, DISPLAY ELEMENTS, p. 139, to follow.) The
extent to which various media systems should be employed
within galleries is a subject of debate. The use of
audio-visual techniques in particular is questioned.
One opinion dismisses the effectiveness of such presentations on two counts: the difficulties and cost of
practical application and the creation of conflicts in
the visitor.

*"[Audio systems] compete with the objects and visitors
are often observed watching the floor tiles rather than
the exhibits they are hearing about. Bad reception is
a factor and the system often doesn't cover all objects,
or if it does, not in a selective manner. The cost of
$25,000 per area is high. Scripts are often bad.
Visitors treat the equipment as a toy, necessitating a
good deal of repair. Dealing with sound as an artifact
means that there can be a conflict between two major
sensory systems ... AV is a sixties fad and is often
overdone with a film in every gallery."*[95]

The opposite view proposes that simultaneous presentations reinforce one another, thus increasing communication with the visitor. José Bernardo, for instance,
maintains that presenting the same information several
times through different channels assists the learning
process. He makes a strong case for the view that the
amount of learning increases when information is made

redundant through correlation, as when it is perceived by the brain through different sensor mechanisms.[96]

The multi-dimensional, multi-faceted approach is often considered a suitable way of "involving" the visitor, through its demands for a total sensory response.[97] Supporting this view, the work of Levonian and others underlines *"the importance of subjective feelings in the learning process."*[98] Their evidence suggests that the intensity of an individual's arousal in a learning experience can be directly correlated with his/her learning. In reviewing this, Bernardo concludes that it is the intensity of arousal that is important and not whether the experience is pleasant or unpleasant.[99]

The extent to which multi-sensory stimuli (including effects produced by movement, tactility, sound effects, music, smells, simulated atmospheric change, lighting) can be used in museum exhibits is not well understood. It is clear, however, that additional study could be highly productive. As George Moore has indicated in his article about displays for the sightless, *"work with the blind is not only deeply gratifying, but it stimulates the development of audio, tactile and olfactory interpretive techniques in areas usually considered only suitable for graphic installations."*[100] It would appear that exhibit communication can be enhanced by creative exploration of means of simultaneously stimulating different senses, rather than by abiding by the usual constraints of visual presentation.

ATMOSPHERE

Content and atmosphere

Although it is perhaps the most intangible of all considerations, the general atmosphere of a gallery is of considerable importance. Most museum visitors are casual and make judgments about galleries intuitively and virtually instantaneously. The view from the corridor will often determine whether or not the visitor will enter. With a series of opportunities competing for his/her attention, the visitor will make choices about whether or not to visit a particular gallery on a very different basis than the curator and others involved in the design of a gallery normally imagine. The entrance to the gallery, the overall atmosphere of a gallery or its ambience, and its immediate impact upon the visitor, are very important factors in

determining whether or not there will be an audience
to educate.

Obviously, atmosphere must reflect the nature of the
collection being presented. The atmosphere suitable
for a butterfly collection will clearly be different
from that suitable for a herd of stuffed elephants. A
variety of elements contribute to the quality of atmosphere created. A lack of correspondence between content and atmosphere will limit the effectiveness of any
exhibit.

A major factor, perhaps even the most important single
factor in establishing an atmosphere, is the quality
of lighting. It is not the amount of lighting which is
important but the quality, the way in which lighting
is used to enhance the artifacts and to set the mood.
A very dark, gallery can create a strong effect, either
dull and depressing (such as in many large old galleries with static dioramas on the periphery), or very
dramatic as when artifacts are strongly featured by
creative spotlighting. On the other hand, bright
evenly-lighted galleries can be either bland and unin-
teresting or bright and cheery.

The use of natural lighting and the provision of outside views within a gallery can be a factor in establishing the general visual character of a gallery.
Although sunlight in itself is considered with some
hostility by conservators (and by some designers),
there are excellent examples of carefully provided
views which are not detrimental to the objects being
displayed. The Director of the British Museum notes
one advantage of such lighting for viewing sculpture:
*"There is sufficient natural lighting to make them look
a little different each time one visits them."*[101]

Another contribution to general atmosphere is the sense
of comfort a visitor experiences in a gallery. The
visitor's physical comfort may be increased by the
provision of rails to lean on, seats to allow leisurely
viewing of important artifacts, carpeting to reduce
noise, denote quiet areas, and permit comfortable
standing, and alcoves to provide a sense of privacy.
It is useful to bear in mind that noise, heat and
crowding (human factors) contribute to fatigue and
discomfort, detracting from what could otherwise be an
attractive atmosphere.[102]

The visual atmosphere of a gallery is also dependent upon good maintenance. In order to ensure that a gallery is always in sparkling condition, there should be a *"method of routinely detecting and immediately correcting minor flaws as they occur."*[103] If a gallery is not cared for (e.g. if burnt out light bulbs are not replaced), the visitor can be disproportionately distracted by those flaws.

Telling the story and gallery design

An approach to telling the story forms the basis for gallery design and development. Careful consideration must be given to the four issues discussed above if a concept is to be developed in which it is expected that the story which is being told is in fact being heard. As noted at the beginning of this chapter, the means of conveying information through exhibits is a complex topic and what has been discussed here provides only preliminary background. More detailed discussion of various topics relevant to telling the story is presented in the following chapters, SPATIAL CONSIDERATIONS, PACING WITHIN A GALLERY, DISPLAY ELEMENTS and LIGHTING.

SPATIAL CONSIDERATIONS

Discussion centres on the factors to be considered in the appropriate definition and use of gallery space. These range from the given architectural context of a space within the museum as a whole to the relationship between gallery space and proposed subject matter. In addition, circulation patterns and problems of crowd flow are explored and illustrated.

The use of space

Once a basic approach to a gallery is defined, then the organization of the material within the gallery becomes a major concern. One of the means of accomplishing this is through the spatial organization.

Spatial considerations, while of great significance, are one of the least well understood areas of gallery design. De Borhegyi provides a useful introduction to the subject through a summary of some of the available knowledge about human reactions to space and behaviour in space. He indicates that *"space and design communicate in very much the same way as does the voice ... Unquestionably, people take cues from the space around them. Space can crowd or over-awe."*[104] However, he points out that *"museum people are not sure whether spacious and formal, or small and intimate, lobby areas are better; whether lowered ceilings are better than high ceilings; or whether long vistas are better than winding exhibit corridors"* (p. 18).

Concepts of space

He refers to various categories of space which have become part of our vocabulary - territorial space, personal space, transactional space, sociopetal and sociofugal space - and notes that *"it is the job of museum exhibit hall planners to create the type of space best suited to their exhibit topic"* (p. 19). However, as he also comments, *"in the museum field ... we do not even know the optimum distance between the visitor and the exhibits"* (p. 21). He emphasizes the imperfections of our current state of knowledge, and stresses the need for a *"thorough understanding of human reaction to space"* (p. 21). He indicates some known cultural differences - Japanese visitors in a museum *"head straight to the center exhibit, while our*

North American visitors follow the walls to the right and exhibit confusion and indecision as to just when or how to approach the center exhibits" (p. 22).

He concludes with an indication of the importance of spatial considerations by pointing out that "*when spatial concepts are confusing, the visitor invariably feels out of place, and his irritation with space may subconsciously be transferred against the museum and/ or its mangement*" (p. 22).

Lehmbruck has stressed the need for considering space as part of an integrated approach to gallery design. In his view:

"*A museum is the very place in which perception and behaviour are almost identical, and this means that the exhibits and the space in which visitors move around must be planned together.*"[105]

Stuart Silver has indicated that in his experience people respond differently to the same material in different spatial environments: "*There is such a thing as calm space, a threatening space, a tense space and a transitory space.*"[106]

The impact of spatial arrangement upon museum visitors is obviously great, and our knowledge is admittedly inadequate to provide specific solutions. However, there is some applicable knowledge which, together with an understanding of the specific opportunities and constraints of an existing space and collection, can result in responsive spatial concepts. The development of a spatial concept will therefore be discussed in terms of a physical context, the demands of subject matter, and circulation requirements.

THE SPATIAL CONTEXT

The given spatial configuration of a gallery

The development of a spatial concept for a gallery must start with some awareness of the constraints and opportunities posed by the particular space which is to be made available for that gallery. The conditioning elements include the relationship to adjacent galleries and the architectural quality of the space.

These elements establish the context in which the spatial organization of the gallery can take place.

Obviously, the extent of variation of such enclosing space is endless, and the specific constraints and opportunities are unique to each gallery.

The surrounding galleries and public spaces condition what can occur within a gallery. These include circulation patterns (where people will generally arrive from and where they are likely to go), and aesthetic factors (the brightness or darkness of the gallery and its general atmosphere). Such factors obviously set some basic ground rules which must be considered even before the individual space allocated to the gallery is explored.

Architectural quality and the use of space

The architectural quality of the building depends, of course, on when it was designed and built, and on whether it was intended to provide *"limitless flexibility and undifferentiated space"*[107] for galleries or to form fixed and specific settings for displays. The extent to which a strong architectural "container" is desirable is a matter of some debate. Peter Kimmel, in his study of twelve art museums and galleries, found that viewers seemed to object to any architecturally prominent feature which distracted attention from the paintings.[108] On the other hand, historical buildings have been effectively and dramatically adapted as museums. An excellent example is the Castello Sforzesco Museum in Milan in which *"the design ... relates the exhibition to the historical building which houses it and which ... [itself] has now considerably influenced subsequent museum design."*[109]

In some instances, particular features - elaborately designed entranceways, clusters of columns, arches and domes - can present specific constraints or opportunities. At the Field Museum the current renovation program carefully respects such historical features, resulting in enhancement of the building as a whole, but in some instances creating constraints within individual galleries.

In the case of the Arts and Industry Building of the Smithsonian Institution in Washington, the hundred year old exhibition building is being restored to its original state as a part of a major Bicentennial project. In that case the building becomes a major part of the exhibit, and not simply a container for it.

The Arts and Industry Building, Smithsonian Institution, built
in 1876 and currently being restored, is an artifact itself, as
well as a container of artifacts.

Form of the
space

Beyond the architectural merit of the space the major constraint is its actual form and nature - the ceiling height, the shape of the gallery, the location of entrances and exits, and the sources of natural light. Older museums frequently have very tall ceilings (over twenty feet). These present a number of design options: they allow designers to maintain the full height to display very large objects, to provide a mezzanine where this is felt to be useful, and to provide lower ceiling heights or special cases for the display of smaller artifacts.

The location of entrances and exits of a building or gallery are fundamental determinants of both spatial and circulation patterns, which the overall design of the gallery must recognize from the beginning. Where the location of these elements is not fixed, greater flexibility is possible, with less constraint on the design. Where they are fixed, the implications of their location should be understood (see CIRCULATION, p. 111).

The configuration of a gallery plan sometimes forms natural spatial subdivisions. Where appropriate, these can become part of the spatial organization of an exhibit. According to Lehmbruck, basic shapes are important because various plan forms elicit different responses from the viewer. His work indicates that round or square plan forms are more restful than oval or rectangular ones; and that converging lines or variations in level imply movement, while parallel lines or flat planes suggest repose.[110] In some cases, the opportunities for creating various plan forms are limited by the nature of the enclosure. In other instances, where the enclosure is less definitive, the spaces may be designed to utilize spatial effects.

Some galleries will have opportunities for natural light, while others will not. This can have implications both for lighting effects (see LIGHTING, p. 148) and for spatial effects, sometimes allowing long distance views in contrast to the more limited ones within a gallery.

SPACE AND SUBJECT MATTER

The Fit between Space and Objects: One of the first

*Relationship of
the artifact to
space*

considerations in the spatial organization of a gallery
is the appropriateness of the space or set of spaces
for the subject matter being presented. The relationship between the objects and the space around them is
of particular consequence. Lehmbruck states:

*"Every object needs space if its qualities are to be
brought out. Every visible form projects itself beyond its limits and to a certain extent invests the
'empty' surrounding area with its presence ... Since
the spatial characteristics of the environment determine the shape and the position of the visible object,
space must be organized in a way which is in harmony
with them."* [111]

He suggests that a major design consideration within a
museum is the creation of clearly defined spaces, which
are easily perceived by the visitor. *"As long as the
space is not easily perceptible, the visitor will continue to search, albeit unconsciously. The resulting
uneasiness renders contact with the object more difficult"* (p. 192).

The specifics of how spaces should be arranged to
ensure a fit between object and space is clearly complex. One of the most obvious relationships is that
of scale. In simple terms, small objects and large
objects can look awkward if constrained by available
space. A good illustration of an effective spatial
arrangement is found at the British Museum where long,
high-ceilinged halls housing the magnificent Greek and
Roman collections have mezzanines inserted within them,
creating small-scale areas for the presentation of
small objects. This contrasts effectively with the
large objects in high-ceilinged portions of the rooms.
As a result, the viewer can be at ease in both kinds of
spaces, viewing two scales of objects.

An illustration of a different type of space-object
relationship is the recreation of historical settings
for collections of objects. Period rooms, for example,
can harmoniously combine the decorative artifacts of a
particular age in their appropriate spatial setting,
allowing the visitor to perceive the relationships
between the internal spaces of an era and its furnish-
ings.

Some objects, because of their intrinsic qualities,
demand adequate space, or tensions will be communicated

to the viewer. The space surrounding an object is
further complicated because an object in a case relates to the scale of the case as well as to that of
the surrounding area. The art of spatial fit is based
upon the creative use of both sets of spatial relationships. A small but important artifact carefully placed
in a small case can be made to look grand by the shape
of the surrounding space.

*Spatial
arrangement and
telling the
story*

Space and Story-line: Where a story-line is employed,
spatial organization should obviously be used to reinforce it. In simple terms, the spatial subdivisions
should relate to the subdivision of subject matter.
The degree to which subdivision should be directive
or random is constrained by the extent to which the
story-line is sequential. In the view of Hans
Zetterberg, a sequential layout is necessary since
*"education is not achieved by random exposures, but in
a planned sequence."*[112] However, he also suggests that
no sequence should be so rigid as to be inescapable;
spatial arrangements should allow for choices amongst
viewers - choices which can be based upon varying degrees of interest and involvement in the subject
matter. Shettel's study maintains that exhibits which
place content in a rational sequence will be better
instructional devices than those that do not.[113]

On the other hand, a number of studies indicate that
lineal sequencing does not necessarily make a difference to the effectiveness of the exhibit.[114] In effect,
there is evidence that both approaches are valid.
However, in reacting against the traditional unstruc-
tured presentation of artifacts and in responding to
the opportunity for thematic cohesion, there has been
a temptation to create rigid sequences which are not
necessarily suitable for accommodating the variations
of interest amongst visitors.

One useful reminder by Hal Glicksman is that one should
not forget the end of the exhibit.[115] Care should be
taken to avoid the exhibit merely fading away; some
spatial emphasis should be given to lend a sense of
clarity to the end. This is particularly important as
the visitor's natural tendency is to move more quickly
through the latter part of an exhibit.

*Spatial cues
and direction*

Space and Comprehensibility: The spatial organization
of a gallery should be evident without strain to the

viewer. The visitor should be able to move along the
gallery easily, making logical decisions as to where
he should go. Albert Parr emphasizes the usefulness
of spatial "cues" in assisting the visitor to find his
way. He points out the disadvantages of the traditional grid system of displaying artifacts in a series of
neatly lined up cases:

*"... it does not take much knowledge of psychology to
realize the tiring effect of having to make an endless
series of choices that are without real relevance to
the main purpose or motivation. And the less there is
to choose between at each decision point, the greater
the strain of deciding."*[116]

He indicates that one of the main sources of museum
fatigue is *"our failure to provide adequate spatial
cues for the guidance of our visitors, and the conse-
quent creation of meaningless decision points"* (p. 138).

The same point is made by Hannelore Kischkewitz, who
proposes the creation of a focal point or a series of
focal points to enable the visitor to move through a
gallery easily and with absolute confidence.[117] This
was noted in reference to a gallery which consisted of
a series of rooms. A series of focal points set the
theme for each room within the gallery, and, at the
same time, provided a source of unity for the entire
gallery. A strong element near the entrance can serve
both as a cue and as an orientation device. In suggesting the need for a clear and comprehensible direction through a gallery, Parr indicates that this
does not mean *"that we cannot expose our guest to
unexpected sights and temptations en route"* (p. 138),
but suggests simply that a comprehensible arrangement
of space is less likely to produce irritation and
fatigue in the visitor.

*Subdivision of
space*

Subdivision of Space: Whatever form or sequence an
exhibit takes, there seems to be almost uniform agree-
ment that the subdivision of space is both desirable
and useful. There is some evidence that the scale of
a gallery may attract or repel a visitor: in one study,
a glance from the entranceway revealing a vast space
was found to be a deterrent to entry.[118]

Many advantages can accrue from the subdivision of a
large gallery into small areas, including the creation
of small cul-de-sacs. Small-scale areas create

manageable perceptual environments, reduce movement, and isolate the visitors from remote distractions.[119] In addition, a gallery concept which includes spatial subdivisions can *"make the audience encounter a variety of spaces, which in themselves, are conducive to sharpened awareness."*[120]

Arminta Neal comments on the spatial arrangement of display cases, suggesting that the visitor finds it less exhausting if cases are arranged not in tidy rows but in gently curved lines to take advantage of traffic flows, or are arranged so as to form alcoves to show different divisions within the subject area.[121] In another article which argues for such a spatial organization, the point is made that the division of space created by a grouping of artifacts or a subdivision of theme should, where possible, be directly related to the natural physical spaces created within the available space (e.g. between a corner and a door).[122]

In practice, all of the preceding spatial considerations, as well as whatever practical constraints are involved, obviously form part of the decision about how space should be subdivided.

CIRCULATION

Spatial arrangement and circulation

The other major determinant of spatial arrangement is the circulation pattern, which includes determining the best routes through a space or series of spaces, and recognizing appropriate resting places. Movement patterns should include both primary and supplementary or secondary ones, and should make provision for quiet areas for more lengthy contemplation or detailed examination of artifacts, or simply for sitting and relaxing.

Circulation considerations

A series of basic principles which can be useful in evolving circulation systems are described below:

Entrance: As noted earlier in the chapter on EDUCATION AND LEARNING, it is useful to provide orientation information at the entrance to a gallery to inform the visitor about what is there (so that a decision can be made as to whether to enter or not) and to help the visitor to find his/her way around.

Need for Clarity: An overriding requirement in the development of a circulation system is the need for clarity. Maze-like circulation has the potential for creating confusion and irritation. This is an important reminder in evolving gallery layout, as there has been an increasing tendency to create complex movement patterns in order to take visitors through a highly directive sequential pattern.

Exit Gradient: There is a general tendency for visitors to move through a gallery slowly at first and then gradually more quickly; when the exit sign comes into view they tend to move even more quickly directly towards the sign and out.

Decision Points: It is important to assist the visitor wherever a circulation system presents a number of alternatives within a gallery. At these decision points orientation information should be available to enable the visitor to decide whether to turn to the left or right or whether to go ahead.

Movement to the Right: There is a general tendency for North American visitors to move to the right upon entering a gallery. The typical pattern is described by de Borhegyi: "... *museum visitors almost invariably turn to the right when entering an exhibition hall. They follow the exhibit cases along the wall moving from right to left, reading the labels in each display from left to right.*"[123] This can cause disruption in the traffic flow and confusion in the sequence of didactic material. However the pattern is not uniform and is becoming less dominant as a larger proportion of North Americans are now permitted to be left-handed.

Tendency to Stay at Perimeter: There is a tendency for museum visitors to circulate around the periphery of a gallery. In large galleries, visitors will tend to stay at the periphery of the gallery unless attractions are provided in the centre to attract them. This again is not uniformly the case; Japanese visitors in particular tend to head to the centre exhibit.[124]

Rate of Flow: Another aspect of the pattern of movement within a gallery is the rate of traffic flow. Some useful guidelines concerning the relationship of display presentation and traffic flow are noted by

Stephan de Borhegyi:

"... *areas of constant crowd flow* should have terse, repetitive exhibits that can be quickly understood by the viewers. Such displays are most useful when they include limited introductory material desirable for all visitors.

"*Areas of crowd stoppage,* in addition to displays of a general nature, should have a few exhibits of a conceptual nature which can be absorbed and enjoyed unhurriedly while the visitor waits his turn to move on. Both types of exhibits need to be geared to the educational level of a general audience.

"*Areas of variable crowd flow* should allow the visitor to choose among simple and complex exhibits. Displays here need a single, easily read sentence covering the over-all theme of the display, a lead paragraph or image which communicates the main idea, intermixed with more complex exhibits with longer statements which can be studied at leisure by the more interested visitors."[125]

These are illustrated in his design for the "Hall of Life and Earth Processes" at the Milwaukee Public Museum.

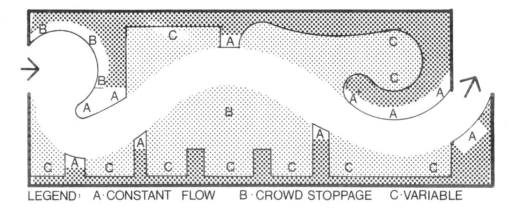

LEGEND: A·CONSTANT FLOW   B·CROWD STOPPAGE   C·VARIABLE

Ease of Movement: Some general circulation guidelines for the blind have been established through experiments in the city of Victoria, B.C., Canada.[126] Such guidelines should be applied more generally, as they also apply to the handicapped and the elderly, as well as providing insight into circulation for galleries in general. The criteria include the following:

+ Changes in elevation should be by means of ramps.

+ Adequate space should be allowed for wheelchairs, including adequate turning radii.

+ Changes in direction generally should not be abrupt.

+ Variations in floor textures are useful to denote changes in division of subject content.

Levels of Interest: Although not necessarily applicable to all galleries, one basis for the organization of circulation is a path system which enables visitors whose interests vary in range and intensity to follow somewhat different paths through a gallery.[127] The most casual visitor would take the quickest route, and the more interested visitor could take a more comprehensive route. The following diagram illustrates a series of paths for varying interests.

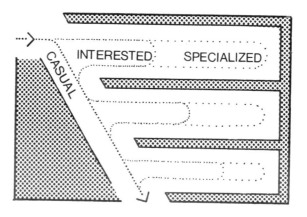

Circulation in relation to a specific gallery

These general principles should be considered in relation to those factors unique to each gallery. These include the following:

+ the shape of the gallery space

+ the locations of entrances and exits

+ the degree of direction or random browsing which is intended.

There are no ideal solutions nor any typical arrangements which can be selected and applied to a gallery. However some examples of circulation patterns and applications of some of the principles just outlined will help to illustrate these issues more clearly.

Illustrative
circulation
patterns

A useful typology of circulation patterns has been evolved by Lehmbruck.[128] He suggests five basic patterns: arterial, comb, chain, star (or fan), and block. Although these are somewhat abstract versions of circulation patterns, they do illustrate some of the organizational considerations.

Arterial: This refers to a circulation pattern in which the main path is continuous and no options exist for the visitor; the path can be straight, curving, or virtually any shape. This type of pattern can be used where the presentation of material is dependent upon a fixed sequence. The major limitation is the rigidity which confronts the visitor.

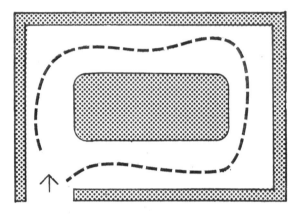

Comb: This refers to a circulation pattern in which there is a main circulation path and optional alcoves which a visitor may enter or by-pass.

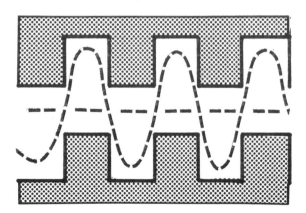

Chain: This refers to a circulation pattern in which
the main path is generally continuous (as in arterials)
but the path leads to a series of self-contained units
which may have a more varied path within them.

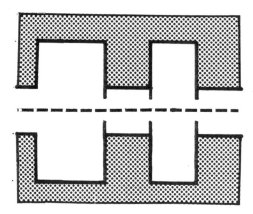

Star or Fan: This refers to a circulation pattern which
presents a series of alternatives to a visitor from a
central area.

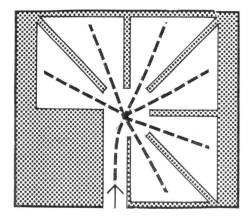

Block: This refers to a circulation system which is
relatively unconstrained and can be as random or as
self-directive as desired by the visitor.

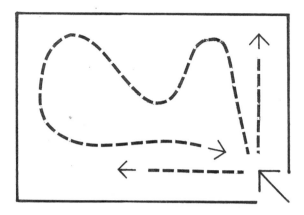

These circulation patterns give some indication of the
possible variety. When they are connected with the
principles previously described, some useful points
became apparent. Some examples of the application of
these principles are illustrated below.

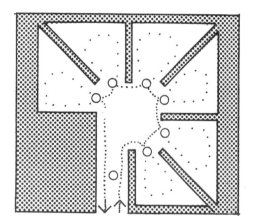

This is an example of a circulation system in which
every decision point is provided with orientation
information which enables the visitor to select a path
through a gallery easily.[129] Orientation information
can also be provided at the entry and summary information at the end.

The following examples illustrate the application to
door placements of the right turn tendency and the
exit gradient phenomenon. (These are based on the work
of Coleman.)[130]

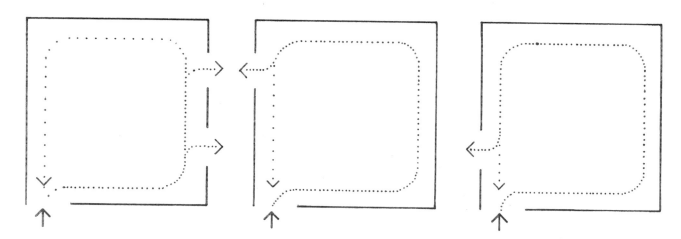

The placement of doors in an axial relationship can result in visitors moving straight through one side of an exhibit as in the following illustration:

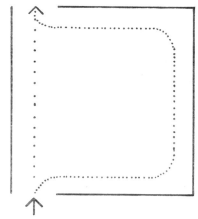

An application of one of the principles previously outlined is demonstrated by a gallery design at the Milwaukee Public Museum, incorporating a deflector to counteract the tendency to move to the right. This tendency *"results in a slow and disrupted traffic flow and the visitors' information retention factor is at a minimum. This problem can be solved by routing the viewers to the left with the aid of a 'deflector' exhibit at the entrance to the hall. Visitors will now move from left to right and read the labels in each display case in the preferred order."*[131]

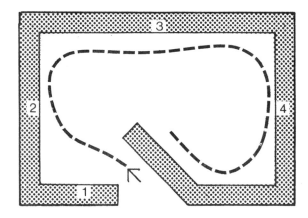

The overall spatial organization of a gallery should
consider all of the three major foregoing considerations: the existing spatial context, the use of that
space in a way which will support and enhance the
presentation of subject matter, and the effect that
circulation paths have on how the visitor moves
through the space and comprehends what is presented.
The chapter which follows - PACING - will provide some
insights into how the visitor reacts to various uses
of space.

PACING WITHIN A GALLERY

The concept of pacing as defined at the scale of the museum is discussed here in terms of its application to the design of a gallery. Methods of arranging the elements in a gallery so as to maintain the visitor's interest and at the same time avoid over-stimulation and fatigue are outlined, together with a series of illustrations of some of these methods in a specific gallery.

Pacing and arrangement of elements within a gallery

The concept of pacing has already been discussed at the scale of the museum (see Section I-A, p. 37), and the present discussion applies the implications of that concept to the development of an individual gallery. An awareness of some of the elements which can assist the visitor to pace his/her visit to a gallery will provide some guidelines for the development of a more satisfying gallery.

Pacing can be a major determinant of the visitor's ability to assimilate and absorb knowledge, and to experience pleasure and excitement. A visitor wandering through a gallery is confronted with a vast array of artifacts, design elements such as textual information, and perhaps audio-visual presentations. The way in which the artifacts are presented (e.g. the spatial contexts, the atmosphere created by the lighting, the use of colour, the sequence, and the circulation patterns) can stimulate, overwhelm, or bore the visitor.

Pacing and choice

Pacing cannot be isolated as an independent technique; it is rather the coordination of basic design principles in order to maintain interest and attention without causing fatigue. This involves providing for sufficient, but not excessive, stimulation for the visitor, providing visual focuses and contrasting areas of visual rest, providing coherence through spatial fit, and presenting a sense of continuity through an organized array of sensations. In this way, choices can be made which reflect individual interests.

It is extremely important that the visitor be able to "self-pace" (in the same manner as the learning approach previously described enables the visitor to learn on his/her own). A gallery arrangement must allow the visitor to select what he/she wishes to see, concentrate on, or ignore. The opportunity to be selective is important, whether a highly directive or more random approach is taken to spatial organization. A museum visitor, no matter how devoted, is unlikely to examine all the artifacts presented and is unlikely to examine them in a predetermined sequence. The organization of a gallery should reflect this fact.

Pacing is complicated by the fact that the visitor is affected not only by the design of the gallery, but by the design of adjacent galleries, by the number of visitors in the gallery, by his/her companions, by the time available for the gallery and by the number of galleries visited previously. However, accepting all these variables, there is still enough available knowledge and experience to apply some basic principles to the design of galleries. A discussion of some useful pacing considerations follows.

DIVERSITY

Pacing and diversity in presentation

Perhaps the easiest pacing technique is the use of variety in presentation to maintain interest. Of course, the extent of such variety depends upon the nature of the collection being presented. Some collections, like those in the new Islamic Gallery at the Metropolitan Museum of Art (see illustrations later in this chapter), are varied in themselves and are admirably suited to a varied presentation format. Diversity is obviously more difficult to achieve in other collections, such as coins, or large collections of similar vases.

ITEMS OF MAJOR INTEREST

Pacing and placement of items of major interest

The placement of items of major interest within a gallery can also be used to heighten the visitor's interest. Points of interest can act as focuses within a space, or serve as attractions to an adjacent space. This is not to suggest that major items should be uniformly distributed through a gallery, but rather that careful consideration must be given to their

placement. Some of the important considerations are
as follows:

+   The spacing of elements of major interest within an
    exhibit (gallery) should be in balance with the
    remaining or supportive elements, so that the visi-
    tor is always making a new discovery as he passes
    through the exhibit. An excellent example of the
    application of this principle is the Japanese gar-
    dens at Shugaku-in and Katsura Villa, planned so
    that each turn of the path reveals a surprise - a
    vista beyond the trees, a waterfall, reflecting pond,
    or stone lantern.[132] The Islamic Gallery, illus-
    trated later in this chapter, uses this principle
    effectively.

+   The most important piece does not have to be the
    last piece seen. In fact, it is usually an advan-
    tage that it not be, as the visitor can then com-
    pare lesser things with the "great object" just seen.

+   In selecting locations for items of major interest
    it is useful to keep in mind where the visitor's
    attention is likely to focus. In his pioneering
    study, Melton discovered that in a traditional gal-
    lery, visitor attention tends to be highest near
    the entrance and lowest at the exit.[133] Lakota has
    confirmed that maximum visitor interest is at the
    entrance and that *"the shortest route through the
    exhibit from the entrance to exit is also the area
    of greatest visitor attention."*[134]

+   As a result of their inherent attraction, items of
    major interest can easily serve as landmarks, focal
    points, or orientation devices.

 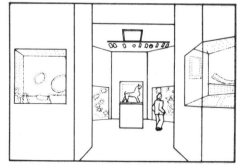

+   Items of major interest can be emphasized through the provision of surrounding "white space". Setting an object in isolation against an uncluttered background in this way, tends to focus attention on the object, especially when its arrangement contrasts with a more visually complex array of artifacts.

+   The arrangements of the major items within an exhibit can affect overall traffic flow (speed, ease of movement, etc.). Major highlights should be spaced adequately to avoid bottlenecks.

DENSITY

Pacing and density of artifacts

Galleries in museums traditionally consisted of large numbers of similar cases, densely packed with artifacts. Following the recognition of design considerations as an important aspect in the display of artifacts, there has tended to be greater novelty in the specifics of artifact display (e.g. variety in case design, creation of habitats and other contextual settings). There has also been a general trend to "thin out" display cases in order to enable each artifact to be more effectively displayed, and to avoid visual clutter. Even the most casual examination of some of the older galleries will confirm the need for more artfulness and less density in artifact display. However, as many observers have pointed out, the tendency to sparseness in artifact display can be at variance with the desires of the visitor. Parsons' study, for instance, concluded that the audience responded better to well-filled exhibits.[135] He suggests that density of artifacts and artfulness of display need <u>not</u> be at variance:

"... a well-designed exhibit may, if desired, display a large number of specimens ... One possible design technique is to balance large clusters of objects with sufficient areas of 'negative' background space. A visually complex exhibit which is well designed can subtly guide the viewer to inevitable associations and conclusions. But it can also allow the viewer to make additional deductions on his own initiative, since a variety of specimens are available for his perusal and comparison."

The desirability of complexity should not however be overstated. Melton's early work confirmed that the number of objects in a gallery affects the visitor's interest in any one particular object. His research suggests that an increase in density can significantly reduce the interest in each individual item.[136] Obviously, some balance must be established between a design preference for sparseness, a desire for complexity and self-selection on the part of the visitor, and the possibility of visual satiation by an over-abundance of artifacts.

SPACING

Pacing and variation in spatial arrangement of artifacts

Variation in the spacing of artifacts is another technique which can be used to help maintain the visitor's interest. This involves arrangement of artifacts to create some spatial diversity independent of the number or density of artifacts used.

The neutral background - white space - provided for the column capitals gives them visual prominence, Metropolitan Museum of Art.

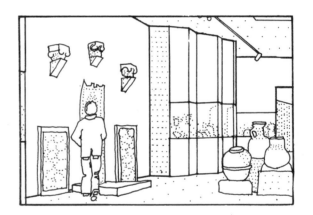

One particularly effective means of varying density is the use of "white space" as mentioned earlier. This can help create spatial variations within any display, with great variations in the spacing of some items with respect to the others. It is especially useful in giving emphasis to a work which is not visually strong, but which is germinal or pivotal to the presentation of an idea.[137]

SCALE

Changes in scale can focus the viewer's interest. Such

Pacing and variations in scale

changes can take place in the context in which objects are set or among the objects themselves. A commonly used device in galleries is change in ceiling heights. In the case of objects, the close juxtaposition of a small piece and a much larger piece can emphasize the boldness of the latter and the delicacy of the former.

A GOOD EXAMPLE OF PACING

Pacing in the Isalmic Gallery, Metropolitan Museum of Art

The best way to describe how these and other techniques can be effectively combined within a gallery is through an illustration. The following description and series of illustrations are of the recently opened Islamic Gallery at the Metropolitan Museum of Art in New York.

The Islamic Gallery consists of a series of rooms housing a superb collection of artifacts ranging from tiny glass vases through pottery, illuminated manuscripts, column capitals and urns, to huge tapestries and rugs and an entire recreated room. The varied nature of the collection and the visual qualities of the individual artifacts would alone make for an interesting gallery. However the quality of presentation makes a visit to this gallery an even richer experience. It is an excellent example of pacing and is used here to illustrate that concept. It is also remarkable for its creative lighting and display case design, which contribute immeasurably to the mood and pace of the gallery.

The accompanying sketches illustrates a sequence of views throughout the gallery. As one enters the exhibit, an elegantly displayed bowl forms a focus in the centre of the moderately lighted room. There are two rooms off this entry, one housing some artifacts from excavations in Nisapur, the other an entire room originally built in Damascus in 1707, and reconstructed as it would have been at that time.

From the moment one enters the gallery one is captivated by the quality of the artifacts and the elegance of the presentation. The contrast of the brilliantly lighted bowl at the entry and the dark rich room on the left begins to illustrate the variety of experiences with which the visitor will be presented.

As one moves through the gallery, there are long low rooms, brightly lighted, high-ceilinged rooms, strongly

n - a large,
cated on
is. The

... provides a directional cue
to the right. The visitor
enters ...

... a more brightly lit
gallery containing miniature
paintings which can be
examined comfortably and at
the visitors' leisure. The
next room ...

... is darker and has a
lowered ceiling. A raised
walkway permits viewing of a
fine rug. The visitor is
drawn naturally ...

ROOM 4A   VIEW G   ROOM 4A   VIEW H   ROOM 4B   VIEW I   ROOM 5

ROOM 9   VIEW P   ROOM 9   VIEW Q   ROOM 9   VIEW R   ROOM 10

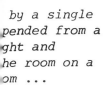

by a single
pended from a
ght and
he room on a
om ...

... also contains a wide
variety of artifacts -
textiles, jewellery - visually
unified through consistent
use of materials and display
techniques. Small
artifacts ...

... are kept in scale with
the gallery by integrating
the display cases with the
walls. Gallery 10 can be
seen ...

... either on entering or
leaving the galleries. It is
a complete reconstruction of
a Syrian room, rich in
detail, and is one of the
highlights of the exhibition.

GALLERY PLAN

1	INTRODUCTORY GALLERY	5	AYYUB AND MAMLUK PERIODS IN EGYPT AND SYRIA AND THE NASARID PERIOD IN SPAIN
2	NISHAPUR EXCAVATIONS		
3	THE EARLY CENTURIES		
4a	SELJUQ AND MONGOL PERIODS IN IRAN AND TURKEY	6	TIMURID PERIOD IN IRAN SAFAVID PERIOD IN IRAN
4b	SELJUQ AND MONGOL PERIODS IN IRAN AND TURKEY	7	TIMURID PERIOD IN IRAN SAFAVID AND POST-SAFAVID PERIOD IN IRAN
4c	THE ART OF THE MOSQUE	8	OTTOMAN PERIOD IN TURKEY
		9	MUGHAL PERIOD IN INDIA
		10	THE NUR-AD DIN ROOM OF 1707 FROM DAMASCUS

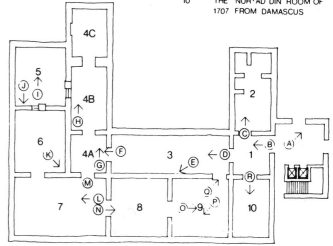

Orientation information is provided at the entrance/exit to the galleries. As the visitor enters the first gallery ...

... a central display, containing a brightly lit bowl, provides a focus. To the right, ...

... a softly lighted room contains many small artifacts displayed simply and without clutter. From the entrance to the third gallery, ...

... an axial view is provided which is framed by continuous and parallel rows of elegant soaring cases. The shape and arrangement of these cases also provide convenient viewing alcoves. On entering this gallery, ...

... a group of urns, centrally located, provide the first focus for the visitor. To the left of the urns, several wall mounted and brightly lit column capitals add to the drama of the gallery. At the far end of this room the visitor reaches ...

... a destinatio[n]
ceramic horse l[eads]
the galleries a[nd]
horse ...

VIEW A

VIEW B   ROOM 1

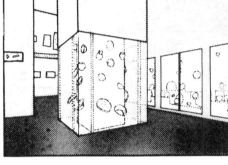

VIEW C   ROOM 2

VIEW D   ROOM 3

VIEW E   ROOM 3

VIEW F

VIEW J   ROOM 5   VIEW K   ROOM 6   VIEW L   ROOM 7   VIEW M   ROOM 4A   VIEW N   ROOM 8   VIEW O

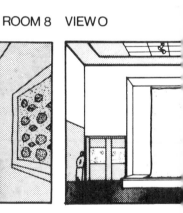

... towards the brightness of the adjacent room. This room ...

... contains pleasant alcoves where the visitor can peruse miniature paintings of the Timurid period. A high ...

... sky-lit room follows. Large carpets displayed on floor to ceiling high panels contrast with the many small artifacts displayed in ceiling height cases. A side glance ...

... brings to view the now familiar ceramic horse. Moving through to the next room, ...

... a series of smaller rugs and artifacts are located around a central display case. Gallery 9, ...

... is dominate[d]
large carpet su[spended]
considerable he[ight]
extending into [the]
plinth. This r[oom]

highlighted (spotlighted) rooms, small alcoves within which one can sit and examine manuscripts, and
large high open rooms with skylights, in which to
view huge rugs. A sculptured horse which may be seen
from several points acts as an orientation device,
turning one at a critical point and upon return, re-
minding one of where one is. There is also a large
dark room with soft spotlights on a recreated ceiling,
part of a porch, and a large rug set in a dropped
floor. The contrasts are deliberate and carefully
designed to maintain interest in the artifacts.

One comes away from a visit having absorbed a great
deal without feeling fatigued or confused, in spite of
having been exposed to a large and varied collection.
Careful examination of the following sketches will
reveal the care and subtlety of the design, but it is
impossible to portray the total impact of this un-
qualifiedly superb gallery.

DISPLAY ELEMENTS

Various aspects of the elements which are used to display arti-
facts and present information in a gallery are discussed.
These elements include cases, walls, text panels, audio-visual
techniques, dioramas, models, reproductions and photographic
material. In addition, some guidelines are provided for ef-
fective design and use of these display elements.

Once the concept for the gallery has been established,
the story-line developed, and the general spatial arrangement determined, the actual process of displaying
artifacts with supporting information involves countless individual decisions. These decisions are commonly
made by museum exhibit designers, based on intuition
and their own often considerable experience in selecting the most appropriate means of displaying a specific
artifact. There is no set of rules which can replace
this experience; however, there is considerable information which can be of assistance to those making such
decisions. This chapter is a presentation of some
relevant observations on several of the common display
elements used within galleries.

The elements which relate directly to the display of
artifacts are discussed below as a series of discrete
items, although obviously they must be considered
simultaneously and orchestrated in an integrated
fashion:

+ cases and walls

+ text panels and labels

+ audio-visual techniques

+ supportive illustrative material.

CASES AND WALLS

Cases and walls are two of the major elements used to
display artifacts. Their design and arrangement is
critical because visually they are related directly to
the objects. They also establish the conditions under

which the viewer sees an object. If a case is inappropriate for an object or if a case is too high or too low for the comfort of the visitor, the object is not being displayed to its best advantage.

Human factors and perception

Knowledge of how the visitor is likely to view displays can be of assistance in ensuring that cases and walls are used effectively.* Available research which is particularly applicable to the design of cases and display of artifacts follows.

An article of Arminta Neal makes two simple but important observations:

+ *"Studies have shown ... the adult museum visitor observes an area only a little over one foot above his own eye level to three feet below it at an average viewing distance of 24 to 28 inches."*[138] These are useful dimensions to consider in designing cases and placing objects. The placement of objects too high or too low makes them less visible and more easily overlooked. (See illustration, p. 127.)

+ One means of reducing the possibility of eye fatigue is to arrange objects in more than a single plane so that the eye must adjust focal depth in viewing the artifacts, rather than maintain a consistent focal depth.[139]

Frank Dandridge has made the following comments on eye movements, based on research at the Visual Research Laboratory of Drake University and the work of Paterson, Tinker and Meldrum.[139]

+ *"The eye tends to move over an observed area in jumps and stops which are termed 'fixations and excursions' ... the majority of persons tested made the first fixation for all media at a point above and to the left of the centre of the observed field. The design or art layout that utilizes this information for placing the starting point at this position will have an advantage as the eye will not be distracted at the beginning of the survey."* (p. 333)

+ *"The periphery of the field of vision is more sensitive to light tones; therefore it is good practice to keep the light tones at the points of interest. Dark and middle tones kept towards the edges of the area help to block any wandering movement of the eye*

---

*The design of all elements, including cases and walls, should be based upon knowledge of human factors. Appendix F includes some checklists and a bibliography to assist in this area.

SOME BASIC HUMAN FACTORS WITH RESPECT TO VIEWING
(This is based on information presented by Arminta Neal in
"Gallery and Case Exhibit Design.")

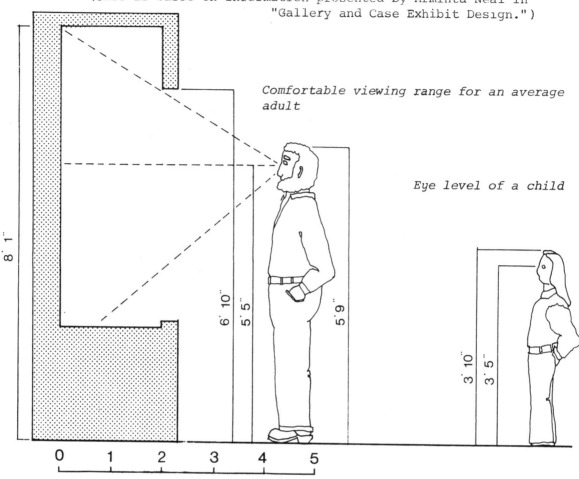

Comfortable viewing range for an average adult

Eye level of a child

The cone of vision below illustrates that the angle of view is greater in a downward direction than in other directions.

Objects placed too high or too low can create unnecessary strain.

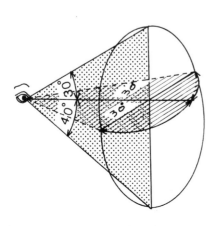

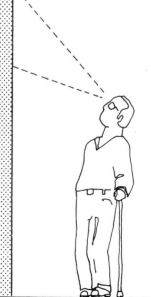

*that tends to move off the exhibit and keeps the
eye centered on the subject matter."* (p. 334)

+ One means of obtaining a sense of unity in a display that consists of a series of separate illustrations is to provide a border which is darker
than the background.

+ *"Tests [on typed matter] showed that lower case
type was read almost twelve per cent faster than
material set in all capitals, and that tested reader
opinion was nine to one in favour of lower case
lettering.*

   *"Attention should be paid to type setting, as dis-
turbances of badly set lines of type can cause word
space eye paths, like rivers of white, that distract
the eye and mind away from the words being read."*
(p. 334)

+ The speed of eye movements can be affected by using
harmonious tones where slow movement is desired and
by using tonal contrast where faster movement is
preferred.

+ When a dark tone is placed adjacent to a light tone,
the eye will move rapidly in the direction of the
light tone.

+ *"A design which has various 'motifs', color patches
and components incorrectly placed and not chromat-
ically in balance, will cause the eye to fluctuate
back and forth"* (p. 335), leading to irritation and
loss of attention on the part of the viewer.

*Cases and
display*

Cases: Most museum objects are displayed in cases,
which therefore must be carefully designed not only to
enhance the objects they contain, but also to ensure
that they themselves are not too great a psychological
and physical barrier between the object and the visitor. One article on cases presents a useful general
classification - tables, upright cases with panels and
drawers, and cases with built-in storage space - and
presents a variety of observations about cases, some
of which are summarized below:[140]

+ With respect to the aesthetic function of cases,
Rivière and Visser note that *"the main function
of the showcase is to set off its contents to the
best adgantage"* (p.7). They recommend a variety
of methods for accomplishing this:

carefully designed glass supports will help to
avoid obstructing the visitor's view; colour should
be used with restraint; careful lighting, including
lighting from a distance and the combining of
fluorescent and incandescent sources, can be helpful.

+ They describe the utilitarian uses of cases as the
protection of the artifacts from dust, insects,
climate, light, theft and carelessness.

+ They note the need for ease of access to service a
case; for case designs which permit flexibility in
arrangements; for designs which permit the movement
of cases when necessary; and for cases which can be
easily maintained.

+ They also describe the need for cases to be designed
with the comfort of the visitor in mind and suggest
that *"well-planned showcases can help to reduce
museum fatigue, especially if they assure the visitor of what may be called ease of vision and physical comfort"* (p. 3). With regard to ease of vision
they refer to angles of vision, the height of artifacts and the relation of artifacts to the rear of
the case. The other important visual consideration
noted is the need to reduce reflections. Two methods are suggested: the careful location of lighting,
and the angling of the glass.

The following are some additional comments on the
design of cases and the arrangement of elements within
them.

+ Cases can be used to *"mediate in scale between the
object and the gallery."*[141] This is perhaps one of
the most critical functions of cases, and it requires great sensitivity to ensure that this relationship is maintained.

+ Arrangement and design of cases can be used to reinforce a theme or to provide visual cohesion. For
example, a continuous display case winding through a
gallery can provide a sense of continuity for a set
of artifacts.

+ With respect to the arrangement of artifacts within
a display case, each *"case should have one area (an
object or small group of objects) as a focal
point."*[142] From this can flow a logical progression
towards other elements in the case.

+ It has been suggested that visual complexity (abundant but organized) can be comprehended, and, to some extent, is even desired by visitors. However, some variation in the amount of complexity in different cases is preferable.

+ Carefully selected textiles can be useful to provide interesting backgrounds. Textiles of natural fibres assist in maintaining a consistent relative humidity within cases.143

+ In reference to an exhibition of Islamic Art at the Metropolitan Museum of Art (see PACING WITHIN A GALLERY, p. 120), the chief designer noted that he had made a particular effort in this gallery to treat the cases as part of the gallery, as an extension of the walls, rather than as pieces of furniture.144 The effect of this treatment, in which cases frequently soared almost to the ceiling, was remarkable. The overall result was elegant, with the cases being completely subordinate to the artifacts on display.

Display cases are incorporated into the walls of the gallery, Metropolitan Museum of Art.

Walls and display

Walls: Walls traditionally have been considered as an enclosing boundary, perhaps used occasionally as a place to mount an object. Walls are now used both to create spatial subdivisions and to act as major display areas. The following comments concern walls as display elements:

+ One function of a wall can be to assist in the provision of "white space." This use of blank areas enables other sectors of a gallery to be in contrast, more densely displayed. Such space can help to keep order in the story-line and provide a resting spot for the visitor's mind.145

+ One specific example of the use of walls as a display element, incorporating the concept of "white space", has been described by Shirley Hartman. In the case, curved screen walls erected within a gallery produced a continuous display surface. *"Each display unit or wall opening is selectively ... placed on the curved facade at the most desirable viewing height for the object within."*[146] This resulted in an interesting wall treatment in which the amount of reflecting glass area was reduced and the restful wall surface area increased.

+ In using walls for display elements, care should be taken not to detract from an artifact by placing it too close to distracting elements such as light switches, grilles, etc. Walls, whether an enclosing envelope or screens added for the purpose of spatial subdivision, form by their presence a major display element and therefore an opportunity which deserves as much conscious attention as any other display element.

+ According to one study, the texture of walls should be related to and can have an effect upon the enclosing space.[147] It was found that a stronger texture appears to make the space seem smaller. This same study found that viewers preferred neutral colours (i.e. tan, grey, beige). Highly textured backgrounds were not satisfactory as backgrounds for paintings and drawings, although with larger paintings, more texture was considered acceptable.

TEXT PANELS AND LABELS

There are two aspects to the conception and design of text panels and labels - the content and the graphic arrangement of information. A set of guidelines for graphic presentation is included in Appendix E. This discussion focuses on some of the issues of communicating to the visitor through text panels and labels.

The role of labels in displays

Labels are one of the most debated issues in museum literature; whether or not labels belong in an exhibit at all is a frequently raised question. On the basis of aesthetic judgments, exhibits with minimal labelling or no labelling have been designed; *"for instance at Trier, whole cases of objects are tastefully arranged but without a single label."*[148] Duncan Cameron argues that *"effective communication between exhibitor and visitor remains dependent on the ability of the visitor to understand the nonverbal language of 'real things',"* implying that language is inherent in museum objects themselves.[149] Another view maintains that printed material plays an indispensable part in the satisfaction of a visitor's cognitive or intellectual curiosity, so that *"learning the language of museums ... is ... learning to see real things, museum things ... in the varied cognitive frameworks of scientific and historical knowledge."*[150]

However, there appears to be a general consensus that objects (and other nonverbal visual aspects of a gallery setting) can communicate with the visitor on the affective level, and to some degree, on the intellectual level as well. Labels and other printed material are considered as means of reinforcing, clarifying or conveying additional information to the visitor. The two are not mutually exclusive.

Organization of label information

Concern over the role of labels seems to have stemmed from an historic misuse of labels, which have often been incomprehensible in themselves and/or have dominated the object. As part of the recent emphasis on the potential of exhibits both as public education and as entertainment, there has been an increasing concern about the most appropriate way to use labels. One generally accepted approach basically consists of a gradation of information, with each portion visually emphasized according to its importance. This approach has been recorded by Wilson, Tynan, Devenish, Neal and de Borhegyi.[151] Of course, variations in this general scheme will occur depending on individual preferences or judgments about spatial arrangement of the artifacts into large, small or interrelated groups, about the amount of information to be divided among headings, sub-headings, etc., and about the particular didactic stress for a specific gallery or display.

Information sheets

This "headline" organization of label information is suitable for didactic galleries. In galleries with a less didactic orientation, an information sheet can identify objects and give pertinent information concerning displays. Although such methods are frequently found in art museums, it has been suggested that they are also appropriate to other types of museums.[152] They have been used successfully in the Milwaukee

Public Museum where such information sheets are available within individual galleries and can be purchased for one cent.

Every artifact may not need to be labelled; the designer, curator and educator must consider which objects can be solely "explained" by their context, or which objects serve a strictly visual purpose and do not require labels. As with other aspects of gallery design, the most careful and judicious thought must be given to the place of labels within the overall concept of the gallery.

Labels and circulation

One particular issue relates to the use of labels and text panels in galleries where a great deal of written information is supplied. When visitors follow a right-handed circulation pattern and must read labels from left to right, this can result in a disrupted traffic flow and inhibit visitor retention of the information presented. When visitors move from left to right (the reading pattern), they read labels more often and remember that information better.[153] Where the amount of textual material in showcases could result in movement constraints, the gallery circulation pattern should be designed with this in mind (see SPATIAL CONSIDERATIONS, p. 106 and p. 102).

Content and Style: Label content is basically dependent on the educator/curator's message about a collection of objects. How such a message can be communicated through textual material is discussed in Appendix G. Some additional comments on content are noted below.

Label content and the visitor

Labels need not be limited to dry, factual texts; they can be intrinsically interesting and/or attention-getting. For example, labels can incorporate or consist of quotations from literature or historical accounts (diaries, letters, etc.). De Borhegyi noted that at the Milwaukee Public Museum exhibit on the Indians of the Northwest Coast, such a method was used very effectively; selections from Kwakiutl mythology texts were used for secondary labels, *"letting the Indians tell their own story through their spokesman, the Kwakiutl Bird Man."*[153]

Labels can also contain information of general interest about who made the artifact, when, where, how and why?

In addition, they might explain how the artifact relates to other items of the same or other periods. Labels can do more than identify; they can build upon the visitor's natural curiosity and interest. On the other hand, it has been pointed out that visitors are interested neither in the donors of the artifacts, nor in the objects' registration numbers. In fact, registration numbers can be confused with a date.[154] Weiner suggests that if included on labels at all, donors' names should be listed *"in type not more than one-half the size of that used for the label text proper, so as not to detract from the label itself."*[155]

Above all, informational content should be couched in a language and style which the visitor can understand. Many have recognized that curators often compose labels too erudite and complex for the general public. Mould proposes that *"the ideal museum writer will be one who can wrote with precision yet warmth, who has a feeling for lean, clear language,"* and suggests that if such a writer were to do all the labels and textual materials in a gallery, the unity of a gallery would be enhanced.[156] At the Smithsonian Institution, a good label editor is retained to revise curatorial labels *"into a form that is as short as the complexity of the subject matter permits, stripped of elevated language ... and fitted into a typographical format that makes reading easy."*[157] Editing label material in this manner would make a similar contribution to the unity of a gallery.

Parsons has suggested that the declarative form of labels, although perhaps *"a somewhat more dependable method of visual communication in that all information is overtly expressed,"* can be varied with question-asking labels, creating a display which implies rather than states.[158] In the results of a study of label forms, he noted that "do-it-yourself exhibits" promoted virtually the same amount of visitor learning, and could perhaps *"provide an added degree of intellectual stimulation and motivation to learn"* (p. 187).

One final point needs to be made about label content: it is unnecessary to state the obvious. For instance, if the visitor can <u>see</u> that the object is a blue plate, there is no reason to repeat that information on the label.

Although the function of label information may be varied (to inform, to amuse, to intellectually stimulate, to excite, etc.) the transmission of a message can be severely impaired if the label is not comprehensible. Numerous factors relating to visual appearance and language level govern a label's overall comprehensibility; these are discussed below.

Testing readability of labels

Readability: Lakota has recommended that labels should be pre-tested for ease of understanding by using the "cloze" procedure, *"a simple and highly accurate way of measuring the clarity and understandability"* of language.[159] Testing written material with cloze involves deleting words from a text, and scoring the readability of the passage by the number of correct insertions readers make.* Different formulas have also been developed which gauge readability by the number of syllables, words, length of line, etc. Klare has reviewed these various formulas with suggestions about how to choose one to satisfy specific conditions and purposes. He cautions, *"the formulas provide good indices of difficulty but do not indicate the causes of difficulty or say how to write readably."*[160] One of these methods, the Fog Index, has been found satisfactory by the National Museum of Natural History at the Smithsonian Institution. It utilizes a formula based upon average sentence length and number of polysyllables.

Length of labels

Length: It must be remembered that the average time a visitor spends before a display case is between 30 and 45 seconds.[161] During that time, the visitor should be able to receive a good general idea of what a display is about, through a quick perusal of the object(s) and any other information which catches his/her attention. For this reason, concise rather than encyclopaedic labels are recommended almost universally.

George Weiner has noted that the main fault of most museum labels is their overwhelming wordiness. At the Smithsonian, where he became label editor, *"a goal was set of not more than 75 words in a main or general text for an entire exhibit case and considerably fewer for individual specimen labels."*[162] Label length, he

---

*This technique is described in detail by G. Klare, H. Sinaiko and L. Stolurow in "The Cloze Procedure: A Convenient Readability Test for Training Materials and Translations," International Review of Applied Psychology, XXI (Feb. 1972); the article also includes a comprehensive bibliography dealing with the development, the uses and the limitations of cloze.

suggests, can often be cut by using illustrations, charts, diagrams or cutaway models; information in excessively long passages of text can often be divided up into several labels. It has also been suggested that simultaneously working up the label copy and the placement of the objects may result in more effective display, since certain groupings of the objects may permit simplification of the accompanying labels.[163] However, making labels comcise and direct does not imply *"that the meat should be thrown away with the fat and gristle."*[164] Over-simplified labels can be useless and misleading.

Label legibility and size

Size of Type: Gauging a successful type size is a particularly complex matter. Consideration must be given to a gallery's crowd flow pattern, to legibility problems, and to creating different degrees of emphasis through variations in the type size. Label illegibility due to inadequate type size is often cited as a visitor complaint. Ideally, label type size should be *"large enough to be read at the distance a visitor usually stands to look at the exhibit."*[165]

The size of type to be used in a specific circumstance is dependent upon a variety of factors (importance of information, location of label, size of artifact, etc.). One system of type size selection is recorded by Weiner in reference to the practice at the Smithsonian Institution:

"We have determined through practice that specimen captions should normally appear in at least twenty-four-point to thirty-point type and that main texts and other general texts should be considerably larger - usually forty-eight to sixty points. We use as high as seventy-two and ninety points when the distance from the eye warrants it. Of course, the size of the specimens must also be taken into consideration, so we have used ten points for coins."[166]

A comment on type size in relation to crowd flow has been made by Schuldes: *"The size and type of display captioning should closely relate to the speed of the crowd flow with short messages in large type when people pass quickly and smaller type where they move slowly or stop."*[167]

Consistent with the "headline" type of labelling, de Borhegyi suggests the use of dramatic labels: *"Large letters can be placed at the focal point of the case to headline the exhibit. They lead the eye to smaller, less conspicuous letters that outline the most important points of the exhibit."*[168] However, he also states that the informative labels for the interested visitors should be unobtrusive but obvious to the searchers, a difficult criterion to manage in practice, where designers will have varied definitions of "obvious" and "unobtrusive".

For the benefit of wheelchair users, Kenney suggests using large size characters, especially to pick out key words in the body of a text.[169] This approach would also benefit those visitors with poor eyesight, such as the elderly. However, labels designed in this manner run the risk of being misleading and may look uneven and unaesthetic.

Label format

Layout: Attention should be paid to the physical form in which the label material appears. Aside from a suitable choice of type size, the communication value of labels can also be affected by the length of each line, punctuation conventions and typesetting. Information on this topic is contained in Appendix E, and only a few observations are noted below.

Making things psychologically easier on the reader by conforming to his expectations seems to be a good rule of thumb. Thus, for long texts, liberal paragraphing with indentations is recommended, and hyphenating should be avoided.[170] Also, it has been proven that exclusive use of capital letters in texts significantly decreases reading speed, although capitalization is acceptable for headings.[171]

The length of a printed line in relation to the type size can impair readability and comprehension, since readers experience difficulty in swinging back to the beginning of successive lengthy lines. Weiner recommends that *"the most desirable line length for the average type face is 1½ picas of width for each point of height."*[172]

Labels and colour

Colour and Contrast: In an effort to make labels more "attractive" or "attention-getting", designers sometimes overlook the fact that certain colour combinations of lettering and background can render the print almost illegible. As Weiner notes, *"psychologists L. Carmichael and W.F. Dearborn report that 'striking differences in readability have indeed been demonstrated depending on the color schemes used in printing' and that 'experiments on the color of the printing surface have supported ... the general recommendation of using black ink on white or cream-tinted paper,'"*173 He feels that it is visually tiring to read for a long time against a dark or strongly coloured background. (See Appendix E for a comment on colour.)

Studies have shown that when perceiving print, *"the eye movement over the whole display is not great and a neutral toned background can be used as a rest period for the eye."*174 If labels are to be unobtrusive, their background colour can be blended with the colour of the case background or they can be mounted on clear plastic or perspex so that only the letters themselves stand out.175

Colour contrast is required to make printed texts readable, and it seems that as a general rule it is preferable to use dark print on a light background.

Location of labels   Positioning: Positioning labels must be considered both in relation to the artifacts they support and in relation to the reader. Opinions differ widely on the first point. One view maintains that identification labels placed in close proximity to the artifacts are visually distracting, and recommends a "key" system.176

Another view holds that visitor confusion is lessened when label information is immediately at hand, and that visitors are also more likely to read a label placed directly beside the object.177 On balance, the possible aesthetic advantages of a key system would seem to be offset by the potential for disatisfaction on the part of the viewer who has to search for information in a remote location.

If a key system is used it should be employed so that the remote label can be readily found and related directly to the key number. For example, the location of the label should be related to the location of the object within the display. (An object on the left side of the case should be related to the label on the same side.)

Positioning labels with respect to the reader should nevertheless be effected with a view to the visitor's comfort and ability to see. Lakota recommends positioning labels at eye level, or below eye level and tilted upwards.178 But with a museum's diverse audience, "eye level" will vary greatly. The mean adult eye level is about 5' 2 1/8".179 (See p. 126 in this chapter for additional comments on the visitor's field of vision.)

For wheelchair users, labels should be set at convenient tilted angles. When objects are placed on the upper shelves of a vertical display, the shelves should be transparent and duplicate labels should be tilted so as to be read from below.180

Labels for the blind

Braile: Wherever appropriate, consideration should be given to brailling short labels for the blind. This medium would restrict label length to about thirty words since *it's absolutely necessary to be pithy in Braile.*"181

AUDIO VISUAL TECHNIQUES

The role of audio-visual techniques in displays

The use of audio-visual techniques (a-v) within a gallery is a source of controversy among museum professionals. On the one hand, it is lauded as a means of reinforcing learning, of complementing static displays, of attracting visitors, and of maintaining their interest once attracted. On the other hand, a-v is criticized as a "gimmick", as an entertainment device inappropriate to the museum setting, as an expensive toy, and as an undependable and irritating mechanism.

But, in fact, it appears that most criticisms of a-v have resulted from such things as poor selection of equipment, inadequate maintenance, and misuse of a very prominent element. Due to the very prominence and visibility of a-v a good deal of sensitivity and expertise is required for its effective use. Museum professionals are generally not experts in this field and, in many instances, "outside" experts are brought in too late in the process of developing an exhibit to obtain an understanding of its special character.

A catalogue of a-v systems

A detailed catalogue of various a-v systems, including descriptions of hardware, suggested applications and some indication of maintenance, operation and cost

factors, is included in Appendix H. This is intended
to provide an information base which will enable
museum staff to become more familiar with the options
available through a-v and more competent to deal with
a-v specialists. Included below are more general comments on the use of a-v for museum exhibits.

Choice of a-v
techniques

Before a decision to use a-v is made, it must first be
decided what an exhibit is intended to communicate.
Once the message is defined, the best means of communicating that message to the visitor may be found.
Thus programming (or software) is the starting point
for any a-v exhibit, and the selection of hardware can
be based upon what is appropriate to accomplish program
demands. Commonly, the reverse process occurs; hardware is chosen and software must then be tailored to
meet the constraints of the hardware.

As different a-v techniques have different applications, it is essential to know what is wanted before
techniques are selected. Perception research provides
some guidelines. Lakota has pointed out, for instance,
that the visual mode is better suited to the presentation of spatial concepts, while an audio presentation
is more effective if the concept is basically temporal
(e.g. sequential in time). But when spatial and temporal concepts are combined, they are best conveyed
through the simultaneous use of both audio and visual
modes.[182] For example, in examining the designs on
Greek vases, the differences in designs in a series of
vases is a spatial concept, while relating these differences to historical and cultural developments is a
temporal concept.

Uses of a-v
techniques

A-v programs have been successfully employed to inform
and orient visitors at the entry to a gallery. In
addition, a-v techniques can incorporate many educational methods (e.g. arousal, stimulus contrast,
information redundancy through correlation, freedom of
choice, etc.) which ongoing research suggests are
important to the learning process.

A study by Lakota indicated that visitors possessing a
certain level of learning skills* learned more when
guided through an exhibit by an audio script played
on a stop-start cassette tape recorder than they would
have without such a device.[183] Tests were conducted

---

*In order to respond to the audio script and to the testing method
(exposure to previsit questions, a post-test and incentive provided
by the knowledge that a post-test would be given), visitors
required a certain level of verbal ability and self-directed
learning skills.

of visitors who used cassettes and of visitors who did
not. It was found that those who used the cassette
acquired such information as the characteristics of
various periods of art better than those who did not.
(Both groups were aware that they would be tested.) The
script was written by a museum subject matter specialist.
It included statements which directed the visitor to
look at specific characteristics of the paintings and.
asked questions about what he/she was viewing. The
positive results of this type of script led to the sug-
gestion that museums with audio facilities *"might sig-*
nificantly improve effectiveness of that audio, both
affectively and cognitively, by making the message
interactive and exhibit dependent. Apparently, this
can be achieved through the use of attention-directing
statements and questions about what is being viewed,
rather than a narrative which would make as much sense
removed from the exhibit as in the presence of the cor-
responding exhibit stimuli" (p. 96).

Another useful application of a-v is in assisting in
pre-visit preparation. This is most applicable to
visiting school classes. Special preparatory material
can make the actual museum visit more interesting and
more effective by making the students more aware of
what there is to see and to learn. If carefully considered early enough in the design process it is possible that some a-v material prepared for a gallery
(e.g. an orientation device) may be adaptable for this
purpose without great expense.

Location of a-v   The location of a-v elements is of some significance.
elements   The space for certain media techniques involving open
sound may need to be acoustically defined. Sound-
absorbent materials on walls and floors, or alcove
formations, can both be used for this purpose. Because
of the attention-getting potential of a-v techniques,
sound over-spill must be considered so that the impact
of other parts of an exhibit are not lessened. Provision for the necessary electrical capacities and
adequate ventilation for the equipment must also be
arranged. Clearly, a-v techniques can only be successfully integrated into a gallery if planned in relation
to all other exhibit elements.

The location of a-v programs also must relate to circulation patterns and crowd flow. For example, a five
minute a-v program can create a "bottle-neck" in crowd

flow if an adequate amount of space is not allocated for the audience.

It should be cautioned that since certain audio-visual programs are sequentially organized, only those people who are present at the beginning will be able to follow the presentation through. It is therefore advantageous to give the viewer who sees only half the program a basis on which to decide whether he/she wants to move on or wait and see the beginning. This can be simply done by informing him/her of the length of the program.

Maintenance of a-v elements

Once an audio-visual system has been installed, it is essential to establish and carry out a maintenance program. "Out of order" signs are an affront to the visitor. The basis of a good maintenance program is the careful selection of hardware in the first place. Care must be taken to ensure that initial capital savings do not result in excessive maintenance costs later. Where media production is contracted out, it has been suggested that requesting the experts to set up a basic maintenance schedule for their installation can immeasurably assist museum staff to carry out maintenance on a regular basis.

SUPPORTIVE ILLUSTRATIVE MATERIAL

A fourth category of display elements consists of a number of pictorial elements which assist in providing a context for the artifacts. These include traditional diorama or habitat groups, scale models, reproductions of original artifacts and graphic materials such as photographs and transparencies. A brief comment on each of these follows.

The use of dioramas

Diorama/Habitat: Dioramas and habitat groups have been major display elements in natural history museums for some time. In the view of some, the diorama/habitat is an archaic form of display, a nineteenth-century pictorial form. It is argued that artifacts can be better supported now with more contemporary methods, such as audio-visual techniques. On the other hand, a number of museums have indicated that dioramas are very popular with visitors and very effective for school group instruction.

A major criticism of dioramas is that they tend to be static; that they present a "permanent" unchanging image. The traditional arrangement of a series of dioramas on the periphery of a large dimly-lighted hall often creates a somewhat "fusty" and unattractive visual impression. However, this image is not necessary. The more dynamic dioramas at the Milwaukee Public Museum, in which animals are in active rather than stationary poses, and where there frequently is no glass between the visitor and the animals, provide ample evidence that dioramas can be pleasant and even exciting contexts for the portrayal of animals and artifacts. The taxidermy at Milwaukee is a useful measure of the relative quality of the stuffed "teddy bears" which seem to inhabit most museums.

In addition, it has been pointed out that the creation of the traditional diorama is essentially a dying art.184 The preservation of these dioramas as artifacts in themselves would therefore appear to be justified on these grounds alone.

The use of scale models

Scale Models: The scale model is another useful illustrative device which has been used in museum exhibits for some time. Models can be very effective in helping visitors to understand better the place of artifacts in their original contexts. It is useful to remember that scale models can be larger than natural size as well as smaller: one expects to find miniature cities but giant insects and microbes. The larger scale models can also take the form of walk-in exhibits (e.g. a ten-foot-high human heart).

In the experience of many museums, scale models can be very popular, especially with children. Models should therefore be carefully mounted at such a height that youngsters will have a good view.

One caution applies to the use of models, as to audio-visual techniques and to other display elements. Scale models should be used with discretion, as they can compete for attention and thus distract from the artifacts themselves.

The use of reproductions and replicas

Reproductions and Replicas: The display of original artifacts is sometimes supplemented by the use of replicas or reproductions. These are used both to preserve the original artifacts from exposure and to supplement a limited collection.

While from the conservation point of view there are obvious advantages to using replicas, it should be cautioned that incorporating them in displays can have a negative impact upon the visitor. A visitor who expects to encounter "real" objects in a museum, may react negatively to a replica. In his/her eyes, the credibility of the museum may be undermined. Where a replica is used, it should be carefully noted, and accompanied where possible with an explanation of the reason for its use.

Replicas can be usefully employed in an exhibit context as instructional devices. While the original artifact is displayed in a secure location, a replica can be presented in an exposed location where it can be closely examined and handled by the visitor. This can add another dimension to the appreciation and awe engendered by an original object.

The use of photographs and transparencies

Photographs and Transparencies: The use of supportive illustrative material such as photographs and transparencies has been increasing in the last few years. This appears to be a result of both an increased awareness of the need for supportive information and increased facilities for producing such materials easily and inexpensively (e.g. large photostats, etc.). However, the very ease with which large, bold illustrative material can be produced in itself imposes the necessity for great care in the use of such material. The following are some points to consider in the selection and use of such material:

+ *"Selectivity must be exercised"* in order to ensure that the materials chosen *"may prove most suitable for a particular exhibit, [and] assist the objects in the exhibit to tell their story fully and in the most stimulating manner possible."*[185]

+ Graphics are *"interpretative tools"* and *"our chief concern is with the message, the content (software) ... the interpretative message they carry."*[186] Graphics should not in themselves dominate either the subject matter or the artifacts which they accompany. For example, Washburn has commented on an exhibit of Greek vases where large black and white photos of scenes from the vessels were placed on

panels behind each object. *"The exhibit's installation was not keyed to the objects. Indeed, one
did not at first notice that objects were included
in the exhibition. What caught the eye were the
photographic panels."*[187]

+ At the same time, if graphic materials are successfully integrated with the artifacts, they can immeasurably enhance an exhibit. Small objects which
   are not visually prominent can be strengthened.
   Graphics can also create a comprehensible context
   for artifacts by indicating the locale from which
   they come (e.g. through maps) or by presenting the
   object in its natural setting (e.g. with photographs
   or transparencies). In addition, in collections of
   objects of similar type and size, graphics can be
   used to provide contrast or to establish a focus.

+ Particular care must be taken to ensure that graphics do not distort or misrepresent the subject por-
   trayed. For example, when enlarged and projected
   on a flat plane, a photograph of figures painted on
   the complex geometrics of a Greek vase can distort
   the heads and legs of the figures while accurately
   portraying the torsos.

+ One of the advantages of graphics is that they can
   be produced with relative ease from material available from a multitude of sources, including a
   museum's own collections (e.g. maps and other documents), outside sources (historical archives, government survey and mapping services), public
   resources (e.g. libraries, the National Film Board
   of Canada) and private collections.

+ Used appropriately, graphics can facilitate communication, but used insensitively or too frequently
   they can distort the unique function of the museum
   - the presentation of genuine and original objects.

LIGHTING

Lighting is considered from the viewpoint of its overall importance in museum and gallery design. The use of natural light in museums as well as various other aspects of lighting - adaptation, colour and operational issues - are discussed.

Importance of lighting

Lighting can be an enormously significant aspect of effective communication with the public. Lighting, probably more than any other single factor, can transform a museum environment. But its proper use is a very complex matter requiring both the technical knowledge of a lighting engineer and the talent of an artist.

Since light has the potential for causing deterioration in all substances, its aesthetic function may come into conflict with other considerations. This aspect of lighting is dealt with in the chapter on CONSERVATION which follows, although some recommendations about lighting and conservation are included here for the sake of clarity. Although the effective use of lighting requires a great deal of technical knowledge and tends to be regarded as a technical issue, in reality it should be a matter of much more general concern, since it has a great impact on the museum visitor. The following discussion covers those issues which should be considered by curators, designers, educators, and maintenance people as well as lighting technicians - the overall impact of lighting, the use of natural light in museums, adaptation, colour, and operational concerns. A number of technical concerns are discussed in Appendix I.

OVERALL IMPACT

Lighting and atmosphere

The effect of lighting upon a museum and upon a gallery simply cannot be overstated. As noted in the chapter on ARRIVAL AND ORIENTATION, a museum with an inadequately lighted entry can create an enduring negative impression. Public areas not only msut be adequately lighted, but must reflect the character of a museum.

Within a gallery, lighting is perhaps the most important individual factor in ensuring that the atmosphere is suitable for the most effective presentation of individual artifacts. Many galleries with fine collections and adequate spatial arrangements are seriously flawed as a result of inadequate lighting. Maintenance of lighting must also have a high priority: burnt-out bulbs or incorrect bulb replacement (wrong colour or wattage or incorrectly aimed fixtures) can totally obscure the original intention of a gallery design.

Choice of lighting

It should be emphasized that general rules regarding the use of light sources do not always apply, and that they should be adjusted to suit specific types of displays. There is no simple or general solution to museum lighting. It is always a mixture of many systems and sources, which if properly employed and balanced can immensely increase the enjoyment of the viewing public. A useful method of testing the effect of light is to mock-up portions of displays, and test them with a variety of light fixtures and controls, making an appropriate selection in each specific situation.

Incandescent and certain types of fluorescent lamps are the most commonly used artificial light sources in museums. Incandescent lighting is particularly useful for accent lighting as it is easily directed and filtered. Both are commonly used for general illumination purposes. Applied with discrimination, use of the two sources can produce a system of lighting with enough flexibility and diversity to fulfill the entire range of requirements of a contemporary museum lighting system.

NATURAL LIGHTING

The use of natural light in museums is a somewhat controversial issue for two reasons - the ultraviolet component of natural light has a deteriorating effect on some artifacts, and natural light is difficult to control because of its variability through a day and through the seasons. These concerns have tended to curtail the use of natural lighting.

Use of natural lighting

However, the need for natural light is ingrained in man's nature; he demands it in his home and in his place of work, and the consensus of opinion is that properly

controlled daylight is an asset to any environment.
With proper control of the quantity of light entering
an area, and with the use of ultraviolet filters, one
can meet the requirements of conservation in most areas
and for many objects, and still enjoy the advantages
of natural light. These advantages include not only
its familiar, natural quality but also those variations
in intensity which, although they may sometimes be a
mixed blessing, can create changing views of sculputre
and large artifacts, enhancing their qualities and
lending them life and interest.

*Windows at the Whitney Museum, New
York City, frame an outside view
without allowing too much direct
light into the gallery.*

ADAPTATION

*General Visual
adaptation*

The amount and the nature of the light needed to see
museum displays cannot be arbitrarily established, as
museum viewing consists of seeing appreciably different objects in sequence. The problem is therefore not
only to achieve visual acuity in the illumination of a
single object, but to maintain that acuity over a range
of objects viewed sequentially. This involves consideration of the ability of the eye to adapt. The eye
adapts automatically to changes in brightness pattern;
however, adaptation is not instantaneous and depends on
the brightness levels involved. Generally adaptation
is faster from lower levels to higher levels than in
the opposite direction. This must be taken into account
when designing the lighting system of a museum, which
must make provision for the necessary adaptation of the
visitor's eyes on entering the building and on moving
from gallery to gallery. Rest areas or other activity

areas provided with intermediate lighting and interspersed between the exhibition spaces can help to achieve this purpose.

Visual adaptation within a display

There are two aspects of illumination to be considered in lighting a particular display. The first is the light level preceding the display, and the second is the relative brightness of an object within its visual field. One means of focusing the attention of the visitor upon a display is by having a higher level of illumination on the artifact than on the surrounding background. This means that there has to be time for adaptation to higher levels of illumination as the eye of the moving observer goes from the surroundings to the object and becomes accustomed to the field of view. Even low levels of illumination will appear bright if the eye has previously adapted to even lower levels.

The display background can have a great influence on the final effect of a gallery and can complement or detract from the atmosphere created by direct lighting. Backgrounds can be designed and lighted either to be self-effacing or to enhance particular qualities of the exhibit. Low contrast surroundings tend to create a relaxed mood, while high contrast surroundings produce tautness and a sense of drama. Generally it is better to use lighter untextured backgrounds, which help adaptation and make shadows appear less dense and glare from light sources less severe. There are, however, occasions when the use of dark matte high absorption backgrounds is justified, especially in display areas of highly light-sensitive materials.

Specific applications of adaptation

Some specific applications of the principle of adaptation are listed below:

+ Gradually lower the illumination when coming from the outside or from bright areas.

+ Within the museum guide the visitor from lower to higher levels of illumination, coordinating lighting and signing so that the visitor is guided in the right direction.

+ Use natural light in galleries, where possible, and in relaxation areas. Natural light is ideal in galleries with objects which would normally have been outdoors, such as statuary.

+ Provide visual shielding between galleries to avoid reflection of light sources or light spill from one gallery to the next.

+ Maintain the level of background illumination in galleries so that the contrast between the illumination of the objects and the ambience does not exceed a ratio of 6:1. For example, if the light intensity on the object is 60 footcandles, then the background level of lighting should not be lower than 10 footcandles.

+ Where variety in the intensity of lighting on objects is desired, ensure that the difference between the light intensity on objects and background is maintained.

COLOUR

Colour of light

The effect of the colour of the light on the artifact must also be a major consideration in the selection of a light source. It is important to understand that light sources affect the observed colour of illuminated objects. This effect is referred to as colour rendering. The best colour rendition is from light sources which emit waves from the full spectrum of visible light in proper proportions. Light sources which contain wave lengths primarily from one end of the spectrum will distort the apparent colour of the artifact. In this regard it should be remembered that a colour cannot be added to a light source which did not originally contain that colour. Coloured filters do not add colours; they merely limit which colours penetrate the filter.

Colour for accent lighting depends on the exhibit. For example, tinting with pale blue-white lenses to give a daylight tone to incandescent lamps has often produced outstanding results in objects with delicate hues of unsaturated colours. In general, however, changes in colours must be used with care in order to avoid unnatural effects.

The colour of light is also important because of its effect on the environment and the reactions of observers. Although a colour in an object creates on impression, the same colour in an incident light source can create the opposite impression. For instance green in nature or other objects has the association of pleasing restfulness, whereas in the light source it has an unpleasant and unnatural effect.

Colour temperature

Another aspect of colour perception is the "colour temperature" of light. This is most important for museum lighting purposes. The eye has a different sensitivity to light of lower colour temperature than to light of higher colour temperature. Hence low colour temperature light, such as incandescents, make a room appear bright at low levels of illumination, while fluorescents, which have a higher colour temperature, need a higher level of illumination to make the same room seem equally bright and pleasant.

Colour and light sources

Some specific points of reference with respect to colour and light are as follows:

+ Use low colour temperature light sources so as to reduce the need for high illumination levels.

+ Lamps in all galleries should have good colour rendition. (A colour index of 95 or better is recommended for fluorescent lamps.)

+ Mixing of colour temperatures is a complex matter and unless carefully handled can create unpleasant effects. In public areas, where variations in colour temperatures are less likely to be of value, as a general rule all lighting should have the same colour temperature characteristics.

OPERATIONAL CONSIDERATIONS

Lighting costs and maintenance

The selection of a lighting system for a museum must be influenced not only by aesthetics but also by the owning and operating costs of a system. The operating costs are affected by power consumption and lighting maintenance. The first requires the use of a minimum number of highly efficient fixtures, while the second requires that these be properly maintained so as to develop the same quantity of light during the life of the installation. The combination of fluorescent lamps for background lighting requiring long hours of operation and incandescents for short time accent lighting provides a good combination of quality and efficiency.

It should be noted that the effectiveness of a display is often dependent upon a high density of spotlights;

therefore it can be expected that there will be high power consumption at certain locations. The use of narrow beam, low-wattage spotlighting is a useful solution and is also in full accord with the light intensities recommended by conservation. One means of reducing power consumption is the provision of control systems which enable portions of a lighting system (display, maintenance and emergency) to be turned off at times when they are not needed.

A well-maintained lighting system is one which continues to produce the illumination level it was originally designed for, as anything less will reduce visibility and make seeing more difficult. Dirt accumulations and lamp burnouts can considerably hurt the general appearance of a lighting installation. Since power consumption is the same whether lamps and fixtures are clean or dirty, the cost per footcandle of lighting becomes higher as the effective illumination level is reduced. Such considerations are of particular consequence in a museum, where the average light levels are low to begin with, and where any loss of output through lack of efficiency becomes critical.

Specific operational considerations

Some specific operational applications with respect to lighting follow:

+ Choose light sources and levels of illumination which are efficient in their output and consume a minimum amount of energy for a given result.

+ As much as possible without unduly constraining the range of lighting choices, limit the number of different types of light sources used in order to simplify maintenance and stocking.

+ Provide three levels of illumination: for display, for maintenance, and for emergency purposes.

+ Provide emergency lighting using the same type of fixtures as those used for general illumination, dimmed and controlled so as to be in balance with the regular lighting.

+ Provide for flexibility in light level adjustments within each gallery by installing dimmers in all general and accent lighting circuits.

+ Maintenance of lamps in the gallery areas, both on the ceiling and in the showcases, is an extremely delicate operation and should be made as hazard-free as possible.

+ A spot re-lamping procedure for incandescent lights (when used for accent lighting) is recommended in gallery spaces, while group re-lamping for fluorescents may be advantageous.

+ Provide access points for electric power within each gallery to permit flexibility in the location of showcases and spotlights. Provision of continuous wireways on the walls at different heights and multiple track facilities in the ceiling are highly recommended.

+ Provide adequate power for anticipated lighting and power demands. As a general rule, 5 to 15 watts per square foot of gallery space should be provided. In addition, allow for temporary electrical loads created by photographic and television lighting needs.

CONSERVATION

Lighting and conservation

The conflict of lighting with conservation is a complex matter, and is dealt with in some detail in the chapter on CONSERVATION which follows. Below are some points to consider with respect to lighting and conservation. (These are included here as they should be considered when lighting decisions are made.)

+ In galleries containing light-sensitive objects, the lamps used should have a minimum of ultraviolet radiation content in their spectrum. The ambient illumination should be low and diffuse, so as to allow sufficient contrast between exhibits and the space around them.

+ Wherever possible eliminate light sources in cases.

+ Where it is essential to have light sources within cases, the cases should permit heat dissipation and provide for easy access to lamps and ballasts for servicing. Where spotlights are used in cases, they should be of a type that eliminates infrared radiation from the main light beam.

+ Illumination levels for particularly sensitive objects should be limited to 50 lux. Most museum objects may be illuminated to a level of 100 lux, while those objects that are not sensitive to light may be illuminated to a level of 300 lux.

CONSERVATION

This chapter discusses those conservation issues which are pertinent to the display of objects: temperature, relative humidity, light, and contaminants in the air. Methods of monitoring and controlling the deterioration of artifacts on display are also suggested.

Conservation and display

The need for conservation of artifacts poses a particular problem in connection with their presentation to the public. The nature of the problem is perhaps most obvious in relation to lighting:

"... there will often be some conflict between the requirements of conservation and display. For example, conservation may call for low lighting levels and display for high levels. The curator, whose function is separate from that of the conservator, must decide with the help of the architect, conservator and lighting designer, between the rival claims and propose the necessary compromise. While accepting the importance of conservation, he has to recognize that a primary function of a museum is to make its exhibits available to the public to an extent sufficient to reveal their essential significance. He must be concerned at all times to develop and maintain the interest of visitors by a lively but controlled variation in the lighting throughout the museum and must often try to do this in a building designed long before modern display techniques were developed."[188]

Conservation is further complicated because individual artifacts vary considerably in their conservation requirements. These will vary from display to display, sometimes from artifact to artifact within a display. Some artifacts require a minimum of care, while others require considerable attention for their preservation.

This chapter of the report discusses four aspects of conservation in relationship to the display of artifacts:

+ temperature and humidity

+ lighting

+ contaminants in the air and air movement
+ monitoring and handling

TEMPERATURE AND HUMIDITY

Temperature change and relative humidity

Temperature and humidity can seriously affect some artifacts. Changes in temperature can result in expansion
or contraction to an extent which is dependent upon the
expansion coefficient of the material. If artifacts
are constructed of substances with very different expansion coefficients, they can quickly deteriorate
under expansion strains inflicted by abrupt changes in
temperature which cause the surface to be temporarily
hotter or cooler than the inside. However, the most
potentially deteriorating effect of temperature is its
effect upon relative humidity. The dimensional stabil-
ity and physical properties of many substances are
dependent on moisture content, and changes in the moisture content of some materials can change both their
dimensions and their physical properties.

As the moisture content of any substance will be affected by the availability of moisture in its environment, a major conservation issue is the control of the
moisture content of the gallery. A commonly used
measure of moisture content in the air is relative
humidity (R.H.), which is noted as a percentage. With
respect to changes in temperature, it is useful to
understand that as the air temperature increases, its
ability to hold moisture also increases and a higher
moisture content is required to maintain a constant
level of relative humidity. Conversely, as the temperature falls, the same moisture content in the air
results in a higher relative humidity.

Relative humidity and conservation

Much has been written about the susceptibility of
various substances to changes in relative humidity.
For example, wood loses moisture when the relative
humidity drops and re-absorbs it when relative humidity
is increased. *"Changes in relative humidity of compara-
tively short duration can cause dimensional alterations
of sufficient magnitude to be damaging."*[189] In fact,
most objects can adjust to a wide range of temperature
and a fairly wide range of relative humidity, <u>provided
that changes in relative humidity do not occur too
quickly</u>. One major consideration in museums, then, is
ensuring that changes in relative humidity take place

gradually over an extended period of time.

*Optimum range
of relative
humidity*

It appears to be generally agreed that the optimum
range of relative humidity within the general museum
environment is from 45% to 65%, with 50% as the median
target. Ideally, R.H. should not vary more than 4%
above or below the accepted norm, at whatever point
that may be established. Morever, this 4% change
should not be allowed to occur quickly.

*Achievable
ranges of
relative
humidity*

This general museum relative humidity level (subject
to special exceptions for particularly sensitive materials) is neither easy nor inexpensive to attain. It
requires very sophisticated heating, cooling, and
humidifying/dehumidifying systems, with particular
attention paid to air distribution and control systems
so that localized variations beyond tolerance do not
occur. The closer the tolerances of temperature and
relative humidity required, the more expensive the
mechanical systems will be to purchase and to operate.
Indeed, very close tolerances may simply be impossible
to achieve with the usual equipment. It is important, then, that the standard conditions and tolerances
to be adopted be very carefully considered in relation
to the overall needs of the bulk of the collections,
so that mechanical systems designers may have as much
latitude as possible consistent with good conservator-
ial practice.

A further very important consideration is that, while
R.H. levels of 50% and above may be splendid for the
collections, they are much higher than normal for inside winter conditions in cold climates, and they have
very serious effects on the structural fabric of museum
buildings. Under cold exterior conditions, interior
moisture driven by high vapour pressure migrates
through the building walls, condenses, freezes, and can
do very serious structural damage. In new construction,
this problem can be minimized by careful attention to
the proper placement of vapour barriers and insulation.
When introducing high R.H. levels to old buildings not
designed for them, the greatest care must be taken in
considering the probable effects. Indeed, the cost of
the necessary vapour barrier and insulation provisions
in old buildings is likely to be prohibitive, and a
compromise may be required in which relative humidity
levels substantially below those theoretically desirable are accepted, with enhanced attention to

specialized microclimates for particularly sensitive
objects.

It should be pointed out that no general environmental
condition will ideally suit all artifacts. A suitable
level of R.H. for any object is that to which it has
already become acclimatized. Some objects are best
conserved at an R.H. below 35% (e.g. metals), and some
objects will be so sensitive to relative humidity and
changes in relative humidity that they will require
special treatment.

*Means of
controlling
relative
humidity*

Relative humidity can be controlled by changes in
temperature, and by humidification or dehumidification.
Both methods are very much dependent on mechanical
equipment, such as heating, air-conditioning and humid-
ifying systems. While mechanical systems are effective
in establishing a stable level of relative humidity
over the long term, they are less likely to be effective in countering a short-term change in conditions
such as might be created by gusts of wind on very cold
days at the entrance areas. For the short term, static
means of maintaining relative humidity are effective in
assisting and supplementing mechanical systems. For
example, natural-fibre carpeting and textiles within
galleries can be used to help maintain a stable level
of relative humidity because they absorb and/or release
moisture and will tend to maintain equilibrium in their
environment. Depending on the volume of space relative
to the amount of textile or carpet used, this can be an
effective means of limiting the extent of short-term
fluctuations in relative humidity.

The use of cases is most effective in counteracting the
effects of changes in the surrounding environment; just
as the museum building mediates against short-term
fluctuations in outside temperature and relative humidity, so the case can mediate against fluctuations in
temperature and relative humidity inside the museum.
This provides the museum artifact with another line of
defense by reducing the exchange of air between the
environment inside the case and the environment outside
it.

In creating a localized environment, a sealed case is
neither necessary nor particularly desirable. It is
preferable to allow air to enter the display case, but
only through a small aperture protected by filters

(e.g. lead acetate or activated carbon filters) and contaminant absorbers. An aperture of 1" diameter for each eight cubic feet of case volume has been recommended as sufficient for permitting a suitable exchange of atmosphere between the case and its immediate environment.[190] Where humidity needs to be kept high, silica gel may be used in the case. Before being introduced to the case, silica gel must be conditioned to the desired relative humidity and "topped up" regularly. Where the relative humidity should be low, as with some metals, vapour phase inhibitors can be used. (Care should be taken as vapour phase inhibitors which are suitable for certain metals may corrode others.) Alternatively, the case may be heated above room temperature to lower the relative humidity.

LIGHTING

Variations in conservation needs with respect to lighting

One of the most important factors influencing conservation is lighting, as light has the potential for causing deterioration in all substances. However, all substances are not equally sensitive to light nor are they sensitive in the same way. Most organic substances are so sensitive that even short exposure to light will produce a serious change in their appearance or composition. Moreover, substances that are deleteriously affected by light can be affected in different ways. Some substances will fade (pigment or dyestuff deterioration), while others may become brittle (material deterioration). Nor are all light sources equally destructive. Shorter wave lengths of the light spectrum, such as ultraviolet frequencies, are more destructive than the longer wave lengths, although heating by means of infrared radiation can be equally damaging.

The extent to which materials deteriorate under given lighting conditions depends largely on their chemical composition. Most inorganic materials, such as metals and minerals including jewellery, ceramics and the different forms of stone, are virtually unaffected by light. Glass and vitreous enamel can also be regarded as immune to damage, although there have been reports from time to time of slight changes in colour attributable to light.[191]

Organic substance are generally very sensitive. Light-sensitive materials fall into the following groups:

pigments and dyestuffs; textile fibres; paper, wood and other cellulose materials; and thin films of organic materials such as proteins, resins and gums used as paint vehicles and adhesives. Since there is often interaction between pigments and paint media and between dyes and fibres, evaluation of the fading of a pigment or dye in isolation is meaningless. *"A dye may be fast on one fibre and fugitive on another or it may itself be fast but accelerate the light-degradation of the fibre."*[192]

Methods of conservation with respect to lighting

The means of dealing with deterioration from lights within museums vary, but generally involve a careful analysis of the sensitivity of materials and selective application of controls to deal with them. Such assessment of individual artifacts is within the province of the curators and conservators of each institution.

It has been established that the deteriorative effects of light on museum collections depend on the intensity of the radiation, the length of exposure, and the spectral characteristics of the illumination. The measure of this combination of conditions is the foot-candle-hour of exposure.

As far as the spectral characteristics of light are concerned, the major conservation consideration is the reduction or elimination of ultraviolet (u-v) and infrared (i-r) radiation from any light source. This can be done by selecting light sources which produce a minimum of these frequencies, and by using u-v and i-r filters. Within the visible light spectrum, warmer lights (reds) tend to less destructive than the cooler lights (blues), and should be used with light-sensitive materials.

Damage caused by light intensity is a product of illumination level and length of exposure. For example, an object exposed for one hour to a hundred footcandles of illumination will show the same amount of deterioration as an object exposed to one footcandle for one hundred hours. Both the lighting level and the length of exposure should therefore be kept to the lowest practical level. Reducing the length of exposure can be accomplished in various ways, including turning off lights at night; using timelag switches; and alternating artifacts on display with those in storage. Illumination levels for substances which are light-sensitive should be kept to a low level. (Once the eye has accommodated itself to low levels, the highlighting of light-sensitive objects can be achieved at a relatively low brightness.) The recommended maximum illumination levels within galleries for various categories of artifacts are as follows:[193]

Maximum illumination levels

Object	Illumination Level
Sensitive items (textiles, watercolours)	50 lux*
Most museum objects	100 lux
Metal and stone	300 lux

Heating effect of light

It is generally agreed that light sources should not be mounted inside display cases unless the light source is *"an extremely low intensity (less than 25-watt) incandescent lamp, with dimmers where heat build-up is significant."*[194] Light produces ambient as well as radiant heat. The heating effect of light, where air movement is limited, as in a display case, will raise temperatures and affect the relative humidity. The exclusion of the light source from the display case and the reduction of radiant heating effects by the filtering of infrared wave lengths or the use of "cold beam" lighting will do much to reduce the heating effects of lighting. It is suggested that the latter is preferable because *"filters often don't get put back after re-lamping."*[195]

The heating effect of light has led to some disagreement in the literature as to whether lights should be turned off at night. The argument is made that turning off the lights also turns off the radiant heating effect and results in a decrease in temperature and a harmful fluctuation in relative humidity. However, if the light levels are relatively low, the heating effect of the light sources will also be low. The argument for leaving lights on is also countered by the argument that turning off lights will arrest the deteriorating effects. The relative sensitivity of the artifact to light and to changes in relative humidity should be considered in determining which approach will be followed. Where objects are known to be sensitive to relative humidity, thermohygrographs can be used to check this against the effects of turning lights on and off.

*Lux is a unit of measurement of illumination level which indicates the quantity of light falling on a given surface; to illustrate, an unshaded 100-watt bulb has an illumination level of about 14 lux on a surface 10 feet away. The illumination level would increase as the distance was reduced or as the wattage was increased.

CONTAMINANTS IN THE AIR AND AIR MOVEMENT

Methods of removing contaminants from the air

Conservation of artifacts within a museum requires control of the number and type of pollutants in the air. The most effective means of removing solid atmospheric pollutants is through the use of mechanical dry filters. Filters can be used as part of an air-cooling system or an air-cleaning system (which may be used where there is no air-cooling system), or in particular parts of a museum, such as the entrance areas, where air pollution problems are most intense. Filtration systems are available which can remove 99% of all particles of 10 microns and over, and 97% of all particles of 1 micron and over. These are expensive in terms of first cost, maintenance, and the energy needed to circulate air through them. Activated charcoal filtration can be effective in controlling sulphur dioxide, ozone, oxides of nitrogen, and gaseous contaminants commonly generated in museum laboratories.

In addition to air pollution, dust and dirt are tracked into a museum at the main entrance. In the winter (in northern climates), salts are used to melt snow, and this also finds its way into the museum with the visitor. Carpets can be used effectively to trap dust and other contaminants, provided that they are cleaned well and often, although poor quality rugs will deteriorate under heavy usage and can contribute to dust. However the main problem associated with rugs and dust lies with the vacuum cleaners. Special cleaners, with dust entering the vacuum bag from above, are better at making sure that most of the dust is picked up rather than blown about. Vacuum cleaners with pressure gauges to measure a pressure drop should be used to indicate to the janitorial staff when it is time to change the bags. Where mechanical systems permit, a special "wall" of moving air, or a slightly higher atmospheric pressure may be created inside the lobby to encourage movement of air from inside to outside at heavily-used entrances.

Reducing air movement

Depending upon the quality of the air, it might be necessary to establish localized climates (by means of display cases) for particular artifacts. Display cases can also protect particularly delicate objects from air movement as a result of gusts from entrance areas or from air-cooling or cleaning systems. Obviously, careful placement of artifacts can also help to solve these problems.

MONITORING AND HANDLING

*Conservation
programs and
procedures*

Conservation is an ongoing process involving the care
of artifacts in storage as well as on display. It
needs to be emphasized that the most significant causes
of damage to artifacts are neglect and carelessness.
As stated by Robert Organ, Chief of the Conservation-
Analytical Laboratory at the Smithsonian Institution:

*"Man is the greatest single source of damage to objects
unless he has been alerted. Clean cotton gloves should
be worn whenever objects are handled, except where objects have decoration that could be caught in textiles.
In these cases, plastic gloves, dusted inside with talc
(baby powder) should be used instead. Nothing should
be touched without reason and then for the shortest
time compatible with the task. Objects should be carried on padded trays, covered if possible with a transparent dust cover. Their journeys should be brief and
not subject to violent accelerations (bumps or shock)
nor risk of spraying water, spilled drinks, etc."*[196]

There are a variety of techniques and devices which
should be used as part of an effective conservation
monitoring program. Conservation is dependent upon
conscientious attitudes as well as effective programs
and procedures. These should include regular inspection of artifacts to ensure that there are no changes
in conditions which could deleteriously affect them.

MAINTENANCE

The need for good maintenance is emphasized, along with the advantages of considering maintenance requirements in the initial stages of gallery design.

Maintenance and communication

A museum cannot be too well maintained. As Bernardo indicates, the effect of maintenance is felt by the visitor immediately upon his arrival.

*"Entering into a museum hall where dust has accumulated for years and where objects are poorly lighted is a bad museum experience. On the other hand, entering a museum environment that is neat and clean and properly lighted, predisposes the audience to a successful interest in the object."*197

However a predisposition to learning involves more than cleanliness and good lighting. Interaction between the museum visitor and exhibits can also be impaired if the visitor is physically uncomfortable. Proper care of mechanical systems is an equally important aspect of general maintenance.

One of the by-products of good maintenance is an appreciative and respectful audience, which lessens the possibility of spontaneous vandalism and theft. As Howard has noted, *"spotless maintenance is a remarkable aid to security."*198 Dusty cases, dirty floors, and peeling labels are invitations to carelessness, indications of neglect which the public is quick to recognize.

A full treatment of maintenance issues is beyond the scope of this report. Since the general maintenance of a museum is really no different than that of any other building, it will not be discussed here. Those issues having to do with exhibit maintenance are the main concern here. (The care and maintenance of the artifacts themselves is primarily a conservation issue and this is discussed in Section II-A, p. 155.)

Maintenance and design

Decisions made during the development and design of a gallery or exhibit can establish conditions that determine whether maintenance is easy or difficult, cheap or expensive. With early planning, maintenance considerations can often be accommodated without undue difficulty. The following are some specific issues which should be considered and resolved during the design phases of gallery development.

Cases   There are a number of maintenance concerns in the design of cases:

+ Ease of access to the inside of cases (and in some instances to internal lighting) is critical.

+ The normal hazards of wear and damage should be considered in the choice of finishing materials for cases. Wherever possible, these should be chosen with a view to strength, durability and ease of cleaning. Projecting edges of materials which might chip, split or be torn away are both a hazard and a potential cost.

+ Glass substitutes have been found to be useful for temporary exhibit case construction but they have a number of drawbacks when used on a long-term basis: "Some may turn yellow and cloud, they are easily scratched, and - a serious defect - they are electrostatic and attract dust."[199]

All of these issues must be considered together with the aesthetic and security considerations involved in the design of cases.

Dust   A major maintenance concern is dust. The removal of dust from the air before it comes into contact with the artifact is obviously the most useful approach. The most effective starting point can be an air-conditioning system with good filtration. In addition, when sensitive artifacts are involved, cases can be designed to prevent dust from entering them. (If vents are necessary, filters should be provided to keep dust migration to a minimum.) Dust-proofing major design elements such as dioramas by air pressure has been suggested, particularly for "large and complex installations such as habitat groups, in which most items are immovably attached [and] cleaning, even with the best equipment, is very costly."[200]

The relationship between rugs and dust is somewhat more problematical. Under very heavy usage and as they wear out, they can actually be a dust source; on the

other hand, they can form an excellent dust trap.
Used in conjunction with good vacuum cleaners* and a
regular maintenance program, rugs can be effective in
removing dust from the gallery environment.

Walls   Exposed wall coverings should be easily washed, repair-
ed or painted. Choice of surface colours or textures
should consider the extent to which they highlight
every smudge or fingerprint. It has been suggested
that the use of carpets on walls, in art museums in
particular, eliminates the problem of hanging marks.
Vinyl wall coatings have been found to be durable and
easy to maintain both within cases and on display
walls.

Maintenance and   In order to ensure that adequate attention is given to
process   maintenance issues, maintenance staff should be involved in the process of exhibit development from the initial concept through to day-to-day operation. This can
also have the advantage of creating greater personal
involvement and commitment to maintenance as part of a
larger responsibility. Alternatively, maintenance can
be the responsibility of staff who are directly involved with the production of an exhibit. At the
Metropolitan Museum of Art, for example, carpenters
are responsible for the continuing maintenance of the
work they have constructed.

An overall approach to maintenance obviously includes
the need for constant monitoring of all maintenance
activities from cleaning, to replacing burned-out
light-bulbs, to ensuring that special equipment is
working properly. This should also include a method
of monitoring artifacts to ensure, for example, that
artifacts out on loan are returned. (Little notes in
cases indicating that artifacts have been loaned out
for years are an affront to the visitor.) Effective
monitoring should ensure that exhibitions are maintained with the same integrity and spirit in which they
were conceived.

*Vacuum cleaners designed so that dust enters the vacuum bag from
above, equipped with pressure gauges to measure a pressure drop,
should be used.

PART B · PROCESS FOR AN INDIVIDUAL GALLERY

INTRODUCTION

As described in Section I, Part B, one of the aspects of an overall museum communications strategy is the initiation of individual projects. This part of the report deals with the process by which an individual project - a gallery, hall or exhibit - is developed and implemented after it has been initiated. The discussion includes an indication of the nature of a project team, its composition, organization and leadership. In addition, the context in which the design process occurs and the sequence of stages which a display process should take are discussed. Although the stages of the process can vary with jobs of varying size and complexity, there are a series of steps which should be followed in carrying out even the smallest job. The value of a well organized process applies equally to a small museum or a small project and to more obviously complex ones. In fact limitations of resources may make the organization of a small project more difficult than that of a larger one.

To illustrate the nature of the issues to be considered at each stage of the process a checklist follows the discussion of each of the stages. In addition a chart is included which illustrates the various stages of the display process and several of the typical activities at each stage.

The other aspect of a process for developing an individual gallery is evaluation. This is normally thought of, if at all, as a post-facto consideration. The concept is discussed here as an ongoing one which should be an inherent part of the decision-making process.

Whether the process is informal or formal, it is

essential that there be an ordered framework for
making decisions and monitoring progress. As indicated in the first part of this section, the design
of a gallery involves countless decisions; there are
a broad range of contributions from various people
representing competing interests. The value of an
effective process is to ensure that issues are considered at the right time; that decisions are based
on the available information from all relevant sources;
that crucial decisions made early on in the process set
a framework for later decisions and activities; that
actitivities are undertaken in an orderly sequence,
eliminating needless delays and ensuring the allowance
of adequate time for each activity.

A PROJECT TEAM

This is a discussion of the nature of a project team for developing a gallery - its composition, its organizational structure, the selection of its members, and the need for leadership.

Composition of a project team

On the basis of the literature and the experience of several museums, it is clear that the design of a gallery requires an interdisciplinary team effort. The nature of the team will vary depending on the museum and the scale of the individual project, but the concept of a team working in concert to effect a design is essential. The "team" in a small museum may be an individual who will require a series of resources in order to carry out this function.

A basic team for gallery or exhibit development would include curator, designer and educator. Other participants might include conservators, media experts, preparators, artists, carpenters, maintenance staff, etc. Such a group needs at its head a person with considerable leadership qualities and managerial skills.

The nature of the project will determine which people should participate and at which stages of the process they are needed. If, for example, an exhibit is to be interdisciplinary, then more than one curatorial department will have to be involved and the responsibilities of each established. If, on the other hand, the subject matter is entirely under one curatorial department, then it may simply be a matter of determining the appropriate person for each task. In any case, the people involved should be aware of the time required to participate in the project, and administrative provisions should be made so that they can participate to the necessary extent.

Organizational structure of a project team

An important aspect of a successful process is the organization of the team. People involved should have clearly defined roles. Effective teamwork requires the establishment of formal relationships which permit both leadership and a clear direction for collective efforts

in an atmosphere of cooperation. As interviews conducted with museum personnel made clear, an understanding of the display process by the participants
is important to design quality, design production
time, and the avoidance of personal stress. Robert
Inger of the Field Museum pointed out that although
formalizing procedures may be more time-consuming and
may generate large amounts of paperwork, they may be
necessary at the beginning of a project.[201] As noted
previously, this may be a one-time experience for some
of the key people involved in the design of the gallery.
If preconceptions about roles can be clarified at the
outset, effective performance is more probable.

In addition, there must be a direct relationship between the committee responsible for the overall museum
communications strategy and the project team responsible for the development of an individual gallery.
The specific nature of this relationship will vary from
museum to museum; however, as noted in the chapter on
communications strategy, it is essential that there be
a close link between them, so that a gallery does not
deviate from the terms of reference established by the
committee, and so that an understanding of the com-
plexities of scheduling and budgeting is preserved.
In a small museum the membership of the committee and
the project team may largely overlap; in a larger museum it is possible that these will be mutually
exclusive, with the exception of one individual - a
project manager perhaps - who can provide an administrative link between the two.

A common organizational issue is whether the curator
or the designer has the final word about gallery
design. In general, the authority of the curator is
unquestioned on matters of scholarly integrity. The
areas of dispute usually involve overlapping interests:
how something is to be displayed, the number of artifacts, their location, and the relationship of text to
artifact. Frequently the claim is that the curator
wants a display to be attractive to other curators,
and the designer to other designers. There is some
merit in both positions. As one designer has commented:

*"The idea of a curator doing his own exhibits in this
complex age seems approximately as reasonable as
insisting that every novelist also illustrate his own
book."*[202]

Yet curators find that designers frequently make unreasonable demands to meet their own working styles.[203] Obviously a great deal of cooperation is necessary. If the means of resolving disputes is clearly defined in advance, unpleasantness can be avoided.

Selection of the members of a project team

The careful selection from among museum staff of prospective team members is extremely important. Selection should not be an arbitrary or authoritarian process; it should be based primarily upon the need to create a climate in which commitment, involvement and motivation are fostered.

The way in which these matters are handled will vary from museum to museum. At the National Museum of Natural History, the Exhibits Committee, made up of seven curators and the Director, retains an outside scientist (recommended by the appropriate curatorial department but paid by the design department), who is responsible for the script. Some museums appoint a coordinator with managerial capabilities to assist in moving a project towards completion. At the Field Museum an outside manager was brought in for a major exhibit.* His responsibilities included monitoring costs and schedules, as well as ensuring that crucial contributions from participants were made at the right time. The Metropolitan Museum of Art uses an "operation supervisor" who performs a similar function. He has little actual authority but acts as a catalyst, monitoring activities and ensuring that schedules are met.

The need for supportive personnel and the extent of their roles can sometimes be clarified only as a project proceeds. As the purpose of an exhibit is analyzed and broken down into units, it may appear, for example, that the services of an audio-visual expert or graphics illustrator are required. The involvement of conservators, carpenters, etc. will also vary. An exhibit of highly sensitive artifacts may require that a conservator be part of the process from the outset. In other instances conservators may not need to be involved in the early stages. But a major error in many projects is delaying consultation with specialists until their usefulness is seriously curtailed.

Although most gallery design is done by museum staff,

*This exhibit - "Man and His Environment" - was a concept-oriented exhibit and involved curatorial resources from more than one department.

outside designers are occasionally retained by institutions. Some museums have found that external designers provide a challenge and impetus to in-house design work. External designers may also be hired to supplement the museum's own design department when it is fully occupied with other projects. An additional reason may be simply to avoid an obvious personality clash.

Leadership of a project team

The total membership of the team must be carefully constructed to suit the specific needs of the individual project. However there is one essential common factor to all teams, whatever their size or composition. There is a need for leadership. The team will not function without a quarterback: that is, one individual whose prime responsibility is to see that the conceptualization, design, and implementation process goes ahead in an orderly, controlled manner, as discussed in Section I-B, p. 64. The management functions which should be undertaken by this crucial coordinator are planning, organizing, implementing, communicating, controlling, and evaluating. The careful selection of this individual is critical: he/she should be picked solely on ability to carry out this catalytic role effectively. It is a rare skill.

Once appointed, the coordinator must immediately establish the process mechanisms: regularly scheduled meetings, graphic portrayals of key steps and interdependencies, coat and time control procedures, and project files. Museums with significant new exhibit programs should standardize these management mechanisms to a substantial degree, so that they are applied consistently in each case.

CHECKLIST OF ISSUES

Issues concerning a project team

+ *Who will be part of the project team? For example, curator(s), designer, educator, evaluator, preparator, conservator, lighting specialists, maintenance men, writer, and media specialists?*

+ *Of those, who will be major participants with ongoing long-term time commitments?*

+ *Who will be the leader and coordinator of all activities?*

+ *What specific roles or tasks will be assumed by individual participants?*

STAGES IN THE DISPLAY PROCESS

The display process which is necessary to conceive and mount an individual gallery is explored with emphasis on the sequence of activities and the specific contributions of each member of the project team. Detailed checklists of issues to be considered at each stage are also included.

Stages of the display process

The stages into which the display process can be divided should relate to the decisions which have to be made. There is some degree of arbitrariness in any set of stages, but these can be adjusted to be appropriate to a specific project. In the general model discussed here, the emphasis is on the early stages of the process, as all subsequent actions are dependent upon the effectiveness of initial decisions - decisions which commonly are made quickly and without their later ramifications fully understood. The stages are as follows:

+ program

+ design

+ implementation

+ evaluation and follow-up

Each stage of the process requires careful management to ensure that it is performed in an effective manner within the constraints established (such as budgets and schedules). The main discussion of the management of an individual project is in Section I-B, and it is referred to only peripherally in this part. However, it must be emphasized that without adequate management and without adequate leadership, a process cannot function effectively, no matter how thoroughly it is set out.

The chart which follows shows a simplified schedule of the major activities of each stage of the process to illustrate in a general way their sequence and duration. The activities themselves, and their inter-relationships, will of course vary from project to project. This is intended as an illustration to complement the discussion presented here.

CHART OF ACTIVITIES
- PROCESS FOR AN INDIVIDUAL GALLERY

PROJ. TEAM	ACTIVITY		YEAR 1 (1 2 3 4 5 6 7 8 9 0 1 2)	YEAR 2 (1 2 3 4 5 6 7 8 9 0 1 2)	YEAR 3 (1 2 3 4 5 6 7 8 9 0 1 2)
PROJ. TEAM	ESTABLISH PROJECT TEAM				
PROGRAM	CONTEXT	REVIEW ADMIN. CONTEXT			
PROGRAM	CONTEXT	REVIEW PHYSICAL CONT.			
PROGRAM	CONTEXT	REVIEW COLLECTIONS			
PROGRAM	PRELIMINARY PROGRAM	STATEMENT OF PURPOSE			
PROGRAM	PRELIMINARY PROGRAM	PRELIMINARY SCRIPT			
PROGRAM	PRELIMINARY PROGRAM	PRELIM. SELECT. OF ART.			
PROGRAM	BASIC CONCEPT	DEVELOP CONCEPT			
PROGRAM	DETAIL PROGRAM	FINAL SCRIPT			
PROGRAM	DETAIL PROGRAM	FINAL SELECT. OF ART.			
PROGRAM	DETAIL PROGRAM	SPATIAL LAYOUT			
PROGRAM	DETAIL PROGRAM	SUPPORTIVE MATERIALS			
PROGRAM	DETAIL PROGRAM	LIGHT., CONSERV., ETC.			
PROGRAM	DETAIL PROGRAM	EVALUATION CRITERIA			
PROGRAM	DETAIL PROGRAM	REVIEW BUDGET & SCHED.			
PROGRAM	DETAIL PROGRAM	IDENTIFY SPECIAL PREP.			
DESIGN	DRAWINGS & SPECIFICATIONS				
DESIGN	SPECIALIZED ACTIVITIES				
DESIGN	FINAL BUDGET & SCHEDULE				
DESIGN	SPECIAL PREPARATION				
IMPLEMENT.	CONSTRUCTION				
IMPLEMENT.	FABRICATION				
IMPLEMENT.	INSTALLATION				
IMPLEMENT.	ADJUSTMENTS				
EVAL. & FOLLOW.	EVALUATION				
EVAL. & FOLLOW.	POST-TESTING				
EVAL. & FOLLOW.	REVIEW OF PROCESS				
EVAL. & FOLLOW.	PROGRAM OF CONSERVATION				
EVAL. & FOLLOW.	PROGRAM OF MAINTENANCE				

PROGRAM

Sequence of program steps

The program stage includes the development of an understanding of the context and purpose of the gallery, the nature of the collection, the determination of what is to be communicated and how this is to be done. This is perhaps the most crucial stage of the work of the project team, as an ill-conceived program is unlikely to result in a good gallery, no matter how well the design is executed.

The components of the program stage can vary but it is essential that there be a sequence of steps in order to ensure that issues are considered and decisions made at the appropriate times. This discussion assumes four basic program steps - context, preliminary program stage, basic concept stage, and detailed program stage. Each of these steps involves a gradually more intensive consideration of some aspects of the preparation of a gallery. For example, the selection of artifacts begins with a cursory review of the collection in the first program stage (context), and ends up with a final complete listing of all artifacts in the last stage (detailed program).

The Context: An exhibit or gallery does not exist in isolation, but forms a single component within an institutional setting. While this in itself creates constraints, it can also provide a variety of opportunities. The nature of these opportunities and constraints can vary widely. Some will be administrative (such as budgets, schedules and roles); others will be physical (such as the nature of the space available).

Administrative context

Many administrative decisions may have been finalized by the committee charged with establishing the overall museum communications strategy. These might include terms of reference indicating the basic purpose of the gallery, budgets, schedules, and perhaps the selection of some of the key personnel (see INITIATION OF A PROJECT, p. 74). Such decisions have a major conditioning effect. For example, basic decisions on the size of budget available, and the deadline for completion, can entirely condition what can be done. Even a generous budget will not necessarily compensate for a rigid limitation on the time available to mount an exhibit.

The length of time necessary to develop a complex gallery from concept to opening is often measured in years rather than in months. It is important to develop a concept for a gallery that can realistically be met within a given time-frame. If discipline is not practised regarding time, deadlines become meaningless. Budgets are sometimes influenced from outside the museum. For example, funds provided by government, private foundations, or association may be awarded under specific conditions. If these funds are accepted the conditions must be fulfilled.

Other major administrative constraints concern decisions about the nature of an exhibit. Is it to be a temporary, permanent or special exhibit? For example, certain limitations will be established if a show is set up as a travelling exhibit or with artifacts on special temporary loan. These kinds of decisions obviously are fundamental to the form of the exhibit.

In some cases there may be constraints due to the general educational role defined for a gallery. For example, there might be a policy about the presentation of didactic information (such as the three levels of information presentation developed at the National Museum of Natural History); or about the need for a new kind of gallery to complement others (e.g. the "Man and His Environment" gallery at the Field Museum started with a desire to create a conceptual gallery).

Physical context   One other decision which will probably be made by the communications committee is the allocation of a space for the gallery. Before the concept of a gallery can be developed, the opportunities and constraints created by the location of the gallery and by the size and form of the space must be fully understood.

The location must be considered from the viewpoint of both subject matter and circulation. As noted earlier, the Field Museum has established a master plan which allocates gallery location in accordance with subject matter. This creates some opportunities for conceptual connections between adjacent galleries. The implications on the design of a gallery of an existing circulation pattern cannot be ignored. Again, as mentioned earlier, location can affect not only the number of people who will likely visit a gallery, but also the amount of time they will spend there. Where entrances

and exits are fixed in advance by physical circumstances, these must be considered in the development
and design of the gallery. Such considerations provide a springboard for understanding options and
alternatives.

The collection   The third major aspect of context is the collection itself. In many instances it may be entirely or partially
on display in an existing gallery. In other cases, recent acquisitions may have stimulated the need for a new
gallery. Before any general approach to the gallery
is undertaken, the team should become familiar with
the collection, and understand its major strengths and
weaknesses.

CHECKLIST OF ISSUES

Review Administrative Context:

+   What are the terms of reference provided by the
    committee responsible for the communications strat-
    egy?

+   Is this to be a permanent gallery? a temporary
    exhibit? a special exhibit?

+   What is the preliminary budget? Is the source of
    funds from outside the musem? Are there any con-
    straints related to the type of funding?

+   What is the preliminary schedule?

+   Is there a specific educational function set for the
    gallery as part of the communications strategy? Is
    there a specific approach to the presentation of
    didactic information?

Review Physical Context:

+   What specific space has been allocated for the
    exhibit?

+   What are the adjacent galleries and public spaces
    like? How do they affect this gallery?

+   What is the nature of the space allocated? What is
    the shape of the gallery? What is the ceiling
    height? Does it have serious restrictions such as
    long narrow corridors, low ceilings, small individ-
    ual rooms, narrow doorways, a hidden entrance,
    columns, curved walls, etc.?

Review Collection:

+   *What is the general nature of the collection to be presented? Is it currently on display or in storage, or both? What are the highlights of the collection?*

These are some of the considerations which form the context within which a gallery concept can be evolved. The following stages of the program phase outline the steps necessary for the development of a concept and program within that particular context.

A statement of purpose

<u>Preliminary Program</u>: The preliminary program phase consists of identifying the purpose of an exhibit, establishing a basic or preliminary story-line and making a preliminary selection of artifacts. The first step should be the delineation of a <u>statement of purpose</u> which outlines the basic rationale for the exhibit. The committee responsible for the museum's strategy may have provided some general guidelines to give direction to the development of such a statement; however the responsibility for a detailed statement should lie with the project team.

The importance of articulating the purpose of an exhibit cannot be expressed more clearly than in the simple comment: *"if you don't know where you are going, you won't know how to get there, nor will you know when you have arrived."*[204]   The purpose of an exhibit will, however, have a significant impact on its physical realization only if it is constantly referred to as the exhibit develops. Implicit in the statement of purpose is the content of the exhibit, how this should affect the viewer, and who the viewer is likely to be. A question pertinent to such a statement is: *"Specifically, what do you want whom to do, know or feel after seeing the exhibit that they could not do, know or feel before seeing the exhibit?"*[205]

Shettel has emphasized that, especially for didactic exhibits, lofty aims must be re-stated *"in terms of specific viewer behavior that should be brought under control of the exhibit."*[206]   That is, analysis of the general aim should determine sub-objectives - particular items of behaviour which are evidence of "appreciation" or "understanding." Only then can materials and methods of presentation be selected which would most likely lead to such behaviour. In other words, the definition of specific objectives helps to eliminate ambiguity of intention and permits effective evaluation.

These considerations lead to the problem of who should decide the purposes of an exhibit. Clearly the curator has the major responsibility. However, the contribution of other team members can be extremely important. The educational expert can ensure that instructional objectives are incorporated, shedding light on what categories of visitor can be expected to learn how much about a subject. In this initial delineation of objectives, the inclusion of the designer is also useful in order to ensure that from the beginning he is aware of the goals towards which his efforts will be directed.

There are often other contributors who should be involved from the earliest stages. For example, a preparator might be involved if a project includes difficult, time-consuming preparation (e.g. building a dinosaur). An audio-visual specialist might be necessary. Robert Matthai, at the American Museum of Natural History, noted that in his experience early involvement of a-v specialists is essential for an exhibit with a large audio-visual component.[207] Early involvement will increase the likelihood that specialists are informed of the basic objectives of a project and provide a better opportunity for the development of an appropriate a-v component.

A preliminary script

Once the statement of purpose has been evolved, the next step is usually the development of a preliminary script. This defines in general terms the actual information to be related by the exhibit. The script should bind *"the collection together in a coherent manner."*[208] It will necessarily include the major points and ideas to be conveyed. Because of the concern with content, the major responsibility for its development often falls within the jurisdiction of the curator, the undisputed subject authority. In other instances, it is made the responsibility of the project team. The Metropolitan Museum of Art, the Chicago Historical Society Museum and the Milwaukee Public Museum have all used a team approach to the development of a story-line.

Whatever the educational approach, the extent to which the exhibit is integrated thematically, or the amount

of didactic material to be incorporated, a preliminary
script is a useful way of stating what the exhibit is
to communicate.

A preliminary
selection of
artifacts

Parallel to the development of the preliminary script,
the project team must also make a preliminary selection
of artifacts from the collection. The range of the
collection will obviously affect the story-line or the
script. In some cases, the artifacts available will
omit parts of a possible "story." The extent of a
museum collection thus determines, in part, the ultimate emphasis of a presentation. The planners of the
American Museum of Natural History's gallery on Indians
of the Eastern Woodlands, for example, recognized that
although social organization and mythology were important aspects of Indian culture, little attention could
be given to these subjects in view of the nature of
their collection.[209] Rather than attempting to fill
in the aspects not covered by the collection, they decided to limit the scope of the exhibit.

When choosing artifacts, the designer can make important suggestions about the number and size of objects
to be used; the educator can be consulted on the
desirability of including certain objects for teaching
purposes, or on the possible need for accommodating
study groups in a gallery. In addition, a conservator
should be included in the discussion. He will be able
to acquaint the curator and the designer with the
state of repair and conservation requirements of the
objects - some may need special display conditions;
others may need critical work before being displayed.

Through these close liaisons with the curator, educator,
and conservator, the designer begins to acquire a
familiarity with the subject matter and its complex-
ities - a crucial factor if he is to be able to provide a unique and supportive environment for the
subject. Simultaneously, the curator, although ideally
conversant with the principles of interpretation, begins to appreciate the problems of interpretation and
the problems of translating abstract information into
physical terms. Obviously, a spirit of cooperation
is essential. The result should be a series of solutions, not compromises. The need for an overall
coordinator or team leader, to arrange for all the
necessary meetings and inputs, and to chair discussions,
will be obvious. He/she will keep continuous track of

all the issues to be resolved, and the interdependencies among them.

CHECKLIST OF ISSUES

Statement of Purpose:

+ *What are the main ideas to be communicated?*

+ *What are the specific educational objectives of the gallery?*

+ *What responses to the exhibit are expected from the visitor?*

Preliminary Script:

+ *What specific things does the curator want to say about his collection, his research, new developments, etc.? What are the views of the other members of the team?*

+ *What would the average visitor want to know about the collection?*

+ *Should there be a theme for the gallery? How does it relate to the overall museum theme (if there is one)? Should there be sub-themes for different interest levels?*

+ *If an existing gallery is being redone, what can be learned from the present gallery with respect to a possible story-line for the new gallery?*

Preliminary Selection of Artifacts:

+ *What are the main features of the collection? What are its deficiencies? How are these reflected in the preliminary script?*

+ *Do the artifacts require special security or environmental protection? How will this affect the way in which they should be presented?*

Developing a basic concept

Basic Concept Stage: This should be a brief but critical phase of the program. The products of the preliminary program stage (the statement of purpose, the preliminary script, and the preliminary selection of artifacts) are tested in conceptual form within the allocated space.

Once the message has been firmly established, the

approach to telling the story is examined, including
a more detailed examination of what artifacts should
be displayed and what kinds of supportive material
are necessary to assist in communicating with the
public, and in supporting the visitor's learning process. A preliminary spatial arrangement is useful to
demonstrate the feasibility of presenting the entire
story within the available space.

The development of the concept should include consideration of all the major issues of gallery development.
If all key members of the design team are involved in
the preliminary program stage, acquiring knowledge of
the collection, the subject and the objectives, they
should be able to rapidly move to detailed consideration
tion of these issues. Some of the more obvious of
these are what the artifacts should communicate to the
visitor, the extent of textual information, the extent
to which spatial arrangement (the sequencing of the
story-line) is directive or random, the need for diversity and surprise in presentation, and the general
usefulness of various supportive display elements in
communication.

Interchange among the members of the project team
contributes to a concept incorporating a variety of
ideas generated from different experiences and areas
of knowledge. Those familiar with available research
should ensure that this is applied to assess potential
effectiveness of various aspects of the concept.

When it has been developed, the concept should be reviewed and approved by the entire project team, the
communications committee and the administration. This
review should include a re-examination of budgets,
schedules and manpower requirements to implement the
concept.

CHECKLIST OF ISSUES

+   *Have all the main components of the story been
    established?*

+   *Is the basic information to be presented randomly
    or in a sequential pattern?*

+   *Are there natural subdivisions of the story? Should
    these be reflected in spatial subdivision? How do*

these relate to the available gallery space?

+ *Which major artifacts are necessary to support the story-line? Which other classes or groups of artifacts are to be used, and on what basis will the artifacts from each of these be chosen?*

+ *What major text panels, etc. are needed? What a-v devices will be necessary to support the story? What other supportive materials such as models, transparencies, dioramas, etc. will be useful?*

+ *Have budgets, schedules and manpower requirements been reviewed?*

+ *What approval procedures within the institution must be met before moving on to the next stage?*

Developing the concept into a program

Detailed Program Phase: Armed with a concept, the project team then turns to the task of turning that concept into a useable program which will act as the basic direction for the gallery design and development. The product of this stage of the work should include a detailed script, a final list of artifacts, a listing of all supportive material and techniques, a spatial layout, a preliminary indication of lighting, security and maintenance requirements, a statement of the evaluation criteria, and budgets and schedules. In addition the preparation of artifacts requiring particularly complex preparation should be identified, so that such preparation can be undertaken at an early stage.

The script is frequently quite detailed, identifying the major units of the story-line, establishing each accompanying objective and "informing idea", and then subsequently delineating the smaller, contained subsegments. The relative emphasis desired for the major units should be established and explored with the designer, as he must begin early to *"balance the space available with regard to the relative importance of different sections of the story-line."*[210] For each segment of the story, informational content must be fully defined, accompanied by initial suggestions as to its means of presentation: labels and display of artifacts, map, a-v software, line drawing, text panel, photograph, model, animation, diorama, habitat, etc. This process - developing the detailed script outline - may run to fifty pages or more.

After the final script has been mutually agreed upon,

a final selection and listing of all artifacts, including their dimensions, is prepared. In some cases photographs of each artifact have been included and found to be particularly useful.

A detailed description should also be prepared of all graphics, a-v effects and models to be used. Then, where appropriate, written specification briefs can be prepared in conjunction with the specialists in these various fields, whether in-house or from outside.

After the outline is completed, the designer, in conjunction with the rest of the team, develops the spatial organization, considering, for example, the space for objects (both within and outside cases), projection screens, text panels, graphics, rest areas, etc., in relation to the story-line and traffic circulation. Although the designer may be able to visualize the implications of the story-line, the others on the team will not necessarily have this ability. Through the use of conceptual plans, rough working models, and sketches, the designer can present to the project team an indication of the spatial implications of the script. Alternative spatial arrangements are usually considered until one layout *"having the greatest potential ... is isolated and decided upon for development in the next stage."*[211]

Lighting is one major design consideration which requires detailed consideration at this stage. The basic approach to lighting - the general atmosphere, the means of illuminating the artifact, and any special lighting effects required - must be clarified in order to ensure that it will complement the other aspects of the evolving gallery design.

Once the list of artifacts is finalized, the curator and conservator can specify any particular conservation problems which will influence their method of presentation. Other constraints relating to maintenance and security issues should be detailed, and evaluation criteria should be established in relation to major and minor adjustments of the project; the procedure for evaluation through succeeding stages should be established.

Budgets and schedules should be reviewed and any variation from the preliminary ones discussed with and approved by the communications strategy committee.

CHECKLIST OF ISSUES

Final Script:

+   Is the story to be told in a way which will serve
    visitors with varying interests in the subject?
    Can important artifacts, objects of particular in-
    terest and a-v devices be located throughout the
    gallery to maintain the visitor's interest and to
    assist in his/her pacing?

+   Is there to be an orientation area? What communica-
    tion techniques are to be used and in what combina-
    tion, i.e. a-v, graphics, audio, signs, brochures,
    colour, electronically controlled indicator lights
    and push buttons, numbers?

+   How are the artifacts used to contribute to the
    story-line? Is every selected artifact necessary
    or desirable? Do the selected artifacts represent
    all parts of the collection equally, or do they over-
    emphasize certain areas? Are there gaps in the
    collection which will make the related story-line
    difficult to follow?

+   Are there natural divisions in the collections to
    make grouping of artifacts easier? Should there be
    a separate display case for each group? Can dis-
    similar artifacts be grouped to show comparison and
    contrast? What is the significance of each group
    for the visitor? Does each group tell one complete
    part of the story? Can the group be arranged into
    sections which can be in separate rooms to show
    different time periods?

+   What does the curator want to say about each arti-
    fact or group of artifacts? What does the educator
    want to say?

+   Are cases to be used? If so, what size? Should
    each group be displayed in the same case? Can
    colour be used to identify two or more cases con-
    taining the same group? Can the cases housing the
    groups be built into walls, or are they best stand-
    ing free? Will the artifacts be seen from one or
    more sides?

+   Which parts of the story are going to be communi-
    cated by which technique, i.e. a-v labels, text,

audio, brochures, etc.?　Are open or closed dioramas or habitats to be used?　Are there to be any reproductions on display?

Final Selection of Artifacts:

+ Has each artifact to be used been identified, measured, and photographed?

+ Have all special conservation, security and maintenance measures been identified?

Spatial Layout:

+ Have the spatial requirements of each cluster or group of artifacts, and of all display elements and supporting materials, been established?　Has a spatial sequence of these groupings been established?　Has a preliminary examination been made of the correspondence between the spatial requirements and the available space?

+ Have areas for public spaces, rest areas, orientation devices, mini-theatre, temporary exhibit areas, etc., been allocated in the proposed spatial layout?　Is there adequate space to accommodate groups of visitors at key locations?　Are there locations for teachers or docents to explain the exhibit?　Is a mini-theatre needed for this purpose?

+ Has a preliminary circulation system been established?　Are there adequate provisions for flow-through rate of visitors at a-v presentations, objects of interest, etc.?　Have any changes in level been proposed?　Are there to be ramps to accommodate wheelchairs?

Supportive Materials:

+ Has the function of all text panels and labels been finalized?　What information should be on the labels and text panels?　Should each group be accompanied by a text panel to explain the significance of that specific group?　Should every object be labelled?　Should there be several levels of information?　Have type sizes been selected?

+ Have the purpose and location of media devices been finalized?　Are media devices such as mini-theatres or self-contained projection units to be used to tell part of the story?　Can a-v be used at the end of the gallery to summarize, reinforce, or review what was seen in the gallery?

<u>Lighting, Conservation, Security and Maintenance
Considerations</u>:

+ Are special or dramatic lighting techniques to be
   used to enhance some artifacts? Will the ambient
   light level be kept low? Will fluorescent lighting
   be used in combination with incandescent? Is an
   adjustable track system to be used? What range of
   lights and fixtures is required to achieve the intended effects?

+ Have any special conservation requirements for artifacts been identified? Have the means of dealing
   with these problems been specified and resolved?

+ Have the basic security requirements been considered?
   What type of barriers are required? What type of
   alarms are adequate? Are there enough security
   guards? Are the cases adequately constructed? What
   are the locking requirements? What fire detection
   and control equipment is required? Have the basic
   maintenance requirements been considered? Have
   access requirements for lighting been described?

<u>Establish Evaluation Criteria</u>:

+ Does the script fulfill all the educational objectives originally established? Does the theme, story-
   line, and selected collection satisfy the specific
   educational requirements of all ages and levels of
   interest?

+ How much time is required to examine, read, view
   and learn at each component of the exhibit for the
   casual visitor? for the interested museum "buff"?
   for the scholar? Is this time requirement reasonable?

+ What means are contemplated for measuring the educational effectiveness of the components of the
   exhibit?

<u>Review Budgets and Schedules</u>:

+ Have the man hours required for preparation of the
   artifacts been estimated? Is there adequate staff
   available?

+ Has every display element been identified? Has the
   work to produce it been defined? Have all required

materials been listed and quantified?

+   *Does the budget make allowance for inflation over the period of years needed for construction?*

+   *Has the availability of all materials been ascertained?*

Identification of Artifacts Requiring Special Preparation:

+   *Are there specific artifacts that need special preparation, handling and storage if they are to be displayed? How much time will be required for preparation of such artifacts? Will additional trained technicians be required to complete the work within the schedules established? Can the preparation of some artifacts be started in advance of construction (e.g. in a workshop or lab)?*

DESIGN

Developing a design from the program

At this stage of the process, the project team develops the detailed program into a design. This includes planning in detail such elements as cases; planning the arrangement of objects and information within and upon all display elements; arranging for the lighting of specific artifacts; detailing all those in drawings; and finalizing specifications for all these components.

As the designer works out the detailed designs and sepcifications, he draws on his knowledge of the current availablity and cost of desired materials and manufacturing processes. He should also be aware of the capabilities and availability of in-house construction staff, as this will determine the need for outside contractors and influence construction and installation schedules.

The design should be reviewed by all team members at regular intervals to ensure that the program is being correctly implemented in the design proposals. The stages of design review should progress from general concepts through to detailed considerations. Each is of consequence to the team.

Some specialized activities such as the preparation of software programs for a-v should be undertaken by staff or by consultants.

Evaluation procedures (see EVALUATION, p. 198) should be an inherent part of this design stage. The design should evolve with changes and modifications as the need becomes apparent.

Budgets and schedules and available manpower should be reviewed and altered if necessary, and means of construction and fabrication should be finalized. A system of monitoring all in-house and contract costs must be instituted. Also, at this stage some of the specialized preparation work on previously identified artifacts should be started, to ensure that they are completed when needed.

CHECKLIST OF ISSUES

+ *How are the evaluation procedures incorporated into the design process? Are mock-ups to be built and arranged within the actual gallery space? Are photographs, sketches, etc. of artifacts to be set up to simulate displays? Are text panels, labels, scripts, etc. tested for clarity and ability to communicate?*

Drawings and Specifications:

+ *Are the drawings and specifications sufficiently detailed for the method of construction and fabrication contemplated? Can an outside contractor accurately base his time and costs on these drawings?*

+ *Does the spatial arrangement as designed and detailed meet all the program requirements? Are all of the physical conditions considered - entrances, exits, columns, structural walls, floor and ceiling construction? Are all servicing requirements (e.g. electricity, water, etc.) incorporated?*

+ *Have the sizes of all display elements been checked against available space?*

+ *Has the arrangement and content of every case been determined? Is the location and layout of all labels in cases set? Has the use of case lighting been finalized? Is the access to lighting and to artifacts suitable? Have security considerations in case design been satisfied? Have special conservation considerations been incorporated as required? dust-proofing? R.H. stabilization? Have all human factors and considerations been incorporated?*

+ *Do the design and text of all labels and display elements correspond with the final script? How do the size and type of lettering, colour and design of labels relate to the artifacts being identified or explained? Can the labels be read by people with poor eyesight?*

+ *Has the basic lighting system been finalized? Are the power provisions adequate? Is there enough track and sufficient lighting fixtures to provide the appropriate lighting effects? Has the type of fixtures, bulbs, power costs, been established? Have the number of types of fixtures been selected with design, cost and maintenance considerations in mind? Are there dependable supplies of fixtures and bulbs available?*

+ *Have all special conservation considerations been incorporated? Will the artifacts be exposed to natural light and is this natural light filtered for ultraviolet? Is gallery air-conditioning required?*

+ *Have all maintenance considerations been incorporated? Is there easy access to all parts of the cases or exhibits?*

+ *Have all security considerations been incorporated?*

Specialized Activities:

+ *Have all a-v specialists been thoroughly briefed on the software programs to be developed? Will the final a-v programs correspond to the story-line? Do they explain or reinforce the material that is displayed? Have the scripts been written for the right audience? Are there enough visuals and titles? Has the length of such programs been finalized? Will it be necessary to view the programs in sequence?*

+ *Is the selected a-v equipment suitable for continuous use? Are the physical requirements for all devices checked out against the actual equipment selected?*

Final Budgets, Schedules and Monitoring Procedures:

+ *Has the allocation of in-house staff to perform the construction, fabrication and installation tasks been agreed to? Do in-house work schedules take into account other work to be done in the museum? Do construction times take into consideration museum holidays, staff vacations, curator field trips, etc.?*

Has the procurement of materials been considered for delivery when required?

+ *Have the lists of materials to be acquired been finalized and priced?*

+ *Have estimates been completed of all outside work necessary to implement the design?*

+ *Have overall budgets been established and reviewed in comparison with earlier ones? Does the budget include contingencies for delays due to lack of in-house staff, increase in material costs during the implementation, the needs of staff for over-time work, etc.?*

+ *Is there an adequate system of monitoring all imple-mentation activities to ensure that time and cost constraints can be met? Who is responsible? What techniques are to be employed? Can every phase be realistically scheduled showing when each activity is to take place and how long it is going to take? Will the schedule show the state of each activity on a periodic basis to monitor construction?*

Preparation of Objects:

+ *Can any of the time-consuming preparation tasks which have been previously identified be commenced at this stage? Can an area be made available for this work? Are special services required to enable this to take place in the location extablished?*

IMPLEMENTATION

Phases of implementation

This stage of the process involves the implementation of the design through construction, fabrication, instal-lation and adjustments. The value of having involved such people as preparators, conservators, other tech-nicians and tradesmen early in the display process will become evident during this phase of the work. For example, adequate access to lighting is more likely to be achieved as a result of the involvement of people who will have to maintain it. Moreover, the early commitment of tradespeople to specific display objec-tives is likely to result in a better product.

Construction: This includes the basic structural work necessary to enclose, subdivide and service the gallery. This can be done by in-house staff or by outside contractors.

Fabrication: This includes the fabrication of all display elements (cases, a-v elements, illustrative
material, etc.) which are specifically for the museum
setting. These are usually done by museum staff although some components are done by outside contractors.

Both of these are done in conformity with the drawings
and specifications prepared by the designer. He also
works in collaboration with the in-house fabricators,
setting in motion the acquisition of necessary materials from selected manufacturers. Contracts for any
outside work (e.g. plumbing, wiring) are awarded con-
comitantly. Detailed schedules for fabrication and
installation can be drawn up, identifying all major
time-consuming items.

Whether the designer is working with outside contractors or with the museum's own personnel, it is necessary and productive to establish good working relationships. Hillen has pointed out, for example, that *"if
carpenters fully understand what the designer is trying
to do, they often have excellect ideas for improving
the construction, or solving some difficulty."*[212] He
recommends encouraging the construction crew to *"think
about what they are doing in the same way"* as the
designer does, also involving them in a way that will
make them aware of the importance of their work to the
finished gallery. This is the age-old, but still valid,
maxim that the quality of work improves if those who do
it have an understanding of its purpose and meaning.

Installation: This stage of the implementation includes
the placement and mounting of all artifacts and other
design elements. This work must be coordinated with
the utmost care. For example, it is sometimes necessary to complete the placement of cases, labels, etc.
before any objects are brought to the gallery and
postioned, as extensive handling increases the possibility of accident. The integration of the work of the
preparators with the rest of the display process seems
an obvious and simple idea. However, many galleries
have been completed but unused (in one case, for three
years) because of the lack of advanced planning which
would ensure adequate personnel to complete installation work. As noted in the DESIGN stage, some of the
preparation work can start well in advance of the bulk

of installation work.

Adjustment: An adequate period of time must be allowed for completion and adjustment before the opening of a gallery. This will include such activities as final aiming and adjusting of lights, examination of all artifacts in place, reviewing the positioning of all labels, and trying out a-v, and any special effects.

CHECKLIST OF ISSUES

Construction:

+ *Have the arrangements been made for pre-construction activities? Is a hoarding to be installed? Are artifacts to be removed to a safe storage area? Are all the old display elements removed? Have all the unnecessary wiring and fixtures been removed? Can any major structural repairs be completed before construction begins, i.e. ceilings, floors, walls?*

+ *Have the partitions been accurately laid out to accommodate all display elements? Have large objects - dinosaurs, dimmer boards, etc. - been positioned before walls are built around them? Will the walls be required to support cases, etc., and are they properly supported? Will access doors be required to any area that will be covered by a wall?*

+ *Are there adequate power supplies within the gallery area, or must a new service be installed? Are any existing services to be relocated? Are new services to be provided for future use? Are adequate controls, dimmers, and switches provided in adequate locations? Can lights be adjusted and aimed after artifacts are installed?*

+ *Is air-conditioning to be provided? Are their special filtration requirements? Is the system adequate for the R.H. requirements of the artifacts to be displayed within the gallery? Are the diffusers visually remote from all display elements? Is ventilation adequately designed? Is there easy access to equipment?*

+ *If the finishing materials (dry wall, plaster, special ceilings, etc.) are to be used to support loads (cases, artifacts, etc.) are they adequately reinforced to carry the intended loads? Are ceilings adequately fixed to the structure above?*

+   Is adequate time allowed for painting and finishing
    of all walls, ceilings, and other construction be-
    fore artifacts are installed? Should some painting
    be done early to correspond with complex artifact
    installations? Are colours and finishes tested in
    relationship to artifacts, lighting, etc.?

+   Is the carpet selected to meet the specific needs of
    the gallery? Is the carpet a commercial grade which
    will not give off particles to create dust? Does it
    contain conducting strands of wire in the weave to
    eliminate static build-up? Does the colour blend
    into the gallery yet not show dirt? Does the carpet
    resist stains? Will the carpet be cleaned regularly?
    Does it satisfy all conservation requirements?

Fabrication:

+   Has the fabrication of all display elements been
    scheduled and arranged for? Have all materials for
    in-house fabrication been organized early enough to
    allow for supply and delivery? Have particularly
    scarce materials been identified? Have particularly
    time-consuming activities been identified? Has all
    contracted work been clearly specified, detailed and
    scheduled?

+   Has all work on such complex items as dioramas and
    habitat groups been carefully organized in relation-
    to other activities of the museum? Are there enough
    taxidermists, preparators, and artists to do this
    work? Is the work planned so that installation and
    fabrication are coordinated?

+   Has all the work on graphics, labels, text panels,
    etc., been arranged for?

+   Has the media software been organized so that it wil
    will be completed on time?

+   Has all the preparatory work to recieve display ele-
    ments been arranged for? Are all light boxes for
    rear-lit transparency units, etc., installed? Have
    proper size openings been left for light boxes, pre-
    fabricated cases, etc.? Are elements which may be
    removed for repair attached with proper mounting
    brackets? Are heat-producing elements adequately
    ventilated?

Installation:

+   Has a schedule of all preparatory work been
    completed?

Should some activities commence prior to final design completion? How is preparation work monitored?

+ *Are there sufficient preparators to complete the installation of displays, models, etc. on time? Are sufficient brackets available to secure the models and artifacts in the cases against vibration? Will the positioning of the artifact or model give the viewer the best possible view? Should there be a mirror in the case to expose a significant hidden side? Are the cases securely fastened in place? Are they easily accessible for maintenance?*

+ *Who is responsible for the final check of the content on all labels? Who checks that they identify the correct object? Are the colours correct for the case and its contents? Can labels be changed easily if objects are moved?*

+ *Does the preparator require the artifacts to design, build and fit custom-built brackets, etc.? Will the mount support the artifact, even if there is vibration, without damaging it? Can the mount be designed so that it does not detract from the object itself? Is it being made from material which will not affect the object?*

+ *Who is responsible for the actual installation of artifacts?*

+ *Will installation be handled exclusively by the cuarator, or by the preparators, or by both? What special arrangements are necessary to transport artifacts to the gallery? Is there easy access to the cases for loading? Is each case photographed and the artifacts recorded?*

+ *Can the installation of media devices be delayed to prevent damage from other construction activities? Is there proper ventilation? Is there adequate power? Is it securely attached and protected? Can it be easily removed for maintenance and repair?*

Adjustments:

+ *Have adequate arrangements been made for final clean-up and adjustment prior to opening? Are all dioramas, cases, models, plants, etc. to be cleaned? Are all carpets and wall coverings to be cleaned or protected? Are there paints and fabrics available for touch-up?*

+   *Have arrangements been made for the final adjust-*
    ment of all lighting once the artifacts are in place?
    Are all the labels properly lighted? Are the arti-
    facts properly lighted so they can be viewed from
    all exposed sides? Is the colour temperature of
    the lights correct for the artifacts? Is there
    enough ambient light at ramps and stairs to allow
    people to negotiate them safely? Does the final
    adjustment remove all excess glare?

+   *Can all a-v devices be tested in place? Is there a*
    program to test out the a-v device? Is the screen
    large enough, or does it require a different lens?
    Is the audio clear and at the right level? Is the
    visual sight line correct? Does the machine attract
    dust which may scratch the program or damage the
    audio tape?

EVALUATION AND FOLLOW-UP

The process of
evaluation

Museums tend to think about evaluation, if at all, only
after a gallery has been finished and its doors opened
to the public. This emphasis on post-evaluation can
obscure the fact that evaluation should be considered
at the beginning of the display process and at every
stage throughout the planning of a gallery. As Shettel
has pointed out, *"well-designed and articulated evalua-*
tion studies must be built into the entire development
*cycle and not added on as an afterthought."*213

The initial consideration of evaluation should occur
when objectives for an exhibition are set. In earlier
discussion about the development of a statement of
purpose for a gallery, the point was stressed that
clear and measurable objectives are essential for determining an appropriate evaluative process. Continued
attention to evaluation means that the rationale for
selecting the various display elements and techniques
is expressly related to exhibit objectives.

Direct evaluation (or prevalidation) of all or parts of
an exhibit can be done at various stages of the process. For example, testing the readability of textual
material is an evaluative procedure which can be incorporated into the gallery development process. Moreover, the construction of mock-ups and simulations to
pre-test performance can occur during the process. The
practical value of mock-ups and simulations has been

demonstrated in many other fields (e.g. the automotive industry, Broadway plays, etc.). In an exhibit context, Shettel has found that mock-ups (photographs of displays and information arranged in a three-dimensional circulation sequence) can indeed be valid representation of exhibits, especially for the evaluation of educational objectives. He notes an additional advantage: *"Since the mock-up approach lends itself to design variations, changes in the planned exhibit could be made before costly 'errors' were built into the final product."*[214]

Full scale mock-ups can also serve as an experimenting ground for innovative display techniques.

As well as providing the opportunity to pre-test an exhibit, Lakota has suggested that mock-ups or simulations can generate marketable "by products."[215] A two-dimensional mock-up, for instance, can be done with slides and a type-script of the accompanying text. After testing, such materials can then be used for an outreach program (e.g. as a completely validated school package). Lakota has also suggested that materials used for a three-dimensional exhibit simulation can subsequently double as a travelling exhibit.

Evaluation procedures can also play an important role in ensuring that material produced by outside contractors is consistent with exhibit objectives. For most museums, audio-visual products appear to be the most troublesome display elements in this respect. *"Loose contract specifications and lack of acceptance criteria frequently result in a loss of control and a product that is less than optimal."*[216] Shettel has suggested the following approach for dealing with these problems:

"... insure that ... contract arrangements are thoroughly defined and that contractors meet the same requirements of accountability as the other elements of the system. Acceptance of products being contingent on meeting agreed-to levels of knowledge gain/ attitude change would be one example of how such control could be exerted over this process."[217]

If the concept of exhibit evaluation is viewed as an integral part of the exhibit development process and is consciously applied through such methods as the above, a museum will have a degree of assurance that an exhibit is indeed proceeding towards the successful achievement of its objectives.

The appropriate method for post-evaluation of an exhibit or gallery is essentially determined by those objectives which guided its conception and design.218 In choosing a post-facto evaluative method, consideration also should be given to the purpose of or motive for the evaluation.

Shettel suggests that comprehensive evaluation (including paper-and-pencil methods, direct observation, video, etc.) to assess viewer knowledge, interest, attitude and behaviour, be utilized if evaluation is done with improvement of exhibit effectiveness in mind. Such measures provide *"considerable diagnostic power for determining the relative contribution of the various individual elements within the exhibit."*219 The conclusions of such an evaluation can be applied to that same gallery in the form of design modifications, and to the conceptualization of other new galleries. Since practical considerations may sometimes preclude comprehensive evaluations, Shettel recommends selecting a method which is appropriate for testing the summary objectives of the exhibit. For example,

*"the didactic exhibition might best be evaluated solely by paper-and-pencil knowledge tests, and not be concerned with attracting power, interest, and other, less tangible elements. On the other hand, an exhibit designed specifically to 'stimulate interest' might best be evaluated solely by an interest measure plus analysis of viewer behaviour (video tape or direct observation of attracting and holding power)."*220

Bechtel describes an interesting electronic device, the hodometer, which can be used effectively to monitor visitors' exploratory locomotion as they move through a gallery.221 The hodometer consists of pressure sensitive mats laid under carpet and a set of "counters" concealed in a cabinet. The advantages in the use of the hodometer, as stated in Bechtel's article, include the ability to measure preference for objects or spaces without interfering with the visitor; the fact that the device needs neither observers nor technically skilled persons to operate it; the possibility of flexible criteria for evaluating and testing exhibits; and the provision of accurate quantitative data for statistical analysis. If the use of

the hodometer system is decided on in advance, it can
be incorporated into the construction of the gallery.

The specifics of developing accurate evaluation methods and analyzing the results is a technical task
requiring certain skills and experience. A museum can
develop this expertise itself, or consider looking for
outside assistance. There are, however, certain
advantages to the internal development of evaluative
procedures. It has been pointed out that post-evaluation studies done by outside specialists often *"have
almost no impact on the curatorial and design staffs
of the museum."*222 On the other hand, it has been
suggested that museum educators with a minimum of
training could provide effective evaluative research
for their museum.223 In a large museum, it is more
efficient and often more effective to separate responsibility for evaluation from the curator and designer;
however, a small museum may prefer to combine such
functions. In any case, the evaluator must be a
member of the team, to ensure that evaluation is an
integral part of the process. Whoever is responsible,
he/she must make an institutional commitment to
correct identified deficiencies, for evaluation undertaken without such a commitment is of little value.
It is important that an adequate budget be made available for this purpose.

One advantage of maintaining the involvement of the
design team is assessing the gallery and in establishing the appropriate modifications, is that the integrity of the original design is not destroyed. The
spirit with which evaluation is undertaken is critical, and the "threat" of exposure of design "errors"
should not be used to inhibit creativity and experi-
mentation, but rather to foster them. Evaluation
undertaken as an integral part of the process becomes
a design tool rather than just an independent examination of the results of the process.

Once the gallery has opened, the design process itself
might be worth evaluating from the viewpoint of its
success and failures. This would particularly benefit
the processes in other galleries. There are usually
strong parallels between galleries and useful insights
would certainly be presented as a result of such an
evaluation.

Finally, the project team could usefully establish an ongoing program of conservation and maintenance, in conjunction with the relevant departments. This would help ensure that these departments are sensitive to what the specific needs of the gallery are and how they should be dealt with.

CHECKLIST OF ISSUES

+   *Although major evaluative procedures should be dealt with during the design of the gallery, are there arrangements for a post-opening test of the exhibit's effectiveness? Does this include funds for any necessary modifications?*

+   *Will there be a review and evaluation of the process to assist in recommendations relating to future galleries?*

+   *Are there regular programs to monitor all conservation considerations once the gallery is in operation? Will relative humidity be checked and adjusted? Will the temperature be checked and adjusted? Will light measurements be taken to protect against powerful light and heat sources? Will case design be checked for air-tightness? Are the cases checked for vibration?*

+   *Is a regular program of gallery maintenance established to ensure that the gallery will continue to function effectively? Does this include lighting, cleaning, a-v, etc.?*

PART C · EVALUATING EXISTING GALLERIES

This entire document has been devoted to an examination of the myriad issues and factors which must be considered when developing an effective strategy for communicating with the museum visitor. Since the most important aspect of such a strategy for any museum will be galleries and exhibits, the issues and procedures related to the conceptualization and design of these have been given major emphasis.

The subject is enormously complex and the authors would have done no service to their readers by trying to make it seem otherwise by oversimplification. As it is, readers with special interests will not doubt feel that their particular fields have been given short shrift. All users of this document will have to extract from the overall survey those aspects which apply particularly to their own needs, while keeping in mind the broad picture which has been painted.

One of the first steps a museum must take in the development of an approach to communicating with the public is an assessment of its existing galleries. This may be carried out for a number of reasons: to identify minor but important improvements which could be made, to establish a priority list for renovation of exhibits, to determine whether a present exhibit is suitable within an overall master plan, to allocate human and financial resources, and so on.

It must be emphasized that galleries cannot be entirely evaluated in isolation. In the first place, the policies which are developed in a Communications Master Plan - such as the educational approach and the relationships among galleries - will provide a framework for making judgments about existing galleries. To the extent that such policies are likely to vary from museum to museum, so will the basis for judging individual galleries.

Given such a framework, evaluation can take place. The issues raised in this guidelines document are generally agreed to be of major importance in effective communication with the public and it is assumed that these issues can form a reasonable basis for assessing an individual gallery.

There is an enormous, almost overwhelming, amount of detail involved in each of the issues raised in this document. It cannot be over-emphasized that a thorough understanding of these issues is essential to any evaluation. However, any attempt to frame a comprehensive list of all the questions that are raised by these issues would be both cumbersome and so unwieldy as to be of little value.

The checklists of key questions which follow are intended for a relatively simple evaluation of an individual gallery or exhibit. There are two separate lists, one for general use and one for the use of individuals with expertise in specific areas such as content, conservation, etc. The purpose of such evaluation may be to develop a preliminary listing of good, bad, and indifferent galleries, upon which priorities for action can then be based.

Just who should fill out the forms, and how the results should be tabulated and interpreted, are of course questions for individual application. Although it would be possible to assign different weightings to the various questions and thus evolve a total point scoring system by which to compare exhibits, this would be misleading and of little real value. The main value of such structured questioning is to assist in forming judgments, not to replace such judgments.

As has been emphasized in the preceding chapter, evaluation is more effective when it is an integral part of an entire design and development process. However, an assessment such as that proposed here also has a place in the development of a communications strategy.

GALLERY AND EXHIBIT EVALUATION SHEET

SHEET NO

NAME OF GALLERY OR EXHIBIT	RATING									DATE:
	INADEQUATE			FAIR				EXCEPTIONAL		EVALUATED BY
	1	2	3	4	5	6	7	8	9	REMARKS

NOTE: THESE ARE GENERAL QUESTIONS
REQUIRING NO SPECIFIC
TECHNICAL SKILL.

1. *Is the gallery attractive, enjoy-*
   able, comfortable?

2. *Does the atmosphere of the gallery*
   enhance the artifacts?

3. *Is the purpose of the gallery*
   clearly communicated to you?

4. *(If there is one), to what extent*
   is the purpose of the gallery
   fulfilled?

5. *If there is no apparent purpose,*
   how well do the exhibits inform
   you about the content of the
   gallery?

6. *How effective is the gallery in*
   raising questions about its
   content?

7. *How well does the gallery serve*
   the casual visitor?

8. *How well does the gallery serve*
   the scholar or expert?

9. *Are the entrance to and exit from*
   the gallery clearly indicated or
   apparent?

GALLERY AND EXHIBIT EVALUATION SHEET										SHEET NO

NAME OF GALLERY OR EXHIBIT	RATING									DATE:
	INADEQUATE				FAIR				EXCEPTIONAL	EVALUATED BY
	1	2	3	4	5	6	7	8	9	REMARKS

10. Is it easy to move through the gallery and see all the parts of it that you wish to see?										
11. Does the gallery have a sense of order?										
12. Does the arrangement of the gallery maintain your interest throughout?										
13. How effective are the following aspects of the gallery:										
- arrangement and mounting of the artifacts?										
- the labels, text panels, etc.?										
- the use of a-v?										
- the use of other supportive techniques, photographs, etc.?										
- other (specify)?										
14. Does the lighting of the gallery enhance the artifacts?										
15. Is the gallery well maintained?										
16. To what extent do security arrangements intrude between you and the artifact?										
17. How effective is the gallery in making you wish to return for another visit?										

GALLERY AND EXHIBIT EVALUATION SHEET

SHEET NO

NAME OF GALLERY OR EXHIBIT	RATING									DATE:
	INADEQUATE			FAIR					EXCEPTIONAL	EVALUATED BY
	1	2	3	4	5	6	7	8	9	REMARKS

NOTE: THESE QUESTIONS REQUIRE SOME SCIENTIFIC EXPERTISE TO ANSWER FULLY.

1. *Does the gallery communicate the present state of knowledge in its subject area?*

2. *Does the gallery illustrate current efforts to expand knowledge in its subject area?*

3. *Is the content expressed in a way which is relevant today?*

4. *Does the content provide useful links to current knowledge in allied subject areas?*

5. *Does the gallery make full and effective use of the museum's resources in the subject area?*

6. *Does the gallery meet good conservational standards?*

   - *temperature and humidity*

   - *light protection*

   - *dust and contamination*

   - *maintenance*

NOTES

IMAGE AND ROLE

1 J.W. Evans, "Some Observations, Remarks and Suggestions Concerning Natural History Museums," Curator, V (Jan. 1962).

2 R.E. Gerald, "A Philosophy on Publicity for Museums," Curator, VI (Feb. 1963).

3 S. Silver, Design Director, Metropolitan Museum of Art (New York), interview held Jan. 28, 1976; M. Snedcof, Assoc. Museum Educator, Metropolitan Museum of Art (New York), interview held Oct. 8, 1975.

4 National Endowment for the Arts, Museums USA: A Survey Report (Washington, D.C.: U.S. Government Printing Office, 1975), p. 127.

5 Metropolitan Museum of Art, Annual Report 1973-1974 (New York: Metropolitan Museum of Art, 1974).

6 D.S. Abbey and D.F. Cameron, The Museum Visitor: II - Survey Results (Toronto: Royal Ontario Museum, 1960).

7 M. Eisenbeis, "Elements for a Sociology of Museums," Museum, XXIV (Summer 1971).

8 B. Dixon, A. Courtney and R. Bailey, The Museum and the Canadian Public (Toronto: Culturcan Publications, 1974).

9 National Endowment for the Arts, Museums USA, p. 135.

10 H.K. Skramstad, "Interpreting Material Culture: A View from the Other Side of the Glass" (paper presented at Winterthur Museum, Wilmington, Del., Autumn 1975).

THEME

11 Field Museum of Natural History, "Exhibit Master Plan (First Phase)," Chicago, May 1974.

12 National Museum of Natural History (NMNH), Smithsonian Institution, "Long-Range Plan for Exhibits Renewal," Washington, D.C., Feb. 1975.

13 J.E. Cruise, "Directors' Memorandum No. 7: Summary of Statement of Intent," Royal Ontario Museum, Toronto, Sept. 29, 1975. This document appears in full as Appendix A.

14 H.K. Skramstad, Director, Chicago Historical Society Museum (Chicago), interview held Feb. 11, 1976.

EDUCATION AND LEARNING

15 S.D. Ripley, "Museums and Education," Curator, XI (March 1968).

16 J.R. Bernardo, "Museum Environments for Communications: A Study of Environmental Parameters in the Design of Museum Experiences" (unpublished Ph.D. dissertation, Columbia University, 1972), p. 3.

17 W.E. Washburn, "Do Museums Educate?" (lecture given at Hagley Museum, Wilmington, Del., May 14, 1969).

18 P.A. Fine, "The Role of Design in Educational Exhibits," Curator, VI (Jan. 1963).

19 M. Snedcof, Assoc. Museum Educator, Metropolitan Museum of Art (New York), interview held Jan. 22, 1976.

20 R.A. Lakota, "Good Exhibits on Purpose: Techniques to Improve Exhibit Effectiveness" (unpublished paper, Washington, D.C., Jan. 1976). Included as Appendix C.

21 Lakota, "Good Exhibits on Purpose."

22 Lakota, "Good Exhibits on Purpose."

23 H.H. Shettel, "The Evaluation Function" (unpublished paper, Washington, D.C., 1975).

24 R.A. Lakota, Office of Museum Programs, Smithsonian Institution (Washington, D.C.), interview held Jan. 19-20, 1976.

25 A.W. Melton, N.G. Feldman, and C.W. Mason, Experimental Studies of the Education of Children in a Museum of Science, New Series, No. 15 (Washington, D.C.: American

Association of Museums, 1936).

26 Lakota, interview held Jan. 19-20.

27 M. Bloomberg, An Experiment in Museum Instruction, New
Series, No. 8 (Washington, D.C.: American Association
of Museums, 1929).

28 Melton, et al., Education of Children.

29 Snedcof, interview held Jan. 22, 1976.

ARRIVAL AND ORIENTATION

30 Dixon, et al., Museum and the Canadian Public, p. 130.

31 Skramstad, interview held Feb. 11, 1976.

32 R.A. Chase, "Museums as Learning Environments," Museum
News (Sept./Oct. 1975).

33 Chase, "Museums as Learning Environments."

34 A. Carnes, Education Department, Field Museum of Natural
History (Chicago), interview held Oct. 21, 1975.

35 C.B. Lusk, "Museum Lighting," Museum News (Nov. 1970).

36 G.H. Winkel, R. Olsen, F. Wheeler, and M. Cohen, The
Museum Visitor and Orientational Media: An Experimental
Comparison of Different Approaches in the Smithsonian
Institution (Washington, D.C.: Smithsonian Institution,
1975), p. i.

37 Winkel, et al., Orientational Media, p. viii.

38 R.A. Lakota, The National Museum of Natural History as
a Behavioral Environment, Part I: An Environmental
Analysis of Behavioral Performance (Washington, D.C.:
Office of Museum Programs, Smithsonian Institution,
1975), p. 87.

39 Winkel, et al., Orientational Media.

40 Lakota, NMNH as a Behavioral Environment, p. 88.

41 Bernardo, "Museum Environments," p. 112.

42 A.E. Parr, "Remarks on Layout, Display, and Response to Design," Curator, VII (Feb. 1964).

43 Winkel, et al., Orientational Media, pp. xi-xii.

44 K. McLay (notes taken at "Knowing Your Museum Audience Workshop," coordinated by R.J. Loomis, Smithsonian Institution, Washington, D.C., March 17-20, 1975).

45 E.P. Lawson, Chairman, Department of Education, Hirshhorn Museum, Smithsonian Institution (Washington, D.C.), interview held Oct. 3, 1975.

46 Lakota, NMNH as a Behavioral Environment, p. 89.

47 R.A. Lakota, The Efficacy of Three Visitor Learning Support Systems in Producing Cognitive and Affective Outcomes in an Art Museum (Washington, D.C.: Smithsonian Institution, 1973), p. 94.

48 Winkel, et al., Orientational Media, p. viii.

PACING

49 A.W. Melton, Problems of Installation in Museums of Art, New Series, No. 14 (Washington, D.C.: American Association of Museums, 1935).

50 Bernardo, "Museum Environments," p. 107.

51 Lakota, NMNH as a Behavioral Environment, p. 64.

52 McLay (notes taken at "Knowing Your Museum Audience Workshop").

53 R. Schickel, The Disney Version: The Life, Times, Art and Commerce of Walt Disney (New York: Simon and Schuster, 1968), p. 321.

54 R.L. Bunning, "A Perspective on the Role of Museums in Community Adult Education," Curator, XVII (Jan. 1974).

55 A.P. Kenney, "Museums from a Wheelchair," Museum News, LIII (Dec. 1974).

56 These three criteria for hall effectiveness are based on the work of Harris H. Shettel. H.H. Shettel, M. Butcher, T.S. Cotton, J. Northrup, and D. Clapp, Strategies for Determining Exhibit Effectiveness,

Technical Report No. AIR-F58-11/67-FR (Pittsburgh, Pa.: American Institutes for Research, 1968).

57 Lakota, NMNH as a Behavioral Environment, p. 87.

58 Melton, Problems of Installation in Museums of Art.

59 B. Lawless, Assistant Director, Design and Production Department, National Museum of History and Technology, Smithsonian Institution (Washington, D.C.), personal communication to Frank Taylor, Director, NMHT (now retired), March 14, 1975.

60 Snedcof, interview held Oct. 8, 1975.

SECURITY

61 J. Chapman, "Physical Security," in C. Keck, et al., A Primer on Museum Security (Cooperstown, N.Y.: New York Historical Association, 1966).

62 Chapman, "Physical Security."

63 S. Weldon, "Winterthur: Security at a Decorative Arts Museum," Museum News (Jan. 1972).

64 R.F. Howard, Museum Security, New Series, No. 18 (Washington, D.C.: American Association of Museums, 1958), p. 7.

65 G. Rivière, H. Visser, and F.E. Herman, "Museum Show-cases," Museum, XIII (1960).

66 Bernardo, "Museum Environments," p. 178.

67 S.F. de Borhegyi, "Visual Communication in the Science Museum," Curator, VI (Jan. 1963).

68 T. Probst, "On Guard," Museum News (Nov. 1965).

69 A.F. Michaels, "Security and the Museum," Museum News (Nov. 1964).

70 A.F. Noblecourt, "The Protection of Museums Against Theft," Museum, XVII (1964).

ROLES, GOALS AND BASIC OBJECTIVES

71 Cruise, "Statement of Intent."

DEVELOPING A STRATEGY

72 NMNH, "Long-Range Plan."

73 Sir John Pope-Hennessy, "Design in Museums," The Royal Society of Arts Journal, CXXIII (Oct. 1975).

74 NMNH, "Long-Range Plan."

INTRODUCTION

75 Pope-Hennessy, "Design in Museums."

76 Pope-Hennessy, "Design in Museums."

TELLING THE STORY

77 S.F. de Borhegyi, "Some Thoughts on Anthropological Exhibits in Natural History Museums in the United States," Curator, VII (Feb. 1964).

78 Pope-Hennessy, "Design in Museums."

79 Shettel, et al., Strategies, p. 156.

80 Lakota, interview held Jan. 19-20, 1976.

81 L.A. Parsons, "Systematic Testing of Display Techniques for an Anthropological Exhibit," Curator, VIII (Feb. 1965).

82 R. Matthai, Director, Special Project, American Museum of Natural History (New York), interview held Oct. 9, 1975.

83 Lakota, Visitor Learning Support Systems.

84 Lakota, Visitor Learning Support Systems, pp. 28-29.

85 Kenney, "Museums from a Wheelchair."

86 R.F. Washburne and J.A. Wagar, "Evaluating Visitor Response to Exhibit Content," Curator, XV (March 1972).

87 Shettel, et al., Strategies, p. 156.

88 Fine, "Role of Design."

89 Fine, "Role of Design."

90 de Borhegyi, "Anthropological Exhibits."

91 Parsons, "Systematic Testing of Display Techniques."

92 A.S. Wittlin, "Hazards of Communication by Exhibits," Curator, XIV (Feb. 1971).

93 Wittlin, "Hazards of Communication."

94 J. Hillen, "The Role of the Designer" (paper presented at the Canadian Museums Association Seminar on Design, Ste. Marie Among the Hurons, Midland, Ontario, Oct. 1973); W.K.F. Schuldes, "Basic Principles of Exhibition Design," Curator, X (Jan. 1967).

95 McLay, (notes taken at "Knowing Your Museum Audience Workshop").

96 Bernardo, "Museum Environments," p. 70.

97 H.W. Parker, "The Museum as a Communication System," Curator, VI (April 1963).

98 E. Levonian, "Auditory and Visual Retention in Relation to Arousal," AV Comm. Review, XVI (Spring 1968); S.L. Becker, "Interest, Tension and Retention," AV Comm. Review, XII (Fall 1964); W.C. Miller, "Film Movement and Affective Response and the Effect on Learning and Attitude Formation," AV Comm. Review, XVII (Summer 1969) acknowledged by Bernardo, "Museum Environments," p. 55.

99 Bernardo, "Museum Environments," p. 55.

100 G. Moore, "Displays for the Sightless," Curator, XI (April 1968).

101 Pope-Hennessy, "Design in Museums."

102 Bernardo, "Museum Environments."

103 H. Glicksman, "A Guide to Art Installations," Museum News, L (Feb. 1972).

SPATIAL CONSIDERATIONS

104 S.F. de Borhegyi, "Space Problems and Solutions," Museum News, XLII (Nov. 1963).

105 M. Lehmbruck, "Psychology: Perception and Behaviour," Museum, XXVI (1974).

106 Silver, interview held Jan. 28, 1976.

107 M. Brawne, The New Museum (New York: Praeger Publishers, 1965, p. 10.

108 P.S. Kimmel and M.J. Maves, "Public Reaction to Museum Interiors," Museum News (Sept. 1972).

109 Brawne, New Museum, p. 41.

110 Lehmbruck, "Psychology: Perception and Behaviour."

111 Lehmbruck, "Psychology: Perception and Behaviour."

112 H.L. Zetterberg, Museums and Adult Education (Paris: Evelyn, Adams and MacKay for the International Council of Museums, 1968), p. 25.

113 Shettel, et al., Strategies, p. 157.

114 Bernardo, "Museum Environments," p. 100.

115 Glicksman, "Art Installations."

116 Parr, "Response to Design."

117 H. Kischkewitz, "New Techniques in Displaying Traditional Objects," Museum, XXVII (1975).

118 Lakota, NMNH as a Behavioral Environment, p. 63.

119 Lakota, NMNH as a Behavioral Environment, p. 90.

120 H.W. Parker, "New Hall of Fossil Invertebrates, Royal Ontario Museum," Curator, X (April 1967).

121 A. Neal, "Gallery and Case Exhibit Design," Curator, VI (Jan. 1963).

122 Glicksman, "Art Installations."

123 S.F. de Borhegyi, "Testing of Audience Reaction to Museum Exhibits," Curator, VIII (Jan. 1965).

124 de Borhegyi, "Space Problems."

125 de Borhegyi, "Testing of Audience Reaction."

126 Moore, "Displays for the Sightless."

127 Zetterberg, Museums and Adult Education, p. 27.

128 Lehmbruck, "Psychology: Perception and Behaviour."

129 Lakota, interview held Jan. 19-20, 1976.

130 L.V. Coleman, Museum Buildings: A Planning Study, Vol. I (Washington, D.C.: American Association of Museums, 1950).

131 de Borhegyi, "Testing of Audience Reaction."

PACING WITHIN A GALLERY

132 D. Pepper, Art Department, Royal Ontario Museum (Toronto), personal communication, Dec. 1975.

133 Melton, Problems of Installation in Museums of Art, p. 93.

134 Lakota, Visitor Learning Support Systems, p. 8.

135 Parsons, "Systematic Testing of Display Techniques."

136 Melton, Problems of Installation in Museums of Art, p. 185.

137 Glicksman, "Art Installations."

DISPLAY ELEMENTS

138 Neal, "Gallery and Case Exhibit Design."

139 F. Dandridge, "The Value of Design in Visual Communication," Curator, IX (April 1966).

140 Rivière, et al., "Museum Showcases."

141 M. Brawne, "Museums," Architectural Design, XLIII (Oct. 1973).

142 Neal, "Gallery and Case Exhibit Design."

143 G. Waddell, "Museum Storage," Museum News (Jan. 1971).

144 S. Silver, Design Director, Metropolitan Museum of Art (New York), interview held Oct. 8, 1975.

145 J. Hillen and F. Brittain, "Some Notes on the Planning and Logistics Involved in Setting Up a New Gallery" (paper presented for Master's Degree Program in Museology, joint undertaking of Royal Ontario Museum (Toronto) and School of Graduate Studies, University of Toronto, October, 1972.

146 S. Hartman, "Designing a Hall of Indian Archeology," Curator, XV (March 1972).

147 Kimmel and Maves, "Museum Interiors."

148 D.C. Devenish, "Methods and Problems of Archeological Display in British Provincial Museums," Curator, IX (Feb. 1966).

149 D.F. Cameron, "A Viewpoint: The Museum as a Communications System and Implications for Museum Education," Curator, XI (March 1968).

150 E.I. Knez and G.A. Wright, "The Museum as a Communications System: An Assessment of Cameron's Viewpoint," Curator, XIII (March 1970).

151 K.M. Wilson, "A Philosophy of Museum Exhibition," Museum News, XLVI (Oct. 1967); A.M. Tynan, "Popular Geology: A New Approach to an Old Problem," Curator, VII (Jan. 1964); Devenish, "Archeological Display"; Neal, "Gallery and Case Exhibit Design"; de Borhegyi, "Anthropological Exhibits."

152 W.H. Bayley, "To Make the Artifact Speak" (paper presented at the Canadian Museums Association Seminar on

Design, Ste. Marie Among the Hurons, Midland, Ontario, Oct. 1973.

153 de Borhegyi, "Testing of Audience Reaction."

154 Devenish, "Archeological Display."

155 G. Weiner, "Why Johnny Can't Read Labels," Curator, VI (Feb. 1963).

156 V.T. Mould, "The Storyline" (paper presented at the Canadian Museums Association Seminar on Design, Ste. Marie Among the Hurons, Midland, Ontario, Oct. 1973).

157 Weiner, "Why Johnny."

158 Parsons, "Systematic Testing of Display Techniques."

159 Lakota, NMNH as a Behavioral Environment, p. 92.

160 G.R. Klare, "Assessing Readability," Reading Research Quarterly, X (1974-1975).

161 A. Neal, "Function of Display: Regional Museums," Curator, VIII (March 1965).

162 Weiner, "Why Johnny."

163 S.A. Freed, "The New Eastern Woodlands Indians Hall in the American Museum of Natural History," Curator, IX (April 1966).

164 Weiner, "Why Johnny."

165 Lakota, NMNH as a Behavioral Environment, p. 92.

166 Weiner, "Why Johnny."

167 Schuldes, "Basic Principles of Exhibition Design."

168 de Borhegyi, "Visual Communication."

169 Kenney, "Museums from a Wheelchair."

170 Lakota, NMNH as a Behavioral Environment, p. 91.

171 Dandridge, "Value of Design."

172 Weiner, "Why Johnny."

173 Weiner, "Why Johnny."

174 Dandridge, "Value of Design."

175 Hillen and Brittain, "Notes on Planning."

176 T.K. Seligman, "Educational Use of an Anthropology Collection in an Art Museum," Curator, XVII (Jan. 1974).

177 Weiner, "Why Johnny."

178 Lakota, NMNH as a Behavioral Environment, p. 91.

179 Neal, "Gallery and Case Exhibit Design."

180 Kenney, "Museums from a Wheelchair."

181 Moore, "Displays for the Sightless."

182 Lakota, interview held Jan. 19-20, 1976.

183 Lakota, Visitor Learning Support Systems, p, 96.

184 Silver, interview held Jan. 28, 1976.

185 Wilson, "Philosophy of Museum Exhibition."

186 Bayley, "To Make the Artifact Speak."

187 W.E. Washburn, "The Dramatization of American Museums," Curator, VI (Feb. 1963).

CONSERVATION

188 Illuminating Engineering Society (IES), Lighting of Art Galleries and Museums, Technical Report, No. 14 (London: Illuminating Engineering Society, 1970).

189 N. Stolow, "The Action of Environment on Museum Objects, Part I: Humidity, Temperature, Atmospheric Pollution," Curator, IX (March 1966).

190 R. Organ, Head of the Conservation-Analytical Laboratory, Smithsonian Institution (Washington, D.C.), interview held Jan. 20, 1976.

191 IES, Lighting of Art Galleries and Museums.

192 IES, Lighting of Art Galleries and Museums.

193 G. Thomson, "A New Look at Colour Rendering, Level of Illumination, and Protection from Ultraviolet Radiation in Museum Lighting," Studies in Conservation, VI (1961).

194 B. Leech, Conservation Department, Royal Ontario Museum (Toronto), interview held Jan. 15, 1976.

195 Organ, interview held Jan. 20, 1976.

196 R. Organ, Head of the Conservation-Analytical Laboratory, Smithsonian Institution (Washington, D.C.). Unpublished notes on conservation issues, 1976.

MAINTENANCE

197 Bernardo, "Museum Environments," p. 178.

198 Howard, Museum Security, p. 7.

199 Rivière, et al., "Museum Showcases."

200 R.C. Morrill, "Dust Proofing Exhibits by Air Pressure," Curator, V (Jan. 1962).

A PROJECT TEAM

201 R. Inger, Assistant Director of Science and Education, Field Museum of Natural History (Chicago), interview held Oct. 21, 1975.

202 S. Silver, "Art as Pleasure in Contemporary Life," The Connoisseur, CLXXII (Nov. 1969).

203 M. Klapthor, Curator, National Museum of History and Technology, Smithsonian Institution (Washington, D.C.), interview held Oct. 2, 1975.

STAGES OF THE DISPLAY PROCESS

204 H.H. Shettel, "Exhibits: Art Form or Educational Medium?" Museum News, LII (Sept. 1973).

205 Shettel, "Art Form."

206 Shettel, et al., Strategies, p. 144.

207 Matthai, interview held Oct. 9, 1975.

208 Hillen, "Role of the Designer."

209 Freed, "Eastern Woodlands Indians Hall."

210 Hillen, "Role of the Designer."

211 J.A.M. Bell, Museum and Gallery Building: A Guide to Briefing and Design Procedure, Information Sheet, No. 14 (London: Museums Association, 1972).

212 Hillen, "Role of the Designer."

213 Shettel, "Evaluation Function."

214 Shettel, et al., Strategies, p. xiii.

215 Lakota, interview held Jan. 19-20, 1976.

216 Shettel, "Evaluation Function."

217 Shettel, "Evaluation Function."

218 Shettel, et al., Strategies, p. 140.

219 Shettel, et al., Strategies, p. 146.

220 Shettel, et al., Strategies, p. 146.

221 R.B. Bechtel, "Hodometer Research in Museums," Museum News, XLIII (July 1967).

222 Shettel, "Evaluation Function."

223 Lakota, interview held Jan. 19-20, 1976.

APPENDICES

APPENDIX A
THE ROYAL ONTARIO MUSEUM STATEMENT OF INTENT

ÖM

Directors' Memorandum

No. 7

September 29, 1975

R.O.M. STATEMENT OF INTENT

This summary of ROM policy intent is a synopsis of the findings of the
Report Review Committee which was established to examine the recommendations
contained in the Guidelines for Planning Report of April 7, 1975. This
summary is in no way intended to conflict with or to supersede the full
Statement of Intent adopted by the Board of Trustees on September 17, 1975.
It is intended simply as a brief review of the policies which have been
adopted, for the convenient reference of participants in the ongoing
organizational, operational, and physical planning of the ROM, as well
as for other interested persons. For more detailed information in any
area, reference should be made to the full Statement of Intent, and to
the Guidelines for Planning Report as appropriate.

OBJECTIVES

The Royal Ontario Museum is unique among the scientific, cultural and
educational resources of Canada. The intent is to maintain the standards
of excellence that have established the Royal Ontario Museum among the
great Museums of the world, and thereby to ensure that for the people of
Ontario, and of the world as a whole, there will be preserved some part
of 'the record of nature through countless ages' and 'the arts of man
through all the years'. This mandate shall be, of necessity, without
geographic limit.

The Goal of the Museum shall be the furtherance of man's understanding of
himself, his society, and the natural world of which he is a part.

The Basic Objectives or purposes of the Museum in and toward the
achievement of its Goal shall be:

a)   the collection and preservation of natural specimens, artifacts,
     documents, books and other relevant materials to document the
     story of the universe and of all living things, including man
     and his brief span among them

b)   the employment of scholars as curators responsible for the care
     and systematic growth of the collections, and for the study and
     interpretation of the significance of those collections and the
     subjects represented by them.

c)   participation in man's search for knowledge through the support
     of scholarly research, field work and publication by the staff in
     order that the holdings in the Museum's collections, and their
     significance, may be known to all men.

d)   the interpretation of that knowledge through gallery exhibits,
     writing, teaching, lecturing, operation of a planetarium and
     other media of communication which will open to all people a
     deeper understanding of man and the universe in which he lives.

- more -

SOCIETAL CONTEXT

The Museum acknowledges its responsibility to maintain awareness of,
and responsiveness to, the various contexts within which it operates:
the opinions and expectations of the people of Ontario with regard to
the ROM; government policies; the local environment; societal trends;
and the general problems of mankind. Conversely, the public and
government must be made more familiar with the Museum and what it does,
through effective information and communication.

Reaction of the public to the Museum generally, and its educational
effectiveness, shall be regularly monitored and assessed in order to
identify and remedy correctable shortcomings, gauge expectations, and
keep the Museum relevant to the needs of the citizens of Ontario.

THEME

A theme shall be adopted to illustrate that the main purpose of the
Museum is to bring the past into the present and future; to emphasize
the interaction and interdependence of man and all things in nature; to
provide a cohesive and integrating thread throughout the Museum and to
demonstrate what the Museum is all about and what it seeks to do. The
expression of the theme shall be subtle and shall avoid stridency, or
dominance over content, design or display. The theme shall be specifically
illustrated in a major exhibition located and organized to serve as an
introduction and orientation to all of the Museum's displays. All other
displays and exhibitions shall contain, implicitly or explicitly, some
recognizable relationship or reference back to the theme and the theme
exhibit, although this need not be specifically explained to the public
at every point.

GROWTH

The Museum accepts the necessity of shifting away from an ethic of
perpetual growth. Future growth shall be carefully planned in accordance
with adopted priorities, and taking into account physical, financial,
legal, and ethical constraints. The emphasis shall be on qualitative
rather than quantitative growth, acknowledging that occasionally the two
are interdependent. Planning for controlled growth must allow sufficient
flexibility to take advantage of important and unexpected opportunities.

For reasons subsequently noted, it is considered essential that the Museum
should retain its cohesiveness on a single site (with the possible exception
of certain support services and storage facilities); and that that site be
the present one. Consequently, the general limits to growth which are seen
as applying to the end of this century, are those imposed by the effective
utilization of the present site.

DECENTRALIZATION AND PROVINCE-WIDE RESPONSIBILITIES

The decision to remain on the present site, rather than moving the entire
Museum or dividing its public galleries onto two or more locations, is
based on the following factors:

- more -

a)   The present location is probably the best served by public transit
      in all of Metropolitan Toronto, and will be even better so upon the
      completion of the Spadina subway. No other location could provide
      such ease of access to so many citizens of Toronto and its
      surrounding communities.

b)   The unique multi-disciplinary nature of the Museum, and its ability
      to demonstrate to staff and visitors alike the interdependencies of
      man, nature, and the arts through the theme described above, as well
      as through various interdepartmental interactions, would be severely
      compromised if the Museum's offerings were fragmented.

c)   Costs of future Museum development can be minimized by making maximum public
      use of the present structures, by avoiding the need to purchase
      additional land on costly sites reasonably accessible to the public,
      and by accepting the present site as the definition of the Museum's
      growth potential for the foreseeable future.

d)   The citizens of Metropolitan Toronto are already well-served by
      over thirty smaller, specialized museums, in addition to the ROM.

The real need for decentralization is in the sense of increasing the
availability of the resources of the ROM to those citizens of Ontario who
cannot conveniently come to Toronto. The Museum shall implement a greatly
enhanced program of outreach to all areas of Ontario, using all available
means including travelling exhibits, film and television, Museumobiles,
long-term loans and displays, visiting lecturers, and the provision of
technical expertise, advice, consultation and training.

Rather than establish branch or satellite museums, in other communities,
the ROM shall encourage and assist the development of local and regional
museums in every practical way, so that they may be indigenous to their
communities and reflect the needs and heritage of the local area. The
ROM will, within the limits of its resources, provide advice, skills,
training and exhibit material as requested in order to assist in the
establishment or development of these local museums.

The ROM will pursue a course of close cooperation with government and
with other cultural institutions in order to ensure that its outreach
programs, and its assistance to local and regional museums, maximize
effectiveness and minimize duplication.

COLLECTIONS AND CONSERVATION

The central fact of any museum, and the thing which sets museums uniquely
apart from other institutions, is a collection of authentic objects. The
collections of the Museum are its central and priceless resource. At
present, a critical shortage of space severely restricts the value of this
resource by limiting display and inhibiting access for reference, study
and research. The amount of public gallery space at the ROM has actually
decreased since 1932.

- more -

It is recognized that, in many instances, collecting in the future will
be substantially influenced by financial, ethical, and legal considerations.
For these reasons, and in accordance with the policy on growth, realistic
policies and criteria shall be established to govern acquisitions, loans,
and disposals so that all may be consistent with the central policies of
the Museum.

The classification and cataloguing systems of the Museum shall be
developed in a fully coordinated manner to ensure maximum useful
utilization of the collections.

All feasible steps shall be taken during physical planning, to correct the
present uncontrolled environmental conditions within the existing structures,
which threaten the well-being of the collections.

COMMUNICATION AND EDUCATION

In fulfilling its obligations as an educator, both within and outside the
institution, the Museum must first strengthen its base by adopting a
strong sense of purpose, establishing an effective internal organization,
and providing adequate human and physical resources. Moreover, the Museum
must strive to eliminate any aspects of its image that are forbidding,
unpleasant or uncomfortable.

Exhibit and display design shall be enhanced to attain a consistently high
level of quality without stereotyped similarity, throughout the Museum, in
order to meet demanding criteria relating to interest, comprehensibility
and relevance to the theme and to the visitor's own experience: and the
Museum's organizational structure shall facilitate the coordination of
skills necessary to attain this high level of exhibit quality.

All departmental gallery areas or groups of galleries shall contain elements
of both permanent and rotating exhibits; each should relate to a gallery
theme and to the main theme of the Museum. Inter-disciplinary or integrated galleries and exhibits shall be encouraged.

Special exhibitions from outside sources shall be encouraged, but shall
be selected with discrimination having regard both to their potential to
reinforce the collections and the theme of the Museum, and to the level of
disruption that is involved.

The educational effectiveness of the Museum related to individual visitors
and to groups, with particular reference to school groups, shall be
carefully evaluated with a view to improvement and enhancement.

As noted under Decentralization and Province-wide Responsibilities a
comprehensive program of enhanced Outreach activity shall be developed,
using a range of proven and experimental methods.

Clear responsibility for education, extension and outreach, and for
cooperation with other institutions, agencies, municipalities, school boards
and local authorities shall be identified in the organization structure.

- more -

RESEARCH

Research within the Museum uses a relatively small proportion of its
financial and other resources, since the bulk of research funds is
furnished by outside granting agencies. Nevertheless, research is a vital
function and basic obligation of the Museum, fundamental to its strength
and reputation, and important to society.

Research suffers from a variety of misconceptions, and its role and results
must be much better explained to the public, to governments, to non-research
staff, and to the Board.

Research projects shall, as a rule, be initiated within Curatorial Departments. They shall, however, be subject to overall review and the application of criteria designed to allow a judgment as to their suitability in
relation to the overall resources and objectives of the Museum.

Inter-institutional cooperation on research shall be welcomed and promoted,
and the Museum shall support all serious efforts to improve communication
and information on the nature and results of research on both national and
international levels.

Shared use of research facilities both within the Museum and outside, shall
be encouraged while maintaining reasonable convenience and flexibility.

The subjects and methods of research shall be important components of
exhibits where possible, particularly in their rotating elements. As
well as scholarly research publications, departments shall be encouraged
to issue publications which interpret their research to the public, and
which provide an overview of their research activities.

INTERNAL ORGANIZATION

The purpose of the internal organization structure of the Museum is to
facilitate the attainment of the objectives of the institution. The present
structure is inadequate in this regard, and must be reconstituted as a
first priority.

The characteristics to be sought in this revised structure are chiefly:

a)   a clear relationship between the objectives and main tasks of the
     institution on the one hand, and the organizational units responsible
     for carrying them out, on the other

b)   reasonable spans of control, so that day-to-day problems do not
     completely squeeze out planning and policy formulation

c)   opportunities for participation and feedback, so that the human
     resources of the Museum may be brought effectively to bear on decisions

- more -

d)   provision of policies and procedures which result in a regular review, as a fundamental duty of management, of the degree of success of the institution in carrying out its main tasks and attaining its objectives and, in the light of this review, of how best to allocate resources to the various programs and activities of the institution.

e)   opportunity and encouragement for the development of management skills amongst the ROM staff.

PHYSICAL FACILITIES

Shortage of suitable space is a critical problem at the Museum, as illustrated by the fact that the general gallery and research space has not increased since 1932. During the intervening years, collections have grown substantially, educational and other activities have expanded, and attendance has grown six-fold. The space shortage, then, is not simply an inconvenience, but a strangling constraint preventing the attainment of the level of service which the citizens of Ontario have a right to expect from the ROM.

Nevertheless, it is recognized that physical development on the present site should take earnestly into account the historical significance of the present buildings, impact on the streetscape, and the concerns of citizens who live in the neighbourhood. For these reasons, contact shall be maintained with local citizens' planning groups through the Toronto Planning Board.

Physical planning will be guided by a general intent to:

- minimize the external impact of physical changes on the site and surroundings

- return as much as possible of the existing space, originally designed for galleries, to public use and add new gallery space as required.

- reduce present vehicular traffic and bus parking problems

- improve convenience of access to public transit, and encourage the use of transit in every practical way

- enhance and make more accessible, available green space

- investigate decentralization of space needs for certain programs and storage

In summary, the Royal Ontario Museum acknowledges its responsibility to serve the people of Ontario in every way which makes good use of the Museum's unique resources, and reaffirms its determination to constantly examine and improve its effectiveness in discharging this responsibility.

James E. Cruise
Director

APPENDIX B
COMMUNICATIONS DESIGN TEAM COMMISSION PAPER

ROYAL ONTARIO MUSEUM PROJECT OFFICE

THE ROM COMMUNICATIONS DESIGN TEAM: COMMISSION

Summary

This paper outlines the need for a Communications Design Team to oversee the conceptualization and design of displays and exhibits, and of visitor orientation
facilities, in the ROM Expansion Program. The assumption is that extensive changes
in the displays, and improvement in visitor orientation, will be made; and that the
quality of these changes is of fundamental importance to the success of the whole
program.

Policy of the Museum

The ROM has engaged in an extensive program of solicitation of opinion on its future,
from its own staff and from the public. In due course, members of the CDT will be
provided with copies of all relevant submissions which have been received as a result
of this program, and of the Museum policy documents which have ensued. For the purposes of this paper, ROM policy in areas of interest to the Communications Design
Team may be summarized briefly as follows:

a) Galleries and Displays

In fulfilling its obligations as an educator, both within and ouside the
institution, the Museum must first strengthen its base by adopting a strong
sense of purpose, establishing an effective internal organization, and
providing adequate human and physical resources. Moreover, the Museum must
strive to eliminate any aspects of its image that are forbidding, unpleasant
or uncomfortable.

Exhibit and display design shall be enhanced to attain a consistently high
level of quality without stereotyped similarity, throughout the Museum, in
order to meet demanding criteria relating to interest, comprehensibility
and relevance to the theme and to the visitor's own experience: and the
Museum's organizational structure shall facilitate the coordination of skills
necessary to attain this high level of exhibit quality.

All departmental gallery areas or groups of galleries shall contain elements of
both permanent and rotating exhibits; each should relate to a gallery theme
and to the main theme of the Museum. Inter-disciplinary or integrated galleries
and exhibits shall be encouraged.

Special exhibitions from outside sources shall be encouraged, but shall be selected with discrimination having regard both to their potential to reinforce the
collections and the theme of the Museum, and to the level of disruption that
is involved.

The educational effectiveness of the Museum related to individual visitors and
to groups, with particular reference to school groups, shall be carefully
evaluated with a view to improvement and enhancement.

A comprehensive program of enhanced Outreach activity shall be developed,
using a range of proven and experimental methods.

Suite 850, Britannica Building, 151 Bloor Street West
Toronto, Ontario M5S 1S4   Telephone (416) 928-6391

b) Theme

A theme shall be adopted to illustrate that the main purpose of the Museum is to bring the past into the present and future; to emphasize the interaction and interdependence of man and all things in nature; to provide a cohesive and integrating thread throughout the Museum; and to demonstrate what the Museum is all about and what it seeks to do. The expression of the theme shall be subtle and shall avoid stridency or dominance over content, design or display. The theme shall be specifically illustrated in a major exhibition located and organized to serve as an introduction and orientation to all of the Museum's displays. All other displays and exhibits shall contain, implicitly or explicitly, some recognizable relationship or reference back to the theme and the theme exhibit, although this need not be specifically explained to the public at every point.

c) Orientation

Orientation of the visitor is of prime importance so that maximum benefit and enjoyment may be derived from what the Museum has to offer. It should be a fundamental aspect of design and layout considerations, using all appropriate methods.

Importance of the Visitor Communication Program

As noted in the Guidelines for Planning report, a basic purpose of the Museum is "By all appropriate methods, to communicate to public and scholar alike the richness and significance of the collections, the results of research, and the full range of the resources and services of the Museum."

Of the various ways of communicating with the public which the Museum uses, the gallery displays are by far the most important. On the quality, effectiveness and interest of these exhibits is based the prime role of the Museum as an educational institution. Moreover, the public image of the Museum, whether dusty den of antiquities or vital source of knowledge and enjoyment, is almost entirely based on the quality of the exhibits themselves and on the clarity with which they are presented.

In Guidelines for Planning, Mrs. Adi Inskeep is quoted as suggesting the following criteria by which to judge the success of an exhibit, in her book "Adapt or Die: Some Thoughts on Museums in the Future":

- Does the presentation, whatever the nature of the material, involve the visitor deeply, and does it evoke his or her curiosity? (the immediate effectiveness of the display)

- Is it as memorable as possible, and does it communicate the complex relationships between objects and their signivicance with absolute clarity? (the lasting effectiveness of the display)

- Do displays establish the connection between reality - past, present, and future - and the material on display?

- Do they help to improve the quality of individual and communal life through aesthetics, experience, and information?

- Do they stimulate emotional and intellectual processes, as an adventure rather than a duty?

- Are the displays understandable to the entire spectrum of visitors?

- Are frequent visitors given enough incentive to return and explore the same subjects more deeply? (through various levels of presentation) and discover new ones? (through temporary or changing displays)

- Finally, do they evoke a sense of pride in the achievements of the Museum and the community?

Several pages of Guidelines for Planning (starting on page 40) are devoted to the importance of displays and exhibits, including expressions of concern about the avoidance of faddishness and gimmickry through over-use of audio-visual technique, comments on the sequential vs. random viewing approach, and the questions of rotating and visiting exhibits. In addition, the critical need for more effective orientation of visitors is pointed out as follows:

"Orientation may be simply described as making the visitor aware of what the Museum has to offer. Unfortunately, it is not so simply implemented. The main point is that, no matter how rich the Museum's resources or how fascinating and informative its exhibits, all is wasted if the visitor does not know what is there, or how best to take advantage of it."

Suggestions are then made on the full range of orientation methods, and on the critical importance of integrating orientation fully with display design and operational aspects.

Two matters are implied in Guidelines for Planning which should perhaps have been more forcefully stated:

1. The Curators must retain absolute control over the integrity of the informational content of all displays

2. Up-grading the quality of displays in no way implies imposed uniformity of technique. On the contrary, sensitive application of the criteria listed above should result in each gallery being totally unique and responsive to its own message and subject matter. Diversity and contrast is essential from every point of view.

The Need for a Communications Design Team

It is clear that the ROM Expansion Program will involve the conceptualization and design of galleries and displays on a scale, and at a speed, which is unprecedented within the institution. It is also clear that, to cope with the extent and pace of the likely changes, present in-house staff will have to be augmented with ouside advisors. In general, the CDT must bring to bear on the problem, the following skills and areas of knowledge:

- Learning processes and communications theory

- Human factors design, and group and individual response patterns

- Integrated display design

- Audio-visual techniques

- Graphics theory and design

- Existing state-of-the-art Museum applications

- Architectural liaison

- Team coordination, administration, procurement, and implementation.

Terms of Reference of the Communications Design Team

1. The Communications Design Team will be responsible for the conception, development, and detailed design of all exhibits at the Museum which are affected by, or considered part of, the Expansion Program.

2. The Curatorial Department involved will be regarded as an integral part of the Communications Design Team for the purposes of design of each exhibit, and the Curatorial Department will retain absolute control over the integrity of the informational content of the exhibit.

3. The Communications Design Team will be responsible for the conception, development and detailed design of the entire visitor guidance, or orientation, program of the Museum, including orientation displays and graphics, handouts, media presentations, written and audio-visual aides, etc.

4. The Communications Design Team will also be available for assistance, as requested and as authorized, in areas of overlapping knowledge such as educational and outreach programs, general graphic and audio-visual advice, and inputs to human factors aspects of architectural design.

5. The Communications Design Team will coordinate its efforts very closely with those of the Architects and of the Architects' sub-consultants, each side being careful to maintain a continuous and clear definition of scope of responsibility as the general design concepts unfold.

The Communications Design Team: Composition and Roles

The CDT will consist of two groups: the Basic Team whose members will attend all regular meetings and work sessions; and the Resource Group, whose members will be requested to undertake specific tasks from time to time.

In due course, when the CDT has established basic guidelines and criteria, it will turn its attention to the evaluation, conceptualization, and design of specific galleries and displays. At that time, special committees will be established for each gallery. These committees will be assembled as appropriate from members of the Basic Team, plus representatives from the Curatorial Department responsible for the gallery.

The initial make-up of the Communications Design Team is shown on the accompanying sheet. A curriculum vitae for each non-ROM member of the group is available for review in the Project Office.

Person/Firm	Role	Area of Special Knowledge

BASIC TEAM

D. H. Scott	Chairman of CDT	
J. E. Cruise	Director of ROM	
T. Valdo	Coordinator of CDT	Audio-visual
J. Anthony - ROM	Member	Design
Architect Representative	Member	Design & Architectural Liaison
D. Abbey	Member	Learning & Communication
E. Llewellyn-Thomas	Member	Human Engineering & Response
A. Fleming	Member	Graphic Communication
D. Barr - ROM	Member	Curatorial Aspects
J. Vollmer - ROM	Member	Curatorial Aspects
Urban Design Consultants	Staff Support	

RESOURCE GROUP

H. Bayley - ROM	Museology
D. Young - ROM	Education
R. Moynes - ROM	Education
B. Leech - ROM	Conservation
I. Lindsay - ROM	Preparatorial Aspects
D. Pepper - ROM	Art
R. Wiele	Learning & Communication
P. Ellard - Architects' Sub-consultant	Lighting/Electrical
R. Tamblyn - Architects' Sub-consultant	Mechanical/Environmental
R. Halsall - Architects' Sub-consultant	Structural

The Overall Work Program

The overall work program of the CDT is expected to involve seven phases, as follows:

Phase 1   Organization and preliminary investigation

Phase 2   Development of Guidelines document

Phase 3   Evaluation of present facilities, and establishment of priority list for change compatible with the overall development concept

Phase 4   Conceptualization and programming

Phase 5   Design

Phase 6   Implementation

Phase 7   Evaluation and adjustment

Phase 1 is essentially complete with the preparation of this paper. Phase 2 now commences, and is scheduled for completion about the end of 1975. Further phases will be scheduled in coordination with the overall Expansion Program master schedule.

In general, then, the approach is: to develop a CDT Guidelines document which will establish success criteria for displays and exhibits as well as providing background material for all key aspects of exhibit design; to use the Guidelines to evaluate existing Museum displays; to compare the results of this evaluation with the overall Museum development concept, in order to establish a priority list for the consideration of individual galleries; and then to proceed with the conceptualization and design of both the central theme/ orientation exhibit and all individual galleries which are to be changed.

The task of the Communications Design Team is to establish a set of standards, policies, and procedures, along with the informational resources to support them, which will become a permanent asset of the ROM. Continuously updated, this asset will not only guide the development of the new or changed galleries which will form part of the Expansion Program per se, but will underlie the continuous upgrading of all ROM displays for the indefinite future. Moreover, properly used, the policies and expertise developed can be of immeasurable help to other institutions who look to the ROM for assistance.

There is no more important single task in the whole range of current activities intended to better equip the ROM to meet its future.

APPENDIX C
GOOD EXHIBITS ON PURPOSE:
TECHNIQUES TO IMPROVE EXHIBIT EFFECTIVENESS

Robert A. Lakota, Ph.D.

Office of Museum Programs

Smithsonian Institution

April 1, 1976

TABLE OF CONTENTS

TECHNIQUES TO IMPROVE EXHIBIT EFFECTIVENESS

The role of museums as educational institutions has been well established. However, in many institutions, that role is often limited to formal programs developed by education departments. The purpose of this paper is to explore exhibits themselves as educational environments for the casually visiting general public, and to present a variety of techniques to improve the effectiveness of exhibits as learning resources.

Learning, in this context, refers to any measurable changes taking place within the visitor which can be directly attributable to the exhibit experience. These changes could include the acquisition of new knowledge, concepts, perceptual skills, or attitudes. This is what impact truly means. It is not sufficient to equate exhibit effectiveness with popularity (visitor count). The mere fact of attendance says nothing about the value of the experience to the visitor.

It is primarily on the basis of this humanistic role (i.e. educating the general public through the interpretation of collections) that museums are seeking greater levels of public fiscal support. Based on the experiences of public school systems over the last 15 years, it is likely that the accountability associated with those tax dollars will question not only who comes to museums but what they leave with.

These notions of impact and accountability raise several questions:

- Are there techniques which will improve visitor learning

  without interfering with the free-choice nature of the

  museum?

- Can any set of techniques be effective for the wide variety

  of visitor knowledge, backgrounds, and objectives which

  characterize the museum audiences?

Based on forty years of educational research conducted in and out of
museums, the answer to both questions is "yes". Furthermore, the techniques
presented below:

- Can be applied to virtually any existing exhibit or designed

  into any new exhibit at a very low cost, and

- Require only existing materials and staff expertise.

The general approach to be presented is one of assisting visitor understanding through a clear representation of exhibit subject matter and organization. Providing this conceptual frame of reference supports the learning skills
visitors have already developed and helps assure that they will make better
visit decisions toward meeting their own objectives.

VISITOR LEARNING SUPPORT TECHNIQUES

Most visitors enter the museum with a variety of learning skills, and
can, under the proper conditions, apply those skills effectively in gaining

information from exhibits. Unfortunately, many museums contain barriers to
visitor learning in the form of insufficient information on the purpose, content
and organization of the exhibits. If there is an organizational plan for an
exhibit, whether it is chronological, conceptual, or any other taxonomic
scheme, the basis for that organization should be communicated directly to
the visitor at the outset.

Keeping this information from visitors forces them to conceptualize and
organize the exhibits themselves, a time consuming process that only few
visitors attempt successfully. By holding on to the romantic notion that
everything must be discovered by visitors to have any "real" impact, we
are not only assuring that fewer visitors will profit from their visit, but
are also avoiding the necessity of being specific about our intentions.

Certainly any exhibit contains information, objects, and relationships
to be discovered by visitors. However, to assure that more visitors will
make those discoveries and understand what it is they discovered, tell visitors
as clearly as possible:

1. What the exhibit is about.

2. What it has to do with them.

3. How it is organized, and

4. What they can expect to learn from it.

Then, restate these points at the appropriate locations within the exhibit
and provide an active review at the end.

This additional orienting information helps visitors direct their attention to critical aspects of the exhibit within a conceptual context that is effective in communicating the message, yet does not prevent or discourage visitors from exploring other aspects of the exhibit according to their interests.

When the content and structure of the exhibit are not clear to the visitor, especially if the exhibit contains unfamiliar or technical material, it is much like tearing pages from a book and presenting them to the reader out of order, without benefit of a title, table of contents, or page numbers. Some "serious readers" who have highly developed learning and organizing skills, as well as a thorough knowledge of the subject matter, would succeed in learning something. Most "casual readers" would not. But would the inclusion of that supporting material be detrimental to our "serious readers"? Not at all. If anything, it would enable them to go directly to the material they are most interested in studying.

Similar support techniques applied to the exhibit as a learning medium would no more prevent a visitor from structuring his own visit, based on his personal interests and learning style, than they would a reader from thumbing his way through a well organized book. Unlike a programmed instruction sequence, exhibits are not designed to control the learning process; but they could provide the information necessary for visitors to apply their own learning skills with greater effectiveness.

Identifying Exhibit Content

Visitors choose a hall based on any available information at the doorway. Without a clear identification of exhibit content, visitors cannot make good decisions based on their own interests and visit objectives.

Title. The selection of the title for the exhibit can make a difference. It should be a clear statement of exhibit content and major focus. Catchy or clever titles should be carefully examined for appropriateness lest they confuse more than clarify.

Personalization. Under the title, it is helpful to state the main points of the exhibit in a way that would appeal to visitors' interests. One technique is to personalize content by answering the visitor's questions: What does this have to do with me; or, Why should I be concerned about it?

Conceptual or aesthetic bridge. Unfamiliar subject matter presents special problems which require maximum learning support to relate the new unfamiliar material to a meaningful structure. A conceptual bridge is a statement which actively associates new subject matter to other, better understood, material. Try to introduce the unfamiliar with the familiar, the technical with the non-technical by showing the functional relationships in common. For example, to introduce an exhibit on Pinnipeds -- a relatively unfamiliar word for most visitors -- functionally link it to the familiar walruses and seals through the image producing characteristics of "flippered feet." To introduce expressionist painting, use the work of a familiar artist such as Vincent Van Gogh and link the two through the common characteristic of heavy paint application and use of color.

Conceptual Orientation

Once inside a hall, visitors spend a disproportionate amount of their time near the exhibit entrance. This is the point of maximum attention to high density information. It is here that visitors are trying to determine the scope and organization of the exhibit to confirm their initial visit decision and determine their subsequent activities.

By initially telling visitors what an exhibit was designed to accomplish, what they can expect to learn from it, and how it is organized, you are providing visitors with some of the tools which are necessary for understanding the entire exhibit.

Objectives. It is not only helpful to tell visitors what the exhibit is all about, but also that something can be learned from it. That simple expectation increases visitor motivation, attention, and therefore, learning. Statements which explicitly state what the exhibit was designed to convey give direction to learning and aid visitors in organizing exhibit content. The availability of a few clearly stated objectives is not only effective in increasing visitor learning, but the very exercise of stating explicit goals for an exhibit gives a continued focus for the designer which can result in better organized and more effective exhibits.

The actual effects of objectives on the learning process depend on their specificity. Highly specific objectives, expressed in terms of observable visitor behavior, lend themselves directly to exhibit assessment, and, are often expressed as the kinds of questions visitors will be able to answer after their visit. With the aid of highly specific objectives visitors will selectively scan the exhibit for relevant material. It is also recommended that objectives be listed in the order in which the visitor is likely to en- counter them following the organizational structure of the exhibit. Further- more, restating these objectives at the appropriate locations within the exhibit can be most helpful.

If an attempt is being made to improve a poorly organized existing exhibit, the use of highly specific objectives can bring very satis- factory results. For example, in a particularly confusing physical anthropology exhibit that required a great deal of support, one set of objectives read:

Look closely at the skulls in this exhibit. By finding their

scientific name, and reading the labels, you will be able to:

● Name each skull when shown its picture,

● Recognize the pictures of each skull when shown the name

● Identify the order in which the skulls appeared from the

oldest to the most recent.

Try it! Test yourself at the end of your exhibit, and see how well you did.

When the objectives presented only represent a small subset of all the important objectives of the exhibit, however, and it is de- sirable that visitors attend to and retain as much of the exhibit material as possible, general high level objectives are a better choice. Objec- tives that are too narrow will greatly decrease incidental learning (learn- ing not directly related to stated objectives or the questions that define them). The following is an example of a general high level objective,

designed to increase visitor motivation and produce incidental learning:

>If you look carefully at the numbered works of art
>
>and read their labels, you will be able to
>
>correctly identify the periods of most modern art
>
>paintings. Try it with some of the other paintings
>
>in this gallery, and see how well you can do.

This objective requires visitors to learn the characteristics of each

period and then apply those characteristics to correctly identify the periods

of previously unfamiliar paintings.

As the examples suggest, the most effective and useful objectives are

those expressed in terms of visitor behavior, i.e. what the visitor can do

after leaving the exhibit that he could not do upon entry.

Affective (i.e. emotional, attitudinal or aesthetic) objectives can also

be expressed with the same precision. For some types of museums, such

as art galleries, where affective objectives are of primary importance, spec-

ifying these objectives is clearly worth the effort. For example, "visitors

should learn to appreciate modern art" can be translated into two objectively

measurable outcomes:

- An increased willingness to view modern art.

- An increased value placed on modern art.

Questions. An effective way to present exhibit objectives and further

increase the active involvement of the visitor is through the use of introduc-

tory questions. A few clearly stated questions at the beginning of an exhibit can be used to full advantage by the most skilled visitor and effectively increase the long-term retention for visitors not as skilled or experienced.

Although they tend to motivate visitors and attract their attention, questions, per se, do not always enhance learning. Responding to questions which are trivial or overly obvious, constitutes boring and tedious tasks to the learner. Questions which are vaguely stated or confusing or deal with tangential concepts or unimportant aspects of the exhibit may actually interfere with the learning desired. To be most effective, questions should:

- Relate to an important aspect of the exhibit and define an important exhibit objective, and
- Maintain visitor focus on the collection, directing attention to the objects themselves.

In addition to motivating visitors, pre-exhibit questions presented to the visitors as they enter the exhibit can effectively orient them to relevant exhibit material. Specific factual pre-questions have highly selective effects on visitor attention and reduce incidental learning. For example, a question related to a specific objective presented above might read: Which form of man came between Australopithecus and Homo Erectus?

General questions, on the other hand, function as instructions to search for classes of information, and they produce more incidental learning. An example of a more general question relating to the same objective as above would be: In what ways did the shape and size of the skull change from earliest man to modern man? For most exhibits, where it is desirable to maintain visitor attention to as much of the exhibit as possible, general orienting "thought" questions are preferable to those which are overly specific.

Orientation questions in the form of a pre-test on exhibit content is a well researched technique. Often in this context, the questions have been presented in a machine which provided push-buttons for responses and, sometimes, feedback. While the attraction on motivational aspects of such devices are well established, machines tend to effectively compete with the exhibit for visitor time and attention. Such devices are, therefore, less effective at the beginning of an exhibit, where visitors are already self motivated to pay maximum attention, than at the end, where visitor attention is at its lowest.

Placing game-like devices within the exhibit tends to accentuate these interference effects with viewing objects and with other visitors who do not wish to participate.

Advance Organizers. Contrary to popular belief, the physical arrangement of an exhibit does not, in itself, affect learning. Even if the juxtaposition of exhibit components does follow a logical sequence that is apparent to the visitor, that organization alone, does not guarantee their examination in the order intended. In fact, in a well organized sequential exhibit, visitors can learn as much proceeding through it backwards as in the direction intended.

So, rather than limiting visitors to one path, simply make sure the organizational structure is made clear so that visitors know exactly what part of the exhibit they are entering. If visitors are given knowledge of

that organization, retention and recall of exhibit material will be increased.
The use of these devices is especially important in exhibits with low
subject matter familiarity and high technical content.

Organizing signs. One type of advance organizer is an introductory
panel which contains clear statements of the conceptual structure and
physical arrangements of the exhibit. If there is any logical reason why
some things are displayed together, others apart; why some are at one
location of the exhibit, and others at another; if there is a sequence and
direction to the pattern of the displays; tell these things to the visitor
directly, and clearly relate this organization and its conceptual basis to the
objectives of the exhibit.

Maps. A simple floor plan map of the exhibit showing all important areas
and displays constitutes a reliable visitor guide. These maps should clearly
reflect the organizational basis for the exhibit, with each section of the
exhibit labeled as to the concept or period it presents, or type of artifact
displayed perhaps depicted by simple line drawings. A large map of this
kind can be displayed on an introductory panel. Such a map could be
useful in providing some new structure to an old exhibit, in which case
the most logical route through the exhibit must be clearly indicated, and
displays or objects numbered in sequence.

Self-Guiding Materials

Various forms of self guiding devices not only orient visitors to
exhibit content, but can effectively restate this orientation information in an

interactive way at the appropriate displays. These generally low-cost techniques can improve the effectiveness of any hall for those visitors who chose that support, without interfering with those who do not.

Brochures. Walking-tour devices (i.e. brochures, pamphlets, booklets, cards) which are dispensed to visitors at the exhibit or museum entrance for their use within are long established as effective techniques in museums. Pamphlets directing visitors to a selected group of paintings within a gallery will increase visitor attention to the entire exhibit, even to those pieces not mentioned in the hand-out.

To be effective, self-guiding materials should:

• Clearly and briefly state the objectives and organizational plan of the particular tour presented,

• Present sufficient directional information for visitors to easily locate the areas mentioned, and sequence their movements,

• Contain a text related to each display which is brief and written to direct visitor attention to the objects themselves,

• Include a minimum of illustrations -- visual information should be contained in the displays, not the hand-out,

• Make the tour interactive by including objects to locate or identify, characteristics to note, or questions to answer, and

• Be small and convenient for the user.

Booklets and catalogues containing rich background material and ample illustrations are quite appropriate for providing "take-home" information or for distribution to those who cannot see the exhibit. Within the exhibit, however, visitors should be viewing and learning from the displays, not reading catalogues.

Although exhibit maps and questions are often included in effective visitor guides, these two devices can also function alone. They increase visitor learning by providing an organizational structure for the exhibit and attracting visitor attention to the information already contained in the objects and labels.

Map hand-outs. If the exhibit arrangement is complex, or, in cases where a choice of objectives or tours is to be presented to the visitor, small hand-out maps could be provided either alone or as part of an informational brochure. These maps should indentify each major exhibit area, and include a clearly marked path for the particular tour covered, with numbered exhibit locations to indicate organization and sequencing. Several such maps might be developed for a single exhibit.

An art collection, for example, could be conceptually viewed from the standpoint of periods, subjects, or artists. If a visitor is interested in understanding the collection through art history, he could choose the appropriate hand-out map. If he wishes to compare the way different artists treated certain subjects or follow the development of one artist's style, he could choose one of the others. In any case, none of the visitors would interfere with any of the others who might be following different objectives, or who have come just to see a few favorite paintings or to enjoy the aesthetic atmosphere.

Question Sheets. In cases where hand-outs are considered preferable to labels, thought questions could be restated on maps or brochures themselves at the appropriate exhibit locations. In addition, more specific attention directing questions could also be included in an accompanying question sheet. For example, visitors would closely examine techniques of applying paint to the canvas when presented with a question comparing brushstrokes on paintings of different periods. Others might require visitors to step back in response to questions concerning the effects of those painting techniques. Such questions maintain their focus on the collection and produce a high level of visitor-exhibit interaction and learning. For exhibits which include text, both maps and question sheets should include a direct statement encouraging visitors to read the labels.

Informational Labels

Since informational labels are important didactic components, it is likely that any exhibit might benefit from improvements to existing labels. Visitor learning cannot expect visitor learning if necessary information is missing from the exhibit. But even if it is technically there, it is no better than missing if it is contained on a dimly lit, illegible label.

There are some well-established rules that, if followed, will improve label effectiveness:

- Label content should be directly related to characteristics of the objects and to exhibit objectives.

- Overly difficult language or technical jargon should be avoided. Even highly complex material can be accurately presented at a 6th grade reading level.

- Labels should be briefly stated in a way that directs visitor attention to the objects themselves.

- Composition should include liberal use of paragraphing, with sufficient line lengths to avoid broken up words.

- Labels should be placed in the closest proximity to their related objects as possible.

- Eye level placement is best, or below eye level and tilted up.

- The type used should be large enough to be read at the distance a visitor usually stands to look at the exhibit, and should be of a simple, clear typestyle.

- Sufficient lighting within the exhibit is essential for easy reading.

- Installation should allow for ease of change to incorporate new information or the results of visitor responses.

Underlining is sometimes used to emphasize important statements in labels. In general, it is a device to be avoided because it tends to over-direct attention, especially that of tired visitors, to the underlined words only, without benefit of the context provided by the additional label material and the artifacts themselves. If the underlined passage represents the only important point in the label, why include the rest? If the remainder of the label contains more detailed or technical content, placing such content in a separate, properly identified label would better assure that those interested would read it.

While some labeling has been proven effective in increasing visitor attention to exhibits, too much labeling can actually <u>decrease</u> attention. This effect is particularly strong for visitor groups which include children under 12 years old. Adults, who usually decide which halls the children will visit, systematically avoid exhibits which contain a large proportion of text and graphics to objects. To avoid the counterproductivity of "over-labeling", make text brief, to the point, and directly related to the collection on display.

If labels meet the above criteria, they will, instead of distracting from the exhibit, make a true contribution to exhibit effectiveness. To be sure that labels do communicate clearly, pretest them with visitors for legibility and ease of understanding as outlined in the "Readability of Written Materials" section below. It is essential that those responsible for an exhibit read all labeling after installation as a final check for accuracy, clarity and legibility from the <u>visitor's</u> perspective.

<u>Question-asking labels</u>. It has been shown that questions, when placed within the material to be learned, tend to reduce learner fatigue. Questions in the form of question-asking labels have been found to be as effective for learning as extensive explanatory labels. When placed within the learning

material, questions have clearly demonstrated, direct instuctional effects on question-related material. This is particularly true in museums when visitors are informed of their use at the exhibit entrance and instructed to "try and find the answers to the questions."

In addition to their motivational and attention directing effects, question-asking labels tend to be very brief. Often a single question can communicate more to the visitor than an extensive text panel that most visitors are likely to ignore. For example, if it is desired to have visitors examine two objects placed side by side and discover their similarities, a simple label containing the question, "How are these alike?" will assure that these similarities will be discovered by many more visitors.

The effects of questions on incidental learning and retention depend upon where they are placed in the material and their type (general or specific, easy or difficult). Meaningful, challenging questions such as those which require the application of exhibit facts, concepts, and principles to new situations are far more effective in maintaining visitor attention as well as increasing learning and retention than simple questions which merely require the location of facts within the exhibit. For example, an application question for a physical anthropology exhibit might read: If the changes that have taken place in the shape and size of man's skull continue, how might the skull of "future man" look several thousand years from now?

Question-label placement. If the traffic pattern through an exhibit is very regular, or some external means of directing visitor movement is provided to assure the sequence in which the displays are viewed, specific effects on learning can be obtained through question placement. Placing question-asking labels just before that part of the exhibit which contains the related material, communicates to visitors what specific things to look for in that exhibit location. The more specific the question, the more selective will be the attention of the visitor when he inspects that part of the exhibit.

Instead of defining specific cues to scan for, post-questions (questions placed just after the visitor is likely to have encountered the question-relevant material) define whole classes of cues within subsequent materials. For example, a post question on a particular tool in a display will increase attention to all tools in subsequent displays, not only the object in question. Post-questions are especially effective with low incentive learners like casual museum visitors. The best results are obtained when the questions are used liberally throughout the exhibit and are placed in the closest possible proximity to the exhibit area they refer to.

In any exhibit where both incidental as well as intentional (question-related) learning is desired, general questions placed just after the material are best.

Area signs. Two of the conceptual orientation techniques mentioned above, statements or questions defining exhibit objectives (learner expectations) and advance organizers (presenting the conceptual basis for content organization and exhibit arrangement) work best when further supported by restatement within the exhibit. A technique for providing that restatement utilizes special purpose signs (large single-statement signs displayed in prominent positions within or perhaps suspended over exhibit areas to which they relate). Organizer labels state the concept or kind of materials displayed at that location in the same way they were stated on an orientation panel. Objective signs restate objectives as a single statement or "thought" question; a general high-level question of an evaluative nature which deals with the significance of the material in that area of the exhibit. By keeping these statements or questions in mind while viewing the exhibit, visitors will maintain a general focus for interpreting exhibit material.

The Readability of Written Materials

Pre-exhibit orientation techniques, "hand-out" materials, and labels all rely primarily on the written word to guide the visitor's exhibit explorations, and communicate information. Before brochures are printed or labels mounted, it is important to determine whether the message is being communicated in a clear and understandable way.

Readability indexes. Fortunately, there are a variety of simple formulas which can be applied to a sample of text to predict reading difficulty. Two of the easiest are the FORCAST readability formula and the SMOG grading formula. Both methods generate reading grade level (RGL) scores:

- FORCAST RGL = $20 - \dfrac{\text{(The number of 1-syllable words)}}{10}$ in a 150 word passage

- SMOG grading = 3 + square root of the number of polysyllabic words in 30 sentences.

The SMOG scores tend to be higher (i.e., indicate greater reading difficulty) than the FORCAST scores. A good procedure is to apply both formulas to generate a reliable range of reading difficulty. Scores for particular hand-out or label scripts are then compared to the reading level that most visitors to a particular museum should be comfortable with.

For most museums with general audiences, a 6th or 7th grade level is a reasonable criterion. Most children in the 5th grade or under are accompanied by an adult (parent, teacher, or docent) who can interpret content for them. Teenagers, however, typically visit in peer groups and utilize their own learning skills. By the age of 12, most children have developed a high degree of conceptual ability. Furthermore, most content can be accurately presented at their reading level. A 6th or 7th grade difficulty criterion assures that a maximum proportion of the visiting audience will understand the message and be able to interpret it to the younger visitors.

A direct measure of comprehension. The indexes presented above while useful are predictive scores, not actual measures of the difficulty visitors have with the material itself. A better, though more time consuming method, is the CLOZE procedure which allows the responses of visitors themselves to determine the clarity and readability of each passage. While CLOZE does produce an overall score related to degree of comprehension, it also furnishes diagnostic information which is very useful as a guide in making revisions.

To apply the CLOZE procedure:

1. Delete every 5th word in the text, replacing each with a
    standard size blank,

2. Present the deleted word version to a sample of visitors, and ask them to fill in the blanks,

3. Score a word as correct only if it is, with the exception of misspellings, exactly the same word deleted from the original text, and

4. Calculate the CLOZE score as the percentage of correctly filled in words.

A CLOZE score between 57% and 61% is roughly equivalent to full comprehension (i.e. a score of 90% or better on an objective test based on the same material). For materials to be used with general museum audiences, over 12 years old, average CLOZE scores of approximately 55% would indicate a high level of comprehension for those visitors.

CLOZE scores can also be calculated as average per-cent correct for each individual blank or group of blanks, thus yielding patterns of strengths and weaknesses which facilitate later revision. Any part of a passage with CLOZE scores of under 35% indicates problems of comprehension of a significant proportion of visitors.

Audio and Response Devices

The techniques presented thus far can be fully implemented without the use of electronic devices or other "gadgets" not common to standard exhibit practices. However, when specifically designed to facilitate visitor interaction, such systems and devices can be effective adjuncts to learning. In deciding to use them, however, be sure to weigh care-fully the cost, in terms of equipment, additional personnel, and upkeep, against the expected benefit.

Audio systems. Many museums already have or are planning to install a broadcast tape cassette or message-repeater audio system. Although they are not among the low cost, simple techniques emphasized in this paper, audio systems can be used much more effectively than is now often the case.

The greatest single improvement can be made in the nature of the messages themselves. Attention-directing techniques, especially questions, can be used to great benefit in audio. Incorporating the following character-istics will result in more effective audio programs:

- Make the content interactive by asking questions and directing attention to the exhibit.

- Have visitors discover answers by guiding their inspection of the collection.

- Use music and sounds only when clearly appropriate, not in an attempt to make a boring narrative more bearable.

- Do not let sequences run too long. Short passages are especially important in broadcast systems.

- Keep professional control over content - do not relinquish that control to a vendor.

The following is an excerpt from an interactive audio cassette sequence concerning a painting of a bridge by Claude Monet:

> Step up to the painting and look closely at the patch of sunlight. Can you find any patches of pure color? Are the pure hues blended or juxtaposed, side by side?
>
> Now step back from the painting. What happens to these individual colors as you look at them from a distance?
>
> That's right, the pure dabs of color appear to be mixed visually. This is how the artist achieved such a rich vibrant effect.

The above sequence not only teaches about Monet and Impressionism, but visually trains the visitor so that he will never look at a painting the same way again.

This approach is also extremely effective in producing attitude changes, in this case in the willingness to accept modern art and value viewing it.

In art museums especially, affective and aesthetic objectives are often primary. The interactive, discovery-based technique presented above, either on an audio system, or set of labels or hand-outs, is a highly effective way of achieving those objectives with visitors. Furthermore, visitors appear to thoroughly enjoy the process. Museums, after all, should be fun.

An important part of any audio system is the hardware itself. The following points should be considered when making a decision:

- Make sure that sound quality is high and, especially in broadcast systems, that interference is low - noise and distortion greatly increase listener fatigue.

- Equipment should be light, comfortable and unobtrusive.

- Cassette systems should provide visitors with an on-off control for self-pacing.

- Message repeaters should be of the "push to start" type.

- "Auto-stop" cassettes and message repeaters are preferable.

- Concept building and programming of content is easier with cassette than broadcast systems or repeater systems.

- Broadcast systems can service more visitors, provide greater choices and flexibility to visitors, and have less equipment for visitors to carry around and attendants to look after.

- Built-in message repeaters do not encumber visitors, but if several visitors are to be accommodated at many stations, they are much more expensive than broadcast systems.

- Any system requires servicing and preventive maintenance - make sure maintenance provisions are adequate.

There are only some museum applications where audio systems seem most appropriate, such as diorama halls, galleries, and period rooms where labels of any kind are deemed unacceptable, and where hall content is too diverse to contain sufficient information on orientation panels. However, even in these cases, hand-outs should not be overlooked as an inexpensive, effective alternative for providing information to visitors. The greatest advantage of audio in these applications is the lack of any additional, potentially distracting visual information. With a good audio system, visitors look only at the exhibits, not at a hand-out.

Audio systems, especially cassette systems with automatic stops, have great potential as an effective "first-aid" technique for poorly functioning exhibits which were completed at great cost. Even though sufficient funds for physically changing the exhibit are not available, there may be enough money to develop an effective audio program which, when superimposed on the existing exhibit, creates an effective learning system.

To develop effective audio programs:

1. Determine the "listenability" of the audio by applying the Easy Listening Formula (ELF) to the script:

   ELF = the average number of syllables <u>above one per word</u> in a sentence.

   A score <u>below 12</u> indicates that the message is suitable for general audiences.

2. Review the script for interactive content (specific attention and movement directing statements and questions), and exhibit dependency (i.e. the audio should not make sense unless you are viewing the exhibit).

3. Observe visitors as they use the system. Note visitor movements and behavior which follows the message, and evidence of inappropriate behavior or confusion.

4. Revise the script and test again until both observations of
    visitor behavior and solicited comments from visitors are as
    expected.

Active responding. Exhibits which involve active responding result
in more visitor interest and learning. The availability of overt responses
to questions (such as pushing buttons) makes it much easier to provide
immediate feedback and can produce a record which is useful as a guide
for making exhibit improvements. However, most evidence in and out
of museums indicates that answering covertly (in your head) is as effective
as answering overtly. Visitor involvement through covert responses would
seem to be as active a process for learning as overt responding. Furthermore,
the role of feedback (being told if your answer is correct), has been shown
to be less essential to the learning process than previously thought:

- Unless feedback conveys new information to the learner, it has
  no positive effect on retention. Trivial or redundant questions
  which the visitor is already certain of answering correctly should
  be avoided.

- Right/wrong feedback is preferable to corrective feedback which
  actually identifies the correct choice.

- Unless it can be assured that the feedback will not be given until
  after the response is made, it is better to provide no feedback at all.

People learn in ways that require the least effort. If the answer is
available, visitors are likely to refer to it, (i.e. cheat) at the expense of
long-term retention.

Response-feedback devices. To take full advantage of the motivational aspects of feedback and to assure that it is response contingent, simple, low-cost devices are available. Both can be used with audio systems or in conjunction with a brochure or other self-guiding device.

The most promising approaches are the punch-board device and self-scoring answer sheets or cards. The punchboard is more flexible and versatile since it accepts answer sheets which you make yourself and can change easily. The punchboard itself can be used alone, or can be plugged into and operate a variety of other equipment such as auto-stop cassettes or slide projectors.

The self-scoring cards are custom printed, most requiring a special crayon or eraser for marking. However, with a new version the visitor responds by scratching the surface of the card with a coin. These devices are better suited to high volume, high demand situations because of their low cost. No monitoring of attendants are required since the cards can be considered "take-home" hand-outs.

Either device can contain answer choices only, when the questions are contained elsewhere (in the exhibit, brochure, or audio message), or, questions and answer choices when used alone as a complete self-guiding system. These sheets could also include a small map of the exhibit with answer choices at the appropriate locations. In any case, answer sheets should:

• Not duplicate any information that is in the exhibit,

- Include a minimum of graphics -- the visitor should be dependent upon the exhibit for visual information, and

- Be limited to a single sheet -- multiple answer sheets can become an unnecessary nuisance for visitors.

Including questions or other exhibit information on the self-scoring answer devices enables them to function as complete self-guided systems.

Question validation. The most important contribution of answer sheets and other response devices is the information they contain about how the exhibit is working with visitors. By collecting the completed sheets and tallying the number of correct and incorrect responses and skips for each question, a diagnostic profile of exhibit strengths and weaknesses can be constructed. If certain questions are missed by most visitors, it is likely that information is lacking or being presented in an unclear way to the visitor.

The visitor response information provides you with a basis for taking effective action by changing the part of the exhibit that relates to often missed questions, the questions themselves, or both. This process of collecting responses, making changes, and testing them by collecting new sets of responses, is called validation, and is an important aspect of instructional technology. As long as you are doing it yourself, at your own pace, within your own budget, it can be a very effective procedure.

After the validation sequence has been repeated and improvements have been made, the use of response devices has lost much of its further utility.

Review Questions and Statements

A review in the form of questions, which define important exhibit objectives, can be presented to visitors just before they leave the exhibit area. In this location, questions, especially those requiring the application of exhibit information, constitute an active review which supports the learning process. Even without feedback devices, review techniques can increase visitor learning. Text panels at the exhibit exit containing "thought" questions which review main points, or even statements reviewing those points, can be very effective if kept brief.

If audio-visual devices are to be used, placement at the end of the exhibit is most advantageous. There it does not interfere with visit time or compete with the exhibit for visitor attention. Providing that access is restricted to those who are leaving the exhibit, a game-like device presenting questions, feedback, and scores will constitute an effective form of active review. The attraction of a game machine and the motivational aspects of the "test yourself" situation it represents will assure ample visitor participation. Furthermore, if scores are recorded, such devices can provide a valuable on-going assessment of exhibit teaching effectiveness. However, for high-visitation exhibits, it may prove impractical to provide a sufficient number of devices to avoid bottlenecks.

SUMMARY

Learning through the examination of objects requires rather different skills than learning through the written and spoken word. However, we need not assume that visitors have suddenly lost their facility for language when entering a museum. Nor is it necessary to remove the emphasis

from the collection as a major source of information. Instead, learning sup-

port techniques take advantage of existing learning abilities as a means of

developing perceptual skills by helping visitors effectively direct their ob-

servations, as well as by providing a basis for understanding what they see.

If you want a visitor to examine objects for certain characteristics, tell them

so. If you want them to make comparisons among specimens, and draw con-

clusions on the basis of those observations, ask them questions which require

those comparisons.

A visitor paying attention to an exhibit because he is interested is

precisely what is meant by visitor interaction. All you have to do is observe

visitors within your own exhibits, reading labels and examining the collection,

to know that interaction is taking place all the time. Visitors do actively

respond to exhibits. The techniques presented in this paper will improve

the quality of that interaction, and thus the learning that results from it,

for a larger proportion of visitors.

If some of the procedures presented seemed rather obvious, stop and

consider whether you actually follow them in developing your own exhibits.

These techniques were selected from the learning literature based on their

cost-effectiveness and ease of applicability to museum environments, and

possess the following major characteristics:

- Efficiency - these procedures are appropriate for a highly
  heterogenous audience. They effectively support the learning
  of those visitors who want and need that support while allowing
  the most sophisticated visitors to take full advantage of their
  own learning skills and knowledge,

● Scope - they are capable of producing incidental as well as specific learning outcomes. That is, they increase attention to other aspects of the exhibit or collection in addition to those related to the stated learning objectives,

● Flexibility - they are able to effectively accommodate large or small numbers of visitors and allow visitors to move in a way that is consistent with their own learning style and at their own pace,

● Reliability - the effectiveness of most of these techniques does not depend upon the operation of equipment which is subject to breakdown (if electro-mechanical equipment must be used, sufficient maintenance personnel and facilities must be provided to assure continuous operation),

● Ease of Installation - these procedures are easily accommodated in a variety of existing spaces without requiring structural or architectural changes,

● Ease of Utilization - these learning support techniques can be applied without excessive reliance on outside consultation, and take full advantage of the museum staff expertise. For the most part, they would require only the exhibitry techniques and materials presently in common use, and

● Cost - since expensive equipment, fancy design techniques, and outside services are not necessary to apply these techniques, the additional cost they represent is minimal.

Museums share with schools the major institutional problem of implementing what is already known to be, or thought likely to be, effective in increasing learning. Techniques which possess the characteristics listed above are the most likely to be assimilated into on-going museum practice. However, they cannot be unless they are successfully tried in a number of museums. Any one of the techniques presented in this paper, if properly applied, is very likely to improve the effectiveness of any of your exhibits. Try them.

APPENDIX D
TYPES OF LEARNING

Extracted from the Background Paper, "Learning and Communications"
prepared by David S. Abbey (Evaluation Research, Toronto).

Here, for example are some 8 types of learning. The curator, designer
and evaluator need to make decisions about what it is they expect will
happen to the learner as a result of being confronted with the exhibit.
If they are using the exhibit as a broadcasting medium they will have
to assume that one of these types of learning is taking place. If they
percieve the exhibit as part of a closed-system which records or
collects feedback from the visitor then they need not assume. They
can know what is happening. These are elaborated here because <u>each type
of learning demands a special set of display characteristics.</u>

<u>Eight Types of Learning</u> - A hierarchy (Gagné, 1965).

1 <u>Signal or Conditioned Reflex</u>

- e.g., The visitor learns to stop in front of exhibits
  bearing a blinking red light.
- The visitor learns to avoid touching the surface of any
  painting.

2 <u>Stimulus-Response Learning</u> (S-R)

- e.g., The visitor learns to call one group of weapons
  "muskets", while another group is called "lunderbuss".
- The visitor learns to call one form of column "Ionic";
  another "Corinthian"; and a third "Doric".

3 <u>Chaining</u>

- e.g., The visitor will learn to find his or her way
  from the front entrance to a permanent exhibit on the
  third floor (without getting lost).
- The visitor will learn to operate multiple-selection
  switches on audio-devices so as to hear mini-lecutres
  in an understandable language.

4 <u>Verbal Association</u> (and Verbal Chains)

- e.g., The visitor will detect those qualities in a
  crystal structure which define it as a "tetrahedron".
- The visitor will learn the chornological sequence of names
  describing various periods of glaciation.
- The visitor will learn to order skulls in terms of cephalic
  index.

5 Multiple Discrimination

- e.g., The visitor will correctly identify a Klee, a Miro
  and a Picasso from a set of three paintings, one by each
  painter.
- The visitor will correctly name the major skeletons in the
  dinosaur exhibit.

6 Concept Learning

- e.g., The visitor will be able to select the "odd-man"
  from the following trios of objects: xylophone, piano, harpsichord;
  whale, porpoise, shark; iron, mercury, lead.
- The visitor will indicate (via test questions) his
  understanding that the pulley, the lever and the wedge
  all provide mechanical advantage.

7 Principle Learning

- e.g., The visitor will be able to conduct an experiment
  to demonstrate the electrical conductivity of various
  sample materials.
- The visitor will select the most correct explanation for
  the Faucault pendulum exhibit from several which are
  provided.
- The visitor will learn that some butterflies, like birds,
  are migratory.

8 Problem-solving

- e.g., The visitor will correctly solve several problems
  requiring specific application of Ohm's Law.
- The visitor will indicate an understanding of harmony by
  filling in various blanks in a musical score.
- The visitor will correctly select several articles which
  would permit survival on the moon for a specific period
  of time.

Each of the above types of learning is distinct from, but related to the
other types above and below it in the list (Gagné's hierarchy). Further,
each type gives rise to specific design requirements; suggests specific
performances required of the visitor; and leads to different froms of
evaluation. Some sample criteria and evaluation questions which relate
to these various types of learning, follow.

Sample Criteria

C.1   Record the statement of intent. (Answer the following questions
      on the basis of the statement as it has been given to you or as it
      is presented as part of the exhibit):

      _____

      _____

      _____

      C.1.1   For whom is the exhibit designed? _____

              _____

      C.1.2   What is the primary outcome which the visitor can expect
              from visiting the exhibit? _____

              _____

      C.1.3   How long should the visitor expect to spend in the exhibit
              in order to benefit fully from it (as defined in C.1.2)?

              _____

      C.1.4   Is this exhibit related to others in the museum or gallery
              or does it stand alone? _____

              _____

C.2   What kinds of stimuli are presented and how are they related to
      the learning which might take place?

Judge the Type of Learning	Is this condition met? (See p. 287)	N/A	Yes	No
C.2.1 ( ) Chain	Clues for each link	( )	( )	( )
C.2.2 ( ) Multiple discrimination	Reward correct; eliminate incorrect responses	( ) ( )	( )	( )
C.2.3 ( ) Concepts	Wide variety of objects representing each class	( )	( )	( )
C.2.4 ( ) Principles	Areas to which they are to apply must be shown	( )	( )	( )
C.2.5 ( ) Problem-solving . . .	Problem situation must be presented by appropriate medium	( )	( )	( )

	N/A	Yes	No
C.3 If there is a known storyline does this linear aspect of the exhibit, i.e., the principle lines of crowd flow - correspond to the sequence of the information required to "read" the story?	( )	( )	( )
C.4 Can the storyline be inferred from a "random walk" through the exhibit?	( )	( )	( )
C.5 Are there aspects of the exhibit which permit the visitor to make responses which are contained in the intent?	( )	( )	( )
C.6.1 If a particular performance or level of knowledge is expected of the visitor prior to his/her exposure to the exhibit is this actually measured?	( )	( )	( )
C.6.2 Is the visitor made aware that some particular level of skill or knowledge is required in order to make use of the exhibit?	( )	( )	( )
C.7.1. If a particular performance or level of knowledge is expected of the visitor after his/her exposure to the exhibit, is this actually measured?	( )	( )	( )
C.7.2 Is the visitor made aware that he/she has acquired a new level of skill or knowledge after exposure to the exhibit?	( )	( )	( )
C.8 If the purpose of the exhibit is to change attitudes or feelings is there provision within the exhibit for the visitor to record these:			
C.8.1 prior to the exhibit?	( )	( )	( )
C.8.2 after the exhibit?	( )	( )	( )
C.9 Does the exhibit contain information or directions which would assist the visitor to engage in follow-up visits or activities, assuming interest is sustained or increased as an outcome of the exhibit?	( )	( )	( )

Each of the eight types of learning is described in general terms as follows:*

Type 1: *Signal Learning.* The individual learns to make a general, diffuse response to a signal. This is the classical conditioned response of Pavlov.

Type 2: *Stimulus-Response Learning.* The learner acquires a precise response to a discriminated stimulus. What is learned is a connection (Thorndike) or a discriminated operant (Skinner), sometimes called an instrumental response (Kimble).

Type 3: *Chaining.* What is acquired is a chain of two or more stimulus-response connections. The conditions for such learning have been described by Skinner and others.

Type 4: *Verbal Association.* Verbal association is the learning of chains that are verbal. Basically, the conditions resemble those for other (motor) chains. However, the presence of language in the human being makes this a special type because internal links may be selected from the individual's previously learned repertoire of language.

Type 5: *Multiple Discrimination.* The individual learns to make *n* different identifying responses to as many different stimuli, which may resemble each other in physical appearance to a greater or lesser degree.

Type 6: *Concept Learning.* The learner acquires a capability of making a common response to a class of stimuli that may differ from each other widely in physical appearance. He is able to make a response that identifies an entire class of objects or events.

Type 7: *Principle Learning.* In simplest terms, a principle is a chain of two or more concepts. It functions to control behavior in the manner suggested by a verbalized rule of the form "If A, then B," where A and B are concepts. However, it must be carefully distinguished from the mere verbal sequence "If A, then B," which, of course, may also be learned as type 4.

Type 8: *Problem Solving.* Problem solving is a kind of learning that requires the internal events usually called thinking. Two or more previously acquired principles are somehow combined to produce a new capability that can be shown to depend on a "higher-order" principle. [pp. 58-59].

Gagne further believed that the most important class of conditions that distinguishes one form of learning from another is its prerequisites, since the types are in hierarchical order, as follows:

Problem solving (type 8) requires as prerequisites:
Principles (type 7), which require as prerequisites:
Concepts (type 6), which require as prerequisites:
Multiple discriminations (type 5), which require as prerequisites:
Verbal associations (type 4) or other chains (type 3), which require as prerequisites:
Stimulus-response connections (type 2). [p. 60]

---

*A résumé of Gagné, taken from M. Knowles, <u>The Adult Learner: A Neglected Species</u> (Housten: Gulf Publication Co., 1973).

APPENDIX E
GRAPHICS, COLOUR AND VISUAL IMPACT

The Background Paper prepared by Allan R. Fleming.

Allan Robb Fleming RCA FGDC AGI FOCA

graphics
colour
and visual
impact

This paper is an attempt to distill a large amount of textual matter through the filter of day-to-day experience and to demonstrate the results in a visual-verbal way. The author would like the reader to consider each point carefully and to act upon the principles described. The result should be an effective graphic system for any display. However, an inspired designer might well contradict several of the points the author has raised, and in the process produce a stunning exhibition. Inspiration is a difficult and transitory blessing which no manual can attempt to provide.

Allan Fleming RCA FGDC AGI FOCA

The first thing one has to consider is the complete alphabet either in capitals (shown below) ...

ABCDEFG
HIJKLM
NOPQRST
UVWXYZ

or in lower case (shown below) ...

abcdefghi
jklmnopqrs
tuvwxyz

or combined together to make a capitals and lower-case setting (shown below).

Many sources, including the Los Angeles Traffic Authority, state categorically that capitals and lower-case settings are by far the most legible, since the ascenders and descenders form the shape of the word.

Exit
Entrance

The second consideration is whether the alphabet has contemporary aligning arabic figures or alternately old-style, non-aligning arabic figures. Incidentally, the aligning figures should always be used in conjunction with capital letters; the non-aligning in upper and lower case text setting.

aligning figures

1234567890

non aligning figures

1234567890

Next one has the choice of categories of letterform design. They can
be broken down into more sub-categories than those shown below,
however the basic divisions are shown.

Bembo (classical)

ABCDEFGhijklm

Century Schoolbook (transitional)

NOPQRSTuvwxyz

Bodoni Book (contemporary)

ABCDEFGhijklm

Helvetica Medium (sans serif)

NOPQRSTuvwxyz

Craw Clarendon (square serif)

ABCDEFghijk

After that comes the problem of size availability; which letterforms are available and in which sizes.

Six point

Sixty point

At this point one must consider what method should be involved in the production of the letterforms. Listed below are five basic methods, starting with stick-down letterforms; moving to strike-on letterforms; from there two methods of metal casting preparations, one line-casting and the second individual letter-casting, and finally a letterform produced from film negatives.

Letraset

This exhibition should be noted for its signage

IBM Selectric Composer (Univers)

This exhibition should be noted for its signage

Linotype

This exhibition should be noted for its signage

Monotype

This exhibition should be noted for its signage

Photosetting

This exhibition should be noted for its signage

Before we leave methods of preparation it should be noted that some
of the typefaces below are available in Letraset up to 192 points. 192
points is roughly two inches in height. The bold asterisks indicate
the number of sizes above 54 point in which the letterform is
available.

Helvetica Light (Medium of Monotype)   6 - 192 pt   *******

Optima Medium   16 - 84 pt   ***

Univers 55   10 - 72 pt   **

Baskerville Old Face   18 - 96 pt   ***

Century Schoolbook   12 - 60 pt   *

Clarendon Medium   10 - 192 pt   ******

Modern 20   14 - 192 pt   ******

Beyond this point, one has to consider large sizes of letterforms (above 192 point in height). There are three basic systems for the application of polyvinyl stick down letters. The first one is Letrasign, the second Letterlign, and the third Spectralegend. I would recommend the latter only because they produce a number of different letterform designs. The first two systems can supply Helvetica only. Letrasign (below)

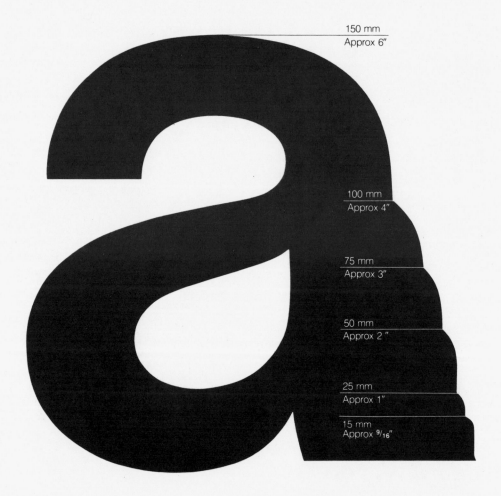

150 mm
Approx 6″

100 mm
Approx 4″

75 mm
Approx 3″

50 mm
Approx 2 ″

25 mm
Approx 1″

15 mm
Approx 9/16″

Letterlign (below)

Spectralegend (below)

Palatino

Design

½–60"

Helvetica

Design

Helvetica Light

Design

Optima

Design

Clarendon

Design

The original line below and the enlargements thereof were made from the IBM Selectric Composer golf-ball system using 11 point Journal Roman. One simply types the information on reproduction proof paper and enlarges the setting through photostatic means. This economical method of preparing text for labels is currently in use at the Boston Museum of Fine Arts.

---

11 pt Journal Roman

This exhibition should be noted for its signage. This exhibit

enlarged x 2

This exhibition should be not

enlarged x 3

This exhibition shou

enlarged x 4

This exhibition

Once a letterform and a method of reproducing it has been chosen, the next consideration is the use of space in relation to the letter. Below you can see mechanical spacing on the left and visual letterspacing on the right. The goal here is to achieve an equality of tone throughout the word through the addition and subtraction of space.

TAVERN TAVERN

wrong   right

Under normal circumstances visual letterspacing should not be used with lower case letters, and never in sizes below 14 point. There are exceptions to this rule; the first being the necessity to cut in letters following the capitals T V W and Y. The second occurs in large display sizes where small adjustments might need to be made.

Warning Turn

wrong

Warning Turn

right

Spacing between words should be kept to an absolute minimum. Ideally the space should be the width of a lower case i of the font size used, plus its two non-printing shoulders. What one is attempting to do through minimum word spacing is to create a uniform horizontal tone to the reading line; one that will reduce the number of vertical rivers of white space throughout the total setting.

This spacing is wrong
This spacing is right

Below are two examples indicating inadequate and adequate leading (or spacing) between individual lines of type. The setting on the left also demonstrates wide word spacing and you can see the white rivers of word spacing starting to form. The leading, or line spacing should always be greater than the word spacing of any line of type.

This leading is
wrong because it

This leading is right
because it creates

In virtually any graphics application it is wise to allow the type to 'fill the field'. It makes for a stronger more forthright statement. In particular, it prevents the background colour, should there be one, from overpowering the message.

This is wrong

This is right

If you decide to do a symmetric design then continue that scheme
throughout the total design. Do not mix symmetry with assymmetry.

This is the way out →

wrong

This is the way out →

right

If you decide to do an assymmetric design, then continue that scheme throughout the total design. Do not mix assymmetry with symmetry.

wrong   right

If you are having difficulty with the arrangement of lines in a design, chances are that you have four lines rather than five or three upon the sign. It is usually easy to readjust the number of lines to an odd number and the result will be more satisfactory.

This
arrangement
is
wrong

This
arrangement
is right

Simplify punctuation wherever possible. Omit punctuation after the following abbreviations and contractions / Mr / Mrs / Ms / Messrs / Dr / St / Co / Ave / Inc / 8vo / No / am / pm

Dr.Jones

DrJones

wrong   right

Wherever possible avoid over-capitalization. The World War I adage of 'when in doubt keep down' applies here.

This Is The Way Out	This is the way out

wrong   right

Use single quotation marks to indicate a primary quotation. If there
is a quotation within that quotation than use double quotation
marks to indicate the change.

The art-nouveau "look"

The art-nouveau 'look'

wrong

right

Raise hyphens and dashes to the optical centre of the capital height when using capitals only or with contemporary aligning figures. Incidentally, always use the fewest possible figures for date or page sequences / 306-9, 1946-7, 1914-18

DROP-IN CENTRE 1975-6

DROP-IN CENTRE 1975-6

wrong   right

Ellipses, a mark of omission, consists of three periods set without spaces, but preceded and followed by the word spacing of the line of type.

and I say the . . . with it

and I say the ... with it

wrong

right

Use small capital letters particularly in text settings for degrees /
LL D, PH D, MA P ENG, B SC, B PAED, D PHIL
abbreviations / BNA USA CBC MP
and roman numerals / Richard III, George V, Chapter X.
Avoid periods wherever possible.

Louis XIV	Louis XIV

wrong   right

These symbols were produced by Cook and Shanosky Associates for the American Institute of Graphic Arts in connection with a just completed study for the United States Department of Transportation by the AIGA. The symbols are to be tested in five cities over the next two years. They are the synthesis of 24 separate symbol projects, and once tested will form the basis of the American National Standard. These, and several additional symbols within the series, are recommended highly.

A great deal has been written about colour psychology, most of which has been ignored in this document. It should be stated here that a north-American can identify at least 12 colours in the spectrum and an African tribe may have only two words to describe the same spectrum. In colour use a great deal depends upon cultural information about the viewer.

The author has given basic facts concerning the use of colour pigments and he feels that the sophisticated choice of colour for display depends upon the skill of the designer of the exhibition. It does not depend upon what the curator's wife thinks would be appropriate.

This is a small demonstration of how reverses (white on black) absorb too much light and are less legible than dark letters on a light ground.

This is the way out

This is the way out

wrong

right

This conclusion is based upon several detailed tests examining male/ female preferences and gives the top choice in the colour spectrum for both males and females.

---

female	male

black on red   black on blue

This is the most visible colour arrangement for day and night viewing in the opinion of north-american traffic engineers.

most visible

black on yellow

On this colour circle, any two colours directly opposite each other are complementary. The physical law of complementaries is exact, and has nothing to do with personal taste. A complementary of one primary colour is the sum of the other two primaries.

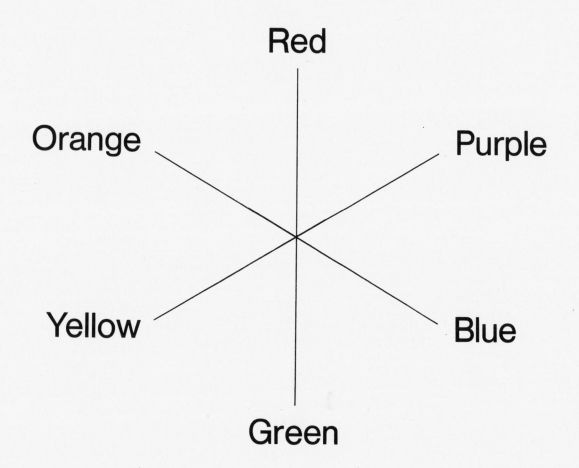

On this colour circle, any three colours equally distant from each other are harmonious. It is called the non-complementary triad colour system.

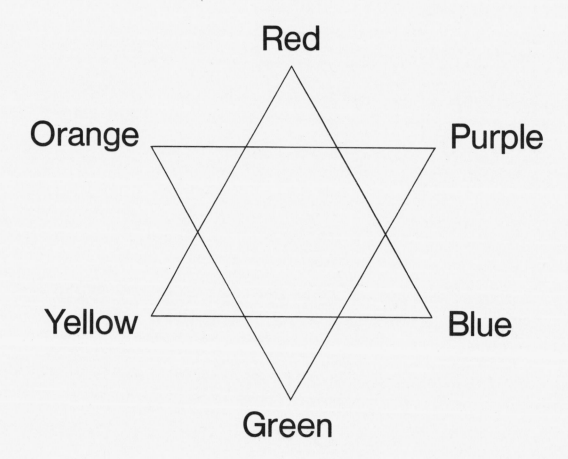

On this colour circle any three colours which are directly beside each other are harmonious. It is called the analogous colour system.

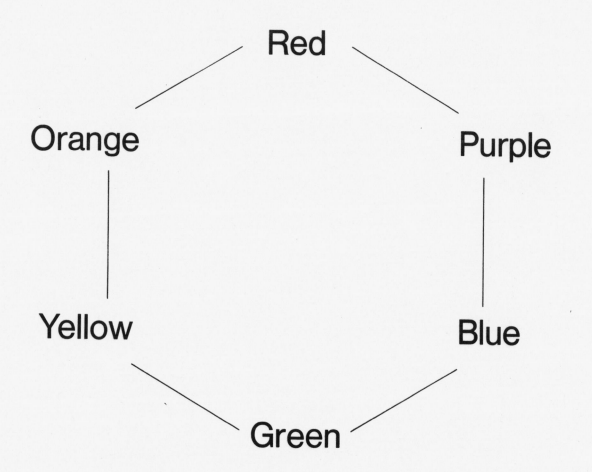

The vertical position of all text signage on walls must fall between 3 feet 11 inches and 5 feet 5 inches in height. This range represents the eye centers of an eight year old child to an adult. All directional signs can go above the 5 feet 5 inches height as long as there is some consistency to their position and providing the letters have an absolute minimum x-height of 1 inch for every 35 feet of viewing distance.

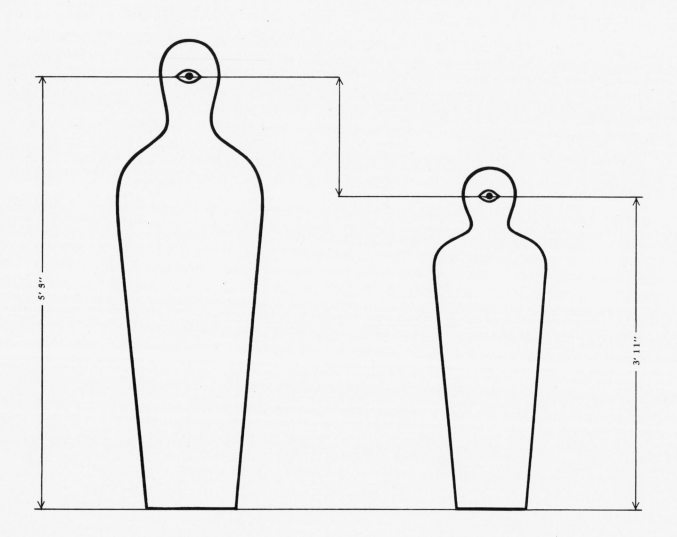

APPENDIX F
HUMAN FACTORS

Extracted from the Background Paper prepared by E. Llwellyn-Thomas
(Faculty of Medicine, University of Toronto). A series of checklists suggests the many ways in which exhibits and public areas
should be examined from the point of view of accommodating people.
An index and bibliography are included to assist in developing
and cataloguing detailed specifications of human factors.)

Check List

Physical

Illumination (light without heat)

Integral, Ambient, Spot, Interfering, Daylight
Direct, Indirect, Diffused, Special distributions
Incandescent, Fluorescent, Other
Glare - Direct, Specular, High Spots
Shadowing and Contrast
Reflectance
Surface Colors, Source Colors
Light Sources: Positions and Intensity - Fixed
                                            Variable preprogrammed
                                            Variable viewer controlled
                                            Variable environment controlled
Signal and Warning lights
Emergency and Escape lighting
Security lighting - potential danger spots and 'dark corners'

Sound and Noise

Sources - Human Voice - Guide, Visitors, Loudspeakers (Pubic Address and
                    Recorded), Earphones (Personal receivers and tape
                    recorders), Telephones
         Display Sound Effects
         Emergency and Warning
Characteristics - Frequency range, Comprehensibility

Interference
         From other signal sources: Floors, telephones, doors, etc.

         From Noise: Quality, Intensity, Pitch, Distinct Tones
                      Frequency, Regularity, Sudden Onset, Prolonged
                      Predictability: Expected and Unexpected
                      Localized or diffuse
                      'Startle' potential
Reverberation, Echoes, Acoustic Damping
Acoustics of rooms and spaces
Acoustical improvement measures
Effects of visitor density on ambient noise and acoustics
Effects of Component changes, e.g. new exhibits) on acoustics
Seasonal changes in noise levels, e.g. air conditioners running up to load,
                          sniffing children and coughing adults)

Temperature, Humidity, Ventilation

    Seasonal and diurnal variations
    Sources of heat, cold, drafts
    Constraints e.g. from nature of exhibits
    User density effects

Ionization

    Effects of positive and negative ions in rooms on Users. (There
    are unproved but supported suggestions that an excess of free
    negative ions tend to exhilarate and positive ions depress people
    in a room. Future experiment?

Interfaces

    Solid, translucent, mesh, grills, bars, rails, air-curtain
    Flat, angled, curved
    Texture, hardness, surface characteristics
    Light, sounds, vibration transmission
    Controls, visitor operated and other
    Floor coverings, wall coverings, steps, stairs, slopes, ridges, etc.
    Seasonal effects on interface, e.g. in winter people cough, spit,
       wear rubbers, drip, carry umbrellas, come in from the cold etc.
    'Wheelability'

Dimensions Focal Interests
               Heights
               Distances
        Shape
        Angles and projections, Steps and wells
        Movement pathways required from viewer

Locations

    Accessability
    Separation from other components
    Potential for physical interference, e.g. visitor viewing one display
       blocks another visitors view of a second display

Access and Escape

    Legal requirements
    Special hazards not covered by above
    Visitors clothing and things carried - hazard potential (bombs also)

Safety

    Hazards, e.g. edges, corners, etc.
    Floors, e.g. slippery? hard?

Installation, Servicing, and Maintenance

Access for personnel and equipment. Standardized parts available.
Reachable facilities (e.g. power points). Room to open covers,
remove panels, use a scredriver, see what you're doing, etc.

Check List

Physiological and Anatomical

Posture demanded: Walking   Climbing
                  Standing   carrying(trays, children, etc.)
                  Stooping
                  Sitting
                  Neck-bending and head turning
                  Leaning
Limb Movements required

Eye Heights

General
Physiological needs: Washrooms
                     Lavatories
                     Food
                     Water
                     Rest
                     First Aid and Recovery

                     Temperature, Humidity, Air Movement, etc.

Physical Demands:
                  Strength, e.g. to open doors
                  Dexterity, e.g. to operate faucets

Anatomical Aspects:
                  Size and Shape of User Populations related to Component

Special Physiological Needs:
                  Diaper changing
                  Infant feeding
                  Disabled visitors
                  Deaf
                  Aged
                  Ill

Check List

Psychological

Demands made on the Perceptual and Cognitive Functions of Users

Visual
        Acuity, near and far vision
        Color discrimination
        Depth perception
        Eye movements and scan patterns

Hearing
        Acuity
        Tone discrimination
        Selectivity (against interference ane ambient noise)

Touch
        Tactile sensitivity
        Tactile discrimination
        Potential for use as communication channel in Component

Olfactory
        Smells - perfumes, odors, and stenches

Multisensory
        Compatability between senses
        Compatability with other Components

Perception & Aperception
        Complexity levels
        Illusions - intended and unintended!
        Gestalts (completeness as perceived)
        Search
        Recognition
        Vigiliance
        Novelty
        Incongruence

Cognition
      Attention Spans
      Language levels
      Complexity of reasoning
      Decision Making
      Adjacent displays/objects
      Feedback from user
      Display/objects component satiation

Affective (Emotional)
      Involvement
      Identification
      Arousal (Exotic, erotic, macabre elements in Component)
      Color (Emotional effects)
      Symbols (Emotional effects)
      Cultural interpretations

Check List

Social

Social Behavior Demanded of the User

Attitude

Cooperation with other individuals

Cooperation with other groups

Cooperation with museum staff

Control of others, e.g. children

Readiness to read instructions, etc.

Non-interference with objects

Target Group

Primary Target Groups   Define in terms relevant to Component
Secondary Target Groups   e.g. age; sex; educational levels;
Other Target Groups   cultural, scientific, and humanistic
                                backgrounds; language skills;
                                occupations (trades, professions, leisure
                                activities)

Cultural/Racial elements in Component, e.g.in display
'Personal Space' allowed
'Social swirl' sociofugal and sociopetal effects
Social compatability with adjacent components (unless 'social shock' is
  sought)
Interaction among age levels - helping relationships

<u>Check List</u>

<u>Educational</u>

Levels of Education demanded of Users

Level of literacy

Language facility

Mathematical ability

Historical knowledge

Geographical knowledge

Scientific knowledge

Artistic knowledge

Local knowledge

Library skills

Religious knowledge

Knowledge of museums in general

Knowledge of other local museums, provincial museums, etc.

Educational Goals of Component

Educational goals defined in objective and subjective terms
Appropriate educational techniques used, e.g. redundancy
Self-testing facilities for users
Cross-referencing to library, other Components (e.g. Exhibits), other
    museums, etc.
Availability of pamphlets, guides, catalogues, leaflets, tapes, etc.
Relevant references near Component (e.g. Exhibit) and a place to read them
    in comfort
Non-verbal, visual and tactile encounters possible with Component
Potential for moving user's imagination to move backward and forward in
    time and place
Has Component an exotic, erotic, or currently relevant potential which can
    be brought out to encourage learning?
Is information available in languages other than English?
Are multi-lingual guides and instructors available for this Component?
What measures will be used to discover Component's success in approaching
educational goals?

<u>Check List</u>

<u>Technological</u>

Technologies involved:

        Curatorial
        Electrical
        Electronic
        Mechanical
        Chemical
        Audio-Visual
        Educational, etc.

Technologies (new and old) which might be involved to advantage

Technical skills demanded of User, e.g. Audio-Visual Controls

Museum technology involved as possible part of Component, e.g. of an Exhibit

Technologies involved to be Overt or Hidden? e.g. machines, operating
    computers, kitchens, lighting fixtures, humidity control in cases, etc.

Relevance to modern technologies? e.g. the traditional forging of a
    Japanese sword and the production of modern razor blades

Check List

Financial

Demands made on museum finances, present and future
(not including initial costs)

Operating costs

Maintenance costs

Repair costs

Rate of deterioration

User wear and tear

Shut-down costs

Maintenance costs if taken out of use

Present financial constraints

Probably future trends

Potential for retrenchment in times of financial stringency

Potential for encouraging gifts and endowments to museum from users, e.g.
    a museum archeological project

Potential for demonstrating social value of museum to tax-paying user

Potential for increasing museum income without betraying museum's primary
    objectives, e.g. interesting and unusual foods in restaurant related
    to exhibits as well as good conventional meals. Encouragement of
    book, catalogue, sourvenir artifact purchases by mentions of avail-
    ability in Exhibit labels. Encouragement in membership of museum
    support groups, etc. (One can imagine some horrible encouragement
    to huckstering at worst; acquiring some devoted museum adherents at
    best.)

Any potential for legal action against the museum? e.g. from falls,
    infringement of copyright, food poisoning, assault, etc.

Potential for offending special religious, political, racial, etc. groups?
    (To be aware of potential, not necessarily swayed by it!)

INDEX

PARAMETERS, SPECIFICATIONS, AND RECOMMENDED PRACTICES

(Initial attempt at a framework on which to develop)

Hearing
>   Description of mechansim
>   Recommendations for Intelligibility
>   Changes with Aging

Illumination
>   Light – Definitions of Units of Measurement
>   Spectral charts
>   Luminance
>   Reflectance
>   Contrast
>
>   Artificial light sources
>   Glare
>   Colored lighting
>   Variable lighting
>   Flicker and Flashing
>   Recommended Levels – Table

Lettering and Signs
>   Recommended alphanumerics – Tables
>   Recommended Symbols
>   Recommended Formats
>   Signing – Good Practice

Noise (Acoustic)
>   Definitions and Units of Measurement
>   Characteristics
>   Expected Levels – Table
>   Recommended Levels
>   Reverberation and Echo

Perception
>   Definition and Description
>   Intersensory Effects
>   Pattern Recognition
>   Search and Identification
>   Illusion and Ambiguity
>   Complexity levels
>   Interest levels

Perception cont.
        Emotional factors, effects on Perception
        Perceptual Spans
        Perceptual Modalities
        Aids to Perception
        Attention, Arousal, and Perception
        Perceptual Defence
        Subliminal Perception

Projection
        Recommendations of Group Viewing - Table
        Types of screen - descriptions
        Critical Angles

Signals
        Recommendations

Stairs and Ladders
        Codes of Practice
        Diagrams

Traffic
        Design Recommendations
        Drawings
        Common Traffic Patterns
        Escape and Emergency Routes
        Traffic Control

Vision
        Mechanism - description
        Visual Acuity - definitions and measurement
        Near Vision - tables
        Accommodation
        Depth Perception
        Visual fields - definitions charts
        Central and Peripheral Vision - description
        Eye Movements - definitions and description
        Visual Angles - definition
        Visual Data - Charts
                        Tables
        Aids to Vision
                        Magnifiers and Minifiers
                        Microscopes
        Visual Changes with Age - description Charts

Visual Displays
        Design Recommendations

Viewing in Groups
        Design Recommendations
        Charts and Figures

Working Areas
        Design Recommendations

BIBLIOGRAPHY

Chapanis, A., <u>Man-Machine Engineering</u>, Wadsworth Publishing co.,
    Belmont, CA, 1965

Chapanis, A., Garner, W.R., Morgan, C.T., <u>Applied Experimental
    Psychology</u>, Wiley, New York, 1949

McCormick, E.J., <u>Human Factors Engineering</u>, McGraw-Hill, New York, 1970

Van Cott, H.P., Kinkade, R.G., <u>Human Engineering Guide to Equipment
    Designers</u>, Superintendent of Documents, Washington, D.C.,
    1964

Woodson, W.E., Conover, D.W., <u>Human Engineering Guide for Equipment
    Designers,</u> University of California Press, Los Angeles,
    CA, 1964

Meister, D., <u>Human Factors: Theory and Practice</u>, Wiley-Interscience,
    1971

Dreyfuss, H., <u>Designing for People,</u> Grossman Publishers; Paragraphic
    Books, 1967

Aerospace Research Applications Center, <u>Databook for Human Factors
    Engineering,</u> Vols. I and II, NASA CR 114271 and CR 114272
    (NAS2-5298), Indiana University Foundation, Bloomington,
    IN 47405

Dreyfuss, H., <u>The Measure of Man</u>, Whitney Library of Design, New York

Gregory, R.L., <u>Eye and Brain</u>, McGraw-Hill Book Company, New York, 1966

Shephard, R.J., <u>Men at Work</u>, Charles C. Thomas, Springfield, IL, 1974

National Design Council, <u>Design for People</u>, Information Canada, Ottawa

APPENDIX G
INTERPRETATIVE TEXTUAL MATERIAL

Extracted (with minor editorial changes) from the Background
Paper "The Curator's Role in the Process of Interpretation"
prepared by David Barr (Associate Curator, Royal Ontario Museum).
(An approach to the conceptualization and development of textual
information is discussed.)

The goal of this paper will be to describe ways of processing textual information so that it can have maximum effectiveness on the Museum visitor.

One basic principle will be emphasized throughout. Only when the visitor's interest is maintained at its highest pitch can understanding of interpretative material, that is, true communication, result. It seems obvious that stimulation of viewer interest is possible only by careful and systematic planning of every aspect of the message to be transmitted.

It is probably self-evident that some of the information to be transmitted in an exhibit concerns basic knowledge of the field of study being presented. In addition, we need to communicate the attitudes, both emotional and intellectual, which knowledgeable people have found most useful and illuminating in integrating this knowledge into their own experience. What is perhaps not so obvious is the fact that this specialized knowledge of a subject is often phrased in a code, what Duncan Cameron refers to as 'the curatorial code' and that this code may in itself be a foreign language to the lay visitor. Therefore, an additional goal must be to try also to communicate an understanding of the code in which a particular body of knowledge is phrased. Thus we expand the visitor's capability of interpreting for himself.

Sources: The sources of basic data for interpretation correspond to all sources of information available to the curator. These include (i) his own internal information file built up on the basis of experience, (ii) the primary or research literature in his field of study, (iii) textbooks summarizing his field of study, and perhaps less obviously, (iv) the body of interpretative publications already available in his field. This last source of information consists of magazine articles,

popular books, lectures, pamphlets, brochures and so on that
most of us accumulate during our working life in the Museum.

The interpretative literature is particularly important because
it represents other people's attempts at communicating the
same types of facts that we deal with. It serves as some sort
of rough guide to what has been found to interest and excite
the layman in others' experience. Even displays in other
museums should be used, for when the goal is effective communication, no source is sacrosanct. There should be no question
of plagiarism, no obsession with being unique or singular.
The exhibit speaks to its audience, not to other curators or
designers. And the majority of visitors to your exhibit will
have access to none of the other sources of information you
will use. The most effective devices (however effectiveness
may be determined), wherever they may have been used previously,
are those that must be employed.

...

The preparation of textual material that adheres to the criteria
good interpretation is in part intuitive and in part an art.
Nevertheless, a compilation of basic principles of interpretation will be useful as a guide to minimum requirements for
most curators preparing a new exhibit.

...

The techniques suggested here are basically those of the author.
Ideas for the principles have come from buides to writers of
books and magazine articles (Fitz-Randolph, 1969; Gilman, 1961),
from the principles of journalism (Flesch, 1974), and from
thinkers who have devoted their major efforts to methods of
interpretation in the museum field (Tilden, 1973). Documentation for many of these suggestions ranges from intuition and
common sense, to rules-of-thumb adopted through experience by

professional writers, to technical criteria of text assimila-
tion established experimentally. Whatever the source of the
information, the curator should regard the guidelines suggested
here not as absolute rules but simply as reliable aids to
achieving desired ends. There will always be room for the
art and genius of the skilled interpreter.

Principles:
a) Effective interpretation relates what is being displayed
    to something within the personality or experience of the
    visitor.
b) Interpretation is revelation based upon information.
c) Interpretation is an art which combines many arts, including
    the art of good writing.
d) The aims of interpretation, in order of importance, are
    excitement, modification of attitude, and transfer of
    information.
e) Good interpretation must be concise and forceful. The
    average museum visitor spends only 30 to 60 seconds view-
    ing any one segment of a display; for example, one exhibit
    case (de Borhegyi, 1965).

...

Context Information: Care should be taken at the very beginning
to explain the context of the entire exhibit to the museum visitor. We must make clear to the audience both the philosophical
and material fore-runners of our collections and the additional
types of studies for which our materials serve as basic information resources. What is the relative position in time and
space of our collections, and what is the relationship to
neighbouring parts of the time/space continuum? This gets us,
I'm afraid into the subject of relevance, for we must inform
the visitor why this exhibit has been done, why its contents

are important, and at the same time, give him a little
guidance as to how it is organized. Only in this way can
the visitor be interested enough in the exhibit to benefit
from the interpretation presented there. It is sufficiently
obvious to be easily overlooked that the exhibit should be
related for the visitor to other parts of the Museum that are
relevant. Context information may be presented in an introductory or orientation section of the exhibit.

...

Textual Materials: The basic levels of textual information
consists of (1) brief and concise labels, (2) expanded labels,
(3) printed handout material (information sheets), (4) audio-
visual scripts,(5) gallery guides, and (6) advertising copy.
Each of these information levels is considered to be interpretative, even the handouts or information sheets which may contain fairly complex types of information. Thus, while the
format of each of these types is beyond the scope of this
paper, the general principles of interpretative writing
suggested here pertain to all of them.

Motivation: Ther term 'motivation' ... is defined here to
encompass any device which increases the visitor's interest,
excitement or mood. Motivation enhances the visitor's emotional
state in order to enhance his appreciation of the information
content of any exhibit. Thus, as Brawne (1965) has suggested,
variety of any type can be motivational. In addition, the
use of humour, metaphor, analogy, evocative vocabulary,
comparisons, allusions and quotations can all impart a strong
motivational element to any information. For motivation by
text we must resort to the wide variety of literary devices,
that is, the language skills that make for good and interesting
writing. (The many non-literary motivational devices -

graphics, colour, lighting - are not treated here.) A
particularly important motivational device is <u>personalization</u>,
the relation of the objects displayed to the visitor and to
other human beings who have handled them: who found the object,
who studied it and what have they learned about it?

...

<u>Final Copy</u>: Final labels for the exhibit may be written by a
professional writer or by a curator with adequate skills.
Labels should make use of all the devices of good writing so
that they communicate as effectively as possible. They must
first, of course, be truly <u>concise</u> (Weiner, 1963) with all
extraneous material pruned out. A journalistic system of
headings (de Borhegyi, 1963) and subheadings can be valuable
in orienting the reader to the information content. Language
should be <u>colloquial</u>, suited to the major target group within
the audience (this is probably lower than you think - probably
Grade V to VIII level), and jargon should either be eliminated
entirely or defined in such a way that useful terms are made
understandable to the reader. Efforts should be made to
include one or more motivational factors in each label and
special effort should be devoted to communicating the scholar's
mood of <u>excitement</u> with his objects of study. Remember that
the time spent in comprehending an individual label is likely
to be 30 seconds or less unless the reader has been motivated
to pay unusual attention to it. Objective standards of label
readability such as any of the several indices developed by
Rudolph Flesch (1973), or the Cloze procedure (Klare and
Sinaiko, 1972), can be used to check the final text.

Information sheets, gallery guidebooks, audio-visual scripts,
and other printed material accompanying an exhibit should also
adhere to the tenets of good writing proposed above. The only

additional principles to be followed are to ensure that
short paragraphs are used and that an outline has been prepared before writing to ensure that the text follows a
logical structure.

The curator should check that after the process of text preparation, the information content of the exhibit remains
intact. There must have been no introduction of error and
no modification the basic concept. This sort of check extends as well to public relations material to be published
or broadcast concerning the exhibit. It would
also be wise to employ a lay critic to read all final copy
and to give constructive criticism as well as pointing out
obvious gaps, inconsistencies and ambiguities from the viewpoint of the non-specialist.

...

A continuing responsibility of the curator associated with
any gallery will be long-term maintenance of copy and story-
line. This means that the informational content of the gallery
must not be disturbed by the removal of an object for study,
by the deterioration of labels or by the eventual obsolescence
of some parts of the information. Each of these conditions
must be watched for carefully and corrected without delay.

APPENDIX H
AUDIO·VISUAL MEDIA TECHNIQUES

Extracted from the Background Paper by Terry Valdo (Media
Consultant). (A discussion of audio-visual programming and
hardware, aimed at the non-specialist, provides essential
information for an understanding of media systems and for the
appropriate selection of a system.)

TABLE OF CONTENTS

SOFTWARE PRODUCTION

The software production (that is the creation and production of a program to be played or shown on the hardware or equipment) is the most important factor when audio visual is to be used successfully in an exhibit. Some of the steps involved in developing a successful slide program are as follows:

Determine the theme of the gallery

- What is the single most important concept that the gallery is to communicate to the public?

Determining the storyline of the gallery

- How does the storyline relate to theme?

How are the objects to be selected for display?

- Has the curator selected a series of objects which show the various aspects of the storyline?

Where should audio visual be used in the gallery?

- Orientation?

What is the purpose of the audio visual?

- As compared with the other means of communication such as the object, labels, graphics, etc.

Type of audience who will use gallery and audio visual

- School groups, tours, individuals, families, etc.?

Duration of visit to gallery

- Will govern number and content of programs.

Topics to be discussed in audio visual

- Should relate to specific objects, groups of objects and concepts illustrated by gallery.

Media selection

- Choice of system dependent on position in gallery, size of audience, size of audio visual, content, etc.

Treatment

- Should the audio visual program pose several questions about the object that the visitor can answer by observation of the object.

Research

- What is the background information on the objects?

Script development

- Content, length, number, purpose, relation to theme, etc.

Script approval

- Curator and designer approves what the writer has finally developed.

Development of visual storyboards

- Visual content and pacing is worked out as well as the shot list for photography and visuals needed for art work.

Location photography

- Shorts taken in the lab, on field trips, and in the gallery.

Production of art work

- Titles, graphics, charts, reconstructions, landscapes, etc.

Studio photography

- Shooting the art work and burning in titles, etc.

Editing the visuals

- Matching exposures, developing visual sequences.

Choosing the announcer and studio

- Announcer's voice should match tone of program.

Choosing the music

- To set the mood.

Choosing the sound effects

- Recording the sounds of digging up bones.

Recording the sound track

- Watching the pacing and pronunciations.

Editing the sound track

- Tightening-up the narration.

Mixing the sound track

- Adding music and sound effects for transition.

Programming the cue track

- To synchronize the visuals.

Testing the completed program

- Checking the pacing and the sequencing of the visuals.

Duplicating the program

- To use in place of the original.

Evaluating the audience reaction

- To see if the program does in fact satisfy the purpose of why the program was designed.

Developing a maintenance program

- To guarantee replacement of faded slides, worn tapes, and equipment wear.

It should be noted that:

- The production of 16mm film and video tape will vary from the above slide production sequence.

SOME CONSIDERATIONS ON WHETHER TO DEVELOP
AN INTERNAL AUDIO VISUAL DEPARTMENT

The question of establishing an audio visual department in an institution
always comes up when an audio visual program is to be produced for an
exhibit. In order to assist those who have to make that evaluation, a
few considerations are listed below:

PROS

-   The establishment of a permanent audio visual department will develop
    an expertise in museum related audio visual programs and programing.

-   It will develop a thorough knowledge of the museum, its people, its
    collections, and its activities.

-   Because of the above, it will be able to initiate the creation and
    development of programs as galleries are planned, developed and maintained.

-   It will be always available to photographically record and file
    activities and events such as field trips, gallery construction,
    research projects, temporary exhibits, etc.

-   The more programs produced, the greater the saving in cost.

-   Maintain and modify programs once they are installed in the galleries
    as well as the associated audio visual systems.

-   Produce title slides, art work, copy slides for internal and external
    presentations such as gallery openings, organizational meetings,
    outreach, etc.

-   Be able to produce programs of varying length and depth using
    existing researched material for different levels of communication.

-   They will be able to plan and supervise outside production of 16mm
    film and video tape thus provide control over the quality and outside
    costs of production.

CONS

- The establishment of an internal audio visual department will require
  the hiring of very skilled - producer
  - writer (could be freelance)
  - photographer(s)
  - recording engineer
  - graphics people
  - administrative people

- Expenses will depend on the number of programs they actually produce
  per year.

- Unless these very creative and skilled people are used to their
  capacity, they will become dissatisfied.

- An internal audio visual department will require the acquisition of:
  - photographic equipment such as cameras, lenses, copy stand,
    slide duplicating equipment, lights, strobes;
  - recording equipment such as professional tape decks, mixer,
    equalizer, sound-proof studio, microphones, transcript player,
    oscillator, tape, etc.;
  - graphic equipment such as drafting boards, art supplies, letraset, etc.

  NOTE: The above will require a sizeable initial investment which
        will be justified if there is a large amount of production
        or a sharing of equipment and human resources with existing
        departments.

- The production of 16mm film or video tape will still require outside
  production.

A FEW CONSIDERATIONS REGARDING
AN OUTSIDE AUDIO VISUAL PRODUCER

- Museum should agree as to the amount of research, planning and production the outside audio visual producer is to be responsible for.

- Outside producer should be brought into the job while the concept of the gallery is being decided on by the curator and designer so that the use of audio visual will be an integral part of the gallery and not an afterthought.

- He should have the responsibility in setting deadlines on background information, on what material from the collections is going to be displayed and what is to be communicated about it.

- He should be required to develop a production schedule showing deadlines for research, rough draft of scripts, final scripts, treatment, approval, visual storyboards, photography, recording duplications, and testing.

- He should be directly responsible to the project manager of the gallery who has the ultimate power to decide on content of scripts, visuals, announcer treatment, etc.

EXAMINATION OF THE MOST COMMON AUDIO VISUAL SYSTEMS

The following thirteen systems have been chosen for evaluation out of
the thousands on the market because most of them are variations of the
thirteen. It should be noted that the systems discussed here are
designed for continuous, heavy duty and automatic operation as opposed
to a system that has to be manually reset. Also, these observations
should only be a guide for a deeper individual examination. Each
system will be discussed in approximately ten sections:

Description of system - describes the simplest system and more complex versions.

Application - describes how each system might be used in a museum
giving specific examples.

Operation - describes how each system mechanically operates.

Maintenance - what sort of problems might occur in continuous operation.
It should be noted that the cost of personnel in maintaining these
systems was not taken into consideration. Also, some maintenance
figures were unavailable at the time of writing.

Software production - the cost of producing a program on each of the systems.

Software duplication costs - the yearly expense of duplicating the
programs on each system.

Equipment costs - these figures can vary depending on the manufacturer
and source of supply.

Equipment maintenance costs - cost of maintaining systems on a yearly
basis. It should be noted that the cost of personnel has not been
considered in this report but should in planning for audio visual in
a gallery. Also, some of the equipment maintenance costs were not
available at the time of writing this report.

<u>Bulb costs</u> - in some systems this figure becomes nearly equal to the cost of duplicating the software.

<u>Evaluation</u> - Some brief comments on how good each system is.

Finally, there is a chart showing six common systems, their cost per year and per day, for: software duplication costs, audio tape, bulb, etc.

16mm FILM STRIP PROJECTORS

DESCRIPTION OF SYSTEM

- A system of self-contained presentation units of various sizes which take a compact cartridge which contains both 16mm film strip and ¼" magnetic sound tape.

- Both 16mm film strip and audio tape are an endless loop and this eliminates the need for rewinding.

- Synchronization of audio track to the film strip is accomplished by cue pulses on the second track of the audio tape.

- A stop cue pulse at the end of the audio program can be used to shut off the whole machine including the bulb or to shut off the machine and leave the bulb on. (To leave the title of the program on the screen.)

- The cartridge will hold up to 18 minutes of audio and up to 250 visuals. This cartridge can be used on several different machines having various screen sizes up to 9" x 12" for small audiences as well as a projector for larger mini-theatre audiences.

APPLICATION

- Designed to run continuously in exhibits or be audience-activated to extend film strip and bulb life.

- To achieve program flexibility, system allows for designing each cartridge to hold several different programs of various lengths or one program that is continuously repeated.

- Compact and self-contained. This unit can be mounted at any reasonable angle within reach of an audience or built into a wall.

- Light can be switched to remain on at the end of each program so that the viewer can see title of next program and choose if he wants to view it.

- Built-in speaker can be disconnected if used with externally mounted speakers mounted in a railing or in a wall.

- A moulded plastic shroud can be obtained to cover the front of the machine's controls and to protect the built-in rear projection screen with a second unbreakable screen.

- Their small self-contained design allows them to be used in a central orientation area where each would form part of a mini-exhibit, one for each gallery. Their purpose would be to indicate to the viewer what he could expect to see and learn if he ventured into that gallery.

OPERATION

- Cartridge is easily plugged into or removed from machine.

- When built-in or remote start button is pushed, machine turns on, starts audio tape running, turns on projection lamp and cooling fan. Inaudible audio cue on tape changes the film frame.

- As both film strip and audio tape are an endless loop, they are ready for replay immediately after a program comes to the end.

- Tape transport and film transport are designed simply and ruggedly for heavy, maintenance-free operation.

- As the film strip change cue is on the same tape as the narration but on a different track, there is no chance of losing sychronization.

- There is, however, a chance after hundreds of pulse activated frame changes that the film strip could get out of synchronization with the audio track. This is rectified by frame advance and frame retard buttons which can quickly resynchronize the program.

- As film strip unit is capable of changing frames as fast as four times per second, limited animation is possible (e.g., to show the movement of a horse).

MAINTENANCE

- Audio system, electronics, film transport and tape transport are built in one module which can be easily and quickly pulled out of back of unit for repair or replacement.

SOFTWARE PRODUCTION COST

- A 16mm film strip program is produced in a similar way to a slide show only that the slides are then reshot onto 16mm film and mounted into a compact cassette containing the audio tape.

- Thus the cost would vary as to the number of location shots, title shots, title burn-in shots, program length, announcer, etc. as well as reducing the 35mm slides in sequence onto a 16mm internegative.

- As the costs are usually based on the script, amount of research, number and type of visuals, etc., only an estimation as to the cost of producing a 16mm program can be given here. Thus for a 120 frame, 10 minute program, may cost from $3,500 to $6,000 depending on the above and the choice and quality of the producer. Note that the above 120 frame, 10 minute program could be made up of four 2½ minute, 40 frame programs or any variation of that.

SOFTWARE CARTRIDGE DUPLICATION COST

- The above software production will result in the production of a 16mm film internegative from which other prints can be made and a ¼" pulsed master audio tape from which the audio portion of the cartridge can be produced.

- Because of the above, the duplication of 16mm film cartridges is very inexpensive (about $35 per cartridge).

- Basing our calculations of cartridge life on the results of film strip programs used in the Dinosaur Gallery of the Royal Ontario Museum for the last 22 months, it is noted that:

    The film strips which contain two or three separate programs have lasted two to three months each whereas audio tapes in those cartridges have lasted up to six months each.

- Bulb is easily replaced via door in top of unit.

- Alignment of bulb is assured by bulb mounting fixture.

- Film and sound cartridge is designed to be plugged in or pulled out to change cartridges or programs.

- Each cartridge is designed so that either the film strip, the audio tape or both can be quickly replaced if they wear out. (Film strips usually wear out faster than audio tapes.)

EQUIPMENT COST

- The 9-3/8" x 12-1/2" screen, heavy duty exhibition unit costs approximately $500.

- A smaller 5-3/8" x 7-1/4" screen, portable presentation unit (which uses the same type of cartridge) costs approximately $400.

- A projector which does not have a self-contained screen like the units above but projects onto a larger separate front or rear projection screen and still uses the same type of cartridge costs about $475.

EQUIPMENT MAINTENANCE COST

- The recommended maintenance of this 16mm film strip projection device consists of cleaning and lubricating the film strip daily and cleaning the tape heads weekly.

- Some adjustments such as changing drive belts and readjusting the sensitivity of the frame change circuit can be done on location.

- The units in the Dinosaur Gallery have not required any type of factory overhaul after 6,696 hours of operation other than three film advance adjustments (including cleaning) at about $14 each.

- There has been in the past an arrangement with the manufacturer to repair any unit for $30 per year.

  Assuming that you would want to replace only what was required:

  Number of film strips per year = 6
  Number of audio tapes per year = 3

  Thus, cost of film strips per year is 6 x $20 each = $120
    cost of audio tapes per year is 3 x $18 each = <u> 44</u>
                  <u>$164</u>

  At worst, six cartridges per year -

  6 times $35 each = $210 per year
  $210 divided by 365 days = $0.58 per day

BULB COST

- Again, basing our calculations of bulb costs on actual gallery experience, we find that a bulb in a 16mm film strip projector lasts about one month.

  Thus, 12 bulbs per year at $9.50 each is
  12 times $9.50 = $114 per year, or
  $114 divided by 365 days = $0.31 per day

SUPER 8mm FILM SYSTEMS

DESCRIPTION OF SYSTEMS

- Increasingly popular film format especially useful for small audiences.

- Built for continuous duty.

- Projector self-contained and compact compared to 16mm.

- Contains solid state audio amplifiers with outlet for external speakers.

- Film cartridge systems contain endless loop film which eliminates threading and rewinding.

- Projectors can be remotely started with a push button and stop automatically at end of film or where the film has been programmed to stop.

- Film capacity for small silent projector is four minutes whereas film capacity for large sound projector is up to 31 minutes in cartridge.

- Large 31 minute capacity projector has either optical or magnetic sound.

- Other models of super 8mm projectors have built-in screens.

- Super loop super 8mm systems incorporate a modified silent super 8mm projector and a cassette player. Cassette tape program when started by viewer will run the film normally until it is stopped by a cue mark on the film. Thus, a 30 minute audio cassette will, by the use of motion and single frame projection, increase the capacity and flexibility of the normally silent projector film capacity of four minutes.

- Another type of super 8mm projector again using a separate super 8mm film cartridge and a separate audio cassette allows for complete control of the super 8mm film, i.e., fast speed to advance over sections, normal speed for regular viewing, half speed to show slow motion, quarter speed for stop action and single frame for titles, diagrams, etc. This machine can be programmed to skip frames that contain information that is not wanted for a particular group of viewers.

- An interesting application of super 8mm film is for video projection through a television monitor. The twenty minute super 8mm magnetic track cartridge would play through a video camera system that uses flying spot scanner, eliminating the need for the normal shutter mechanism.

APPLICATION

- Projector with built-in screens up to 18" x 24" can be built into an exhibit where the ambient light is fairly high to show, as an example, how bees communicate.

- Larger screen sizes of up to 3' wide can be achieved with a super 8mm projector and a separate rear screen to show, for instance, the characteristics and uses of minerals.

- The 31 minute capacity cartridge can have one program up to 31 minutes in length or seven programs of four minutes in length. There would be a stop pulse after every program so that the visitor chooses how many programs to see.

- Each of the seven programs could be about a specific aspect of the display such as: How this vase is made? Why is it significant in transporting food? Why are there different designs? What is the purpose of the curved bottom? etc.

- Because of its compact size, the super 8mm projector with sound can be used to show existing copies of 16mm film to small audiences in portable or mobile exhibits. (For example, a National Film Board ten minute film on archaeology in an archaeology museumobile.)

- The super 8mm projector programmed by a cassette tape recorder or possibly an endless loop lear-type cartridge player could be used where there would be only a few parts of a program that require motion. The rest could be stills. (An example of this would be, a live action film section of a chemical reaction and a series of single frames outlining the formulas and characteristics of the chemicals involved.)

- Super 8mm projection systems with a number of choices of film speeds from fast-forward to single frame are useful in illustrations (e.g., how birds fly by showing wing motion at regular speed and at slow motion, stopping from time to time to point out the aerodynamic features of the wing).

- The ability to skip frames allows the film to contain both English and French titles and by using, as an example, an English version of the cassette program, all the French titles would be skipped and the English titles selected.

- The super 8mm video player allows the use of existing super 8mm magnetic audio track film to be used to feed a television set. The elimination of the mechanical shutter would increase the number of plays of the film far beyond that capable with video tape. Also, because the picture is being projected at a very low light and consequently with a low heat level, into a form of a television camera, there is no colour deterioration. Also, there is the flexibility of changing the intensity and colour by the controls on the television monitor itself.

OPERATION

- Pressing the "on" button on the projector will start the film rolling, turn on the light, and also the audio amplifier.

- The projector can be also controlled remotely by a standard electrical push buttom which would activate an optional custom designed start system.

- Projector will completely shut down when it comes to a set of sprocket holes in the film that have been covered by splicing tape, thus providing flexibility for as many programs and length as desired.

- The projector systems with the choice of projection speeds are controlled by cues recorded on the audio cassette. In this case, the film has already been designed and produced with single French or English titles along with sections of motion picture film. The film is then run with the prerecorded audio cassette and the operator programs the sequence and effects he wants on the second track. This cassette with audio and cue pulses can then be duplicated for other machines.

- The super 8mm film video player may have limitations in that it is: not designed to operate continuously such as an endless loop super 8mm system or to be remotely controlled. In addition, it can only feed one television monitor.

MAINTENANCE

- Projector should be cleaned every seven days to minimize dust build-up which would scratch film.

- Cartridges could be rotated to distribute wear.

- Machine should be overhauled every six months if on continuous operation twelve hours per day, seven days per week.

- Bulbs have an average of 200 hours life and would probably be replaced every 16 days (according to manufacturer's specifications).

- Film cartridges will last an average of 2,000 plays. Thus, a 30 minute cartridge should last 83 days under ideal conditions. (According to manufacturer's information using an estar base film which will definitely not break.)

- Consideration should be given as to whether an optical track or magnetic track is used on the film. The former is part of the emulsion whereas the latter is pre-stripped to the film. Determining which one would wear off first requires further research.

EQUIPMENT COST

- Silent super 8mm projector with four minute film capacity and remote start and automatic stop costs approximately $175.

- Super loop silent super 8mm projector and cassette programmer costs $400.

- The large 31 minute capacity super 8mm projector with optical or magnetic sound costs about $600. Optional remote start would be approximately $150 extra.

- The price for the totally flexible super 8mm systems with fast-forward, normal, slow motion, stop frame, and skip frame action is in the neighbourhood of $650.

- The super 8mm film video player costs about $1,400.

EQUIPMENT MAINTENANCE COST

- A survey should be done on a number of uses of super 8mm projectors as to:

  - the rated and actual life of the projectors,
  - what parts wear out when and cost of replacing these parts (e.g., drive belts, film transport mechanisms, shutter mechanisms, etc.)
  - what constitutes a major overhaul, when required and what is the cots,
  - what constitutes a minor overhaul, when required and what is the cost.

- From these and other statistics, the following could be determined: the cost of maintaining and replacing projectors as well as the skill, time and cost of using outside or staff technicians.

FILM PRODUCTION COST

- Production of super 8mm film will usually be from a 16mm film made up of a 16mm internegative containing the visual material and a 16mm magnetic track of the sound.

FILM DUPLICATION COST

- Assuming the film will be 30 minutes long (for example, one 30 minute segment or several four minute segments making up 30 minutes):

For an optical track super 8mm film

- Optical track work will cost   - $345
  Production work and first film   - <u>180</u>

  Thus, all production work and first cartridge
  loaded and lubricated will cost   - $525

- Cartridges in quantities of 2 to 20 will cost $96 each.

- Assuming the need for 6 cartridges, the cost will be:

        First cartridge - $ 525
        5 x $96 each   -   480
        6 cartridges   - $1,005 per year

- Cost per day is $1,005 divided by 365 days = $2.75 per day.

For magnetic track super 8mm film

- Production work and first cartridge - $188.

- Addition cartridges in quantities of 2 to 20 will cost $129 each.

    Thus for 6 cartridges per year -

        First cartridge - $188
        5 x $129 each   -   645

        6 cartridges   - $833 per year

- Cost per day is $833 divided by 365 days + $2.28 per day.

- Assuming the worst conditions, where a cartridge is replaced every
  month becuase of dust and poor maintenance, the cost of film will be:

Optical cartridges

        First cartridge   - $ 525
        11 additional cartridges at $96 each -   1,056

        12 cartridges $1,581 per year

    or $4.33 per day

Magnetic cartridges

First cartridge	- $ 188
Additional 11 cartridges at $129 each	- 1,419
12 cartridges	$1,607

or $4.40 per day

- The cost of duplicate cartridges for the other super 8mm devices are similar to the above. There will be an additional cost for duplicating the audio cassettes.

Bulb cost

- Assume life of bulb to be 200 hours as per manufacturer's specifications.

    Thus, 22 bulbs per year are needed (for example,
    365 days times 12 hours divided by 200 = 22 bulbs)
    at a cost of:

    22 bulbs at $12 each = $264

    or $0.72 per day.

EVALUATION

- Super 8mm film still must be produced from a 16mm film which has relatively high production cost.

- There is no way of up-dating once film is produced, without going back to the costly production of 16mm film.

- Some super 8mm is produced entirely in super 8mm but considering that the image size is 3/8 that of 16mm film, the quality and colour reproduction is relatively poor.

- Super 8mm, because of its size, has been developed into compact, reliable, continuous, loop systems whereas 16mm has remained reel to reel.

PROGRAMMED DISPLAY LIGHTING

DESCRIPTION OF SYSTEM

-   Several types of systems can be discussed.

-   One system involves a series of switches such as push buttons which directly or indirectly control individual spotlights which are focused on specific objects or transparencies on disply.

-   Another system involves a sequencing switch which continuously switches a series of lights one at a time through an exhibit.

-   A third system combines the sequenced lights with the sequencing of audio speakers.

-   A fourth system makes use of a programmer along with an audio cartridge system to dim down a flood-light display and highlight and compare different objects, change from one colour to the next and even control a slide presentation on the back wall of the exhibit, then return to a normally lit display and wait until another viewer activates the system by pressing one button.

APPLICATION

-   The first lighting system which has a series of push buttons connected to individual spotlights could be developed so that each push button is opposite a specific question about a display in front of it. The viewer then pushes the button opposite the question to discover or check what the correct object is. A variation of this is to have normally dark rear lit transparencies mounted next to the question with the answer printed out so that kids or adults can push a button, light them up, and see the answer.

-   The second system involves a series of lights lighting up one at a time in an exhibit or diagram to reinforce stages that occurred sequentially such as the growth of a butterfly.

- The third system involving the sequencing of lights with the sequencing of sound coming from individual speakers can be used to light up individual birds on a wall display and simultaneously hear their specific call from a speaker directly behind them. Thus, you could have the viewer compare a group of birds and their songs by sequenced light and sound.

- The fourth system involving narration, changing lighting and programmed slides could work as follows: A program would be written for a display of animals in which similarities and differences were compared (for example, physiology, eating habits, habitat, etc.). We can assume that the viewer can see the animals being compared. The program then would be activated by the viewer who would then listen to the first program which compares the physiology of two or three animals. The general lighting would dim somewhat and as the announcer compares the jaw bone and teeth of both, spotlights would come on the jaws of both of these animals. If there were examples of the vegetation each ate in the exhibit, the spotlights would highlight the specific animal and the specific vegetation it ate. The lights could then dim and a dissolve projection system could project examples of the forest conditions on the wall behind the animals to illustrate the dense, lush vegetation that the one animal was used to. This program would then end and the general lighting would return to what it was before the program started. Other programs could follow, each activated by the viewer, each comparing the similarities and differences using audio, prefocus spotlights and possibly audio-visual projection to show visual material not seen in the display.

OPERATION

- The first system of push buttons controlling a set of related spotlights could be strictly heavy duty, high current switches directly connected or low voltage switches, controlling solid state switches which in turn control the lights.

- The second system involves a mechanical drum switch activating relays in a particular order or a solid state logic circuit controlling solid state switches or dimmers.

- The third system, sequencing lights and simultaneously sequencing speakers and audio, involves one cartridge playback machine on which there is a two track tape. The tape has the announcer's voice identifying each bird, followed by the sound of each bird, for all the birds in the exhibit. The cue track would signal a set of relays to switch the light from one bird to the next as well as switch the audio from one speaker to the next. The program would then do each bird in sequence and then shut off until activated again.

- In the fourth system, there would be much greater use of a programmer and programmed magnetic or punch tape to control solid state dimming equipment for spotlights and house lights, slide projectors, additional audio cartridge machines for sound effects and possible rear transparencies built into the railing in front of the exhibit showing label information.

MAINTENANCE

- As with any mechanical switch, audio cartridge playback unit, programmer, etc., continuous operation will quickly show what is not designed properly.

- All of the above equipment if operated in synchronization with some other effect should have some means of automatically resynchronizing itself at the end of each program.

- Note: The above, like other media techniques, should be used to assist in the learning process and should be carefully considered with reference to the whole purpose and theme of the exhibit.

- As regards to the monitoring of spotlights for burned out bulbs, solid state dimming circuits can be designed to turn on a red indicator light if the filament of a bulb is burnt out. Thus, a small red indicator bulb either on one monitoring panel or by each spotlight will be quickly noticed rather than the absence of light in a dark ceiling.

- Also, the use of solid state dimmers to slightly retard the sudden flow of current in a bulb as well as the slight decrease of line voltage will significantly increase the life of bulbs and at the same time cut down on the number of man hours required to maintain bulbs.

EQUIPMENT COST

- The cost of the system can vary greatly depending on the design.

- For example, if the solid state dimmers were all to be located in the same electrical lighting panel, heavy power cables would have to be individually run out to each spotlight in conduit or cable ways resulting in a large installation cost. But, if the dimmers were individual compact units capable of handling the load current of the individual spotlight, they could be mounted beside the spotlight and plugged into a common grid system. The dimmers then would be controlled by a low voltage control signal run via Bell Telephone-type wire. The benefit of this system would depend on whether a grid system was already installed or could be easily installed. The dimmers themselves could be cheaply and easily built.

- Another factor in the cost of a programmed lighting system would be the type of spotlights used and the bulbs required for them (for example, theatrical spotlights with shutters and special focusing condensed lenses or window display type spotlights with standard prefocussed parabolic lamps with built-in reflectors).

- A possible cost reduction factor is the increase in bulb life by the slight reduction in line voltage, if a slight reduction in light output and colour temperature is acceptable (for example, a 120 volt bulb on 115 volts will result in 70% increase in life and 14% reduction in light output).

EQUIPMENT MAINTENANCE COST

- Solid state dimming devices should require no maintenance if designed properly for the expected loads, protected against shorts, etc., and are properly ventilated.

- The electronic control systems should also have negligible maintenance requirements if correctly designed for the system.

- Bulb cost will be the greatest expense depending on the type of bulb, life, light output, how easily replaced, etc.

SOFTWARE COST

- Dependent on complexity and design of system.

BULB COST

- Dependent on lighting system chosen.

EVALUATION

- Lighting can be a very dramatic media technique if used correctly in the right types of exhibits.

RANDOM ACCESS SYSTEMS

DESCRIPTION OF SYSTEMS

- Random access describes any system that can retrieve previously produced visual and/or audio material in any random order, going directly to that selected material without going through unwanted material.

- One type of random access uses a time signal recorded on a track of a tape in minutes and seconds from the beginning. The audio programs would be recorded sequentially on this tape and the starting times noted. Then by programming in the starting time of a particular program, the machine finds the program, then plays it.

- A form of this is an audio random access system in which the listener can choose the program he wants to listen to from a number of pre-recorded audio programs. This system would incorporate a four track, four channel cartridge player or four separate cartridge players connected to a switching device and to a set of headphones or speaker system.

- Another form of this system would be a random access single projector slide system with any of the 80 slides in any order in response to dialling the appropriate number or pressing in the number on a touch-tone type keyboard.

- A variation of this would be a multi-projector random access system in which two projectors would be used to increase the retrievable material to 160 slides. This system can be expanded to up to over 80 projectors operating from the same keyboard.

- Adding sound (we will deal only with the two projector system here but this can be applied to larger numbers of projectors), a program can be dialled up from, as an example, ten audio-visual programs:

the correct audio track would begin to play and its particular cue
track would choose the individual slides in the correct sequence
to follow and illustrate the story.

- A video random access is available for addition to a video cassette
  player. By punching in the tape position of the program on a 3/4"
  video cassette, the control unti then advances or rewinds the video
  tape to that program, then shows the program and stops. Any
  number of programs of any length can be programmed on a cassette
  with a maximum of 60 minutes.

- Random access film devices are also possible and would require
  complex modifications for sensing devices on a 16mm projector that
  is designed to run fast forward and fast reverse.

APPLICATION

- The random access audio systems could be used to give a listener a
  choice of programs or languages about a particular exhibit. For
  example, a series of short programs could deal with different aspects
  of a particular exhibit on Indian tools, or each program could be aimed
  at a different level of comprehension, from pre-school children to adults,
  with the control switch clearly indicating this.

- The random access projector (80 slide capacity and 160 slide capacity)
  could contain the answers in the form of titles, statistics, visuals
  (with or without titles burnt-in), or diagrams (of processes or
  even how to get to a particular gallery). The questions would
  already be listed on a panel adjacent to the control unit and rear
  screen projection unit.

- In an orientation gallery, the addition of sound allows the viewer
  to pick a short (perhaps 2 min. long) audio-visual program which
  tells him what he will find in a specific gallery and how to get
  there. If used in a gallery, this system could provide individual
  programs which a viewer may specifically want to see.

- A random access video system could allow the viewer to watch a specific animal in motion, seeing how it lives in its particular habitat.

- The random access film system would be applied as above.

OPERATION

- The operation of each system is generally described in the "Description of Systems" section.

MAINTENANCE

- There was not enough time to date to search out those people who are presently using these systems to determine their reliability and maintenance requirements.

EQUIPMENT COST

- The random access audio system employing a four track four channel cartridge system would cost about $1,200.

- The random access single projector system consisting of projector, interface unit, and control console would be about $3,500.

- The random access dual projector system consisting of two random access projectors, multiple projector interface unit and control console would be about $6,700.

- The random access dual projector audio-visual system consisting of two random access projector, multiple projector interface unit, N.A.B. cartridge tape decks, audio amplifier, speakers and control console would be about $9,000.

- The random access video tape unit consisting of a 17" colour monitor, video tape cassette player and cassette program locator would cost about $4,500.

- A price for the random access 16mm film retrieval system is not available at this time.

- The above prices are approximate.

EQUIPMENT MAINTENANCE COST

- This is yet to be determined because of lack of data from users.

SOFTWARE PRODUCTION COST

- The costs of software production are similar to those already discussed in the other sections.

SOFTWARE DUPLICATION COST

- The software duplication costs are similar to those discussed in other sections.

EVALUATION

- The retrieval systems can be very effective because they allow the viewer to choose the information he wants to hear and/or see.

AUDIO PLAYBACK UNITS

DESCRIPTION OF SYSTEMS

- Single or multi-channel audio systems may consist of some type of playback unit, built-in or external audio amplifier and speaker system.

- Different types of systems are:

  - Reel to reel tape recorders which have end-of-tape sensing devices to stop and rewind the tape, and to either wait for a command to start or run continuously.

  - Lear-type cartridge playback unit with or without audio amplifier.

  - N.A.B. board cast type cartridge player for the ultimate in fidelity, reliability and continuous operation.

- The above may have one to four discrete tracks or channels with appropriate amplifiers or line feeds (for external amplifiers or programming equipment).

- Above equipment may have built-in external cue-activated stop system which would stop the tape whenever a stop cue is picked up by the playback head.

- Multi-track switching is also available on some machines.

- Some machines could be equipped with remote volume controls and remote start-stop.

- Various types of speaker arrangements, speaker systems and room acoustics.

APPLICATION

- Reel to reel tape recorders, because of their cost, are not normally used just for playback. It is only when the program material is longer than 30 minutes that a reel to reel is considered. For

example, it is used for playback of two-hour reels of background
music so regular staff would only hear the same tune once per two
hours and six times per day.

- The lear-type cartridge playback unit is a very popular unit,
  developing its reputation with eight track home and audio playback
  systems. It is used in audio-visual systems for single channel
  audio playback for one area, two channel audio playback for different
  sound playback in two areas, for single channel sound and cue track
  for single screen and multi-screen audio-visual shows.

- Endless cartridge units can be used to continuously play sound
  effects such as bird calls, animal sounds, wind sounds and fish
  sounds to create effects in certain areas of galleries.

OPERATION

- The tape cartridge player is very simple in design as it is only
  required to drive the tape at one speed in one direction.

- It is designed to play a ¼" endless loop cartridge continuously for
  sound effects or to stop at the end of an audio visual program.

- If used with an audio visual program where it is to play once and
  stop until it is started by a viewer, it can be-programmed to stop
  by either an audio tone signal on the cue track or a piece of metal
  foil depending on the manufacturer.

- The endless loop lear-type cartridge holds up to 18 minutes of tape
  but it is recommended to limit the amount of tape to about 13 minutes
  for continuous use and longer life.

- The cartridge can contain one 13 minute program, or several shorter
  programs which are repeated to make up 13 minutes.

- A N.A.B. broadcast type cartridge system is similar in operation
  except for a pinch roller which is built into the machine and lifts
  up into the cartridge behind the tape (the lear-cartridge pinch
  roller is built into the lear cartridge and cannot be adjusted).
  This roller's function is to press the tape against the capstan
  so that the tape is pulled continuously and at a constant speed
  past the playback heads.

MAINTENANCE

- The cartridge playback is basically designed for long continuous
  operation with no maintenance other than a weekly cleaning of
  capstan and tape heads with the appropriate type of cleaners.

- The reel to reel tape recorder requires more regular maintenance
  because its tape transport system is more complicated: it
  must switch electronically and mechanically from the playback,
  rewind, fast forward and record modes.

EQUIPMENT COST

- A good continuous duty cartridge player with built-in audio amplifier,
  AC off-when-playing, on-when-playing receptacles and projector
  synchronization costs about $200.

- A more expensive single channel message repeater costs about $420.

- A three language message repeater costs approximately $726.

- A four channel N.A.B. cartridge tape deck costs approximately $1,160.

- Each of the above would have various options, frequency responses,
  programming flexibility, life, reliability, built-in audio amplifiers,
  relay contact output on cue track, remote start-stop, etc.

EQUIPMENT MAINTENANCE COST

-   Most of the continuous cartrige playback units are designed for
    heavy duty cycles and long life and require little maintenance
    (for example, cleaning the tape heads, replacing drive belts and
    pinch rollers).

SOFTWARE PRODUCTION COST

-   Production of software may vary from a full audio visual multi-screen
    program to some sound effects repeated continuously. Thus the cost
    of the software for audio playback units may vary from approximately
    $25 to $500 depending on quantity, studio time, editing, mixing,
    number of voices, sound effects, etc.

SOFTWARE DUPLICATION COST

-   Dubbing cartridges involves making recordings from a 7-1/2" per
    second 1/2" or 1/4" master tape onto 1/4", 3-3/4" per second
    lubricated tape. The tape is then trimmed front and back, custom
    wound onto a lear cartridge spool, loaded and spliced. This duplication
    if done in quantity and depending on the length of the tape may cost
    approximately $25 per cartridge. A lear-type cartridge if wound
    correctly and played on good equipment (which is properly maintained)
    can last up to six months.

    Let us assume a cartridge will last only two months -

    Cost per year is 12 months x $25 each = $300 per year
    or $0.82 per 12 hour day

EVALUATION

- Initially developed for broadcasting, the tape transport playback
units have had a long history of success. It is the other parts
of the system that usually cause the problem such as the quality
and reliability of headphones and headsets, choice of speakers, as
well as number and placement in a gallery to minimize acoustical
problems such as reverberation, spill over of sound into other
galleries or areas, frequency response in a cavernous room. Such
things as the use of many smaller speakers in an area each at a low
level may be the answer to good clear sound response for an audience
rather than a few large speakers set at extremely high levels.

16mm CONTINUOUS LOOP FILM

DESCRIPTION OF SYSTEM

- 16mm has a long history of success.

- 16mm projector is designed primarily for running films once to large auditorium audience since most films are 30 and 60 minutes long.

- Well-established industry to produce, process, duplicate, distribute and show a wide range of subjects on 16mm film.

- 16mm projectors standard around the world.

- Continuous loop projectors are usually modified 16mm projectors.

- Film loop devices come in two styles - one that stores film in a horizontal coil on top of projector and one that winds film vertically around a series of spools, housed in a large cabinet.

- Another type of projector actually rewinds the film from reel to reel automatically.

- A two track optical projector is also available which gives you the choice of two different sound tracks on the same film (for example, for English or French or for an adult's version or children's version).

APPLICATION

- A film loop device is designed to run a 16mm film in an exhibit without the aid of a technician to rewind the film.

- Used in museums and exhibitions where audience can see an event in live action such as, the effect of wave action on a limestone cliff or the opening of a tomb containing a mummy.

- It can be used to record in capsule form the techniques of restoring
  a piece of pottery which normally may take a year.

- It could be activated by a viewer who has just seen an ancient tool
  on display but who wants to see the tool actually in operation.

- Basically, it should be used where motion is an absolute requirement
  in presenting the facts.

- Several short subjects that are related and in sequence can be
  presented one at a time with each one initiated by viewer pressing
  a remote start button.

OPERATION

- Regular 16mm projector is modified to take an endless loop cartridge
  which sits on top of machine. Film is fed down through additional
  guide wheels, through the gate like a normal film system and back
  up to the outside loop of the pancake.

- Viewer activates projector by pressing a remote button which
  activates an optional electronic sequencing device which first
  turns on projector to move film, then turns on light, runs sequence
  to end, then turns off bulb, and turns off projector.

- An additional electronic device will, when activated, bring the projector
  speed up to regular running speed very slowly so that there is a
  minimal amount of strain on the film. It likewise gradually
  brings projector to a halt at the end of the sequence. This drastically
  increases the life of the film and projector.

- As it is not normal to show a 30 minute film to a viewing audience
  unless they are seated, most exhibition display films are about
  four minutes in length. The projector is then designed to shut
  off at the end of each four minute segment.

MAINTENANCE

- 16mm film because it is constantly rubbing on itself as well as other parts in a projector, tends to develop a great deal of static electricity especially in a hot, low relative humidity environment. It therefore tends to attract dust in the air which builds up at the gate as well as other rubbing points. This dust build-up can easily scratch the relatively thin emulsion and decrease the life of the film.

- 16mm film should therefore be cleaned daily and coated with silicone lubricant to prevent a build-up of dust.

- The lubricant also prevents the film from drying out and becoming brittle.

- The life of the film could range from only a few passes to over 2,000 passes depending on the maintenance, dust, projector wear, humidity, etc.

EQUIPMENT COST

- A standard 16mm projector usually used in a continuous film loop system costs about $650.

- The addition of a good film loop device plus modifications to the above projector would be approximately $550.

- An electronic remote start unit could cost about $50.

- A variable speed start and stop unit may cost an additional $300 to install.

- To ensure that the system will turn off before damaging the film (or projector, if unbreakable estar-base film is used), a film sensing device is also advisable at $300. This device turns the system off if the film feeding into the projector gets too tight or if the film leaving the projector gets too loose.

- Thus, cost of sample film loop system is:

Projector (with normal lense)	$ 650
Film loop device	550
Variable speed start-stop	300
Film sensing device	300
Press button start	50
Film break switch	175
	$2,025

EQUIPMENT MAINTENANCE COST

- A 16mm projector is operated by numerous moving parts.

  - Its gears, belts, sprockets, sprocket drive shafts, bearings, film guide rollers, motor shutter drive assemblies, sprocket and shutter pawl assemblies must operate 4,380 hours per year.

  - It must drive 9,198,000 feet through the shutter per year.

  - 37,843,200 frames must be individually and mechanically moved up into the shutter, stopped to be projected and moved on per year (for example, 24 frames per second x 60 seconds x 60 minutes x 12 hours x 365 days = 37,843,200 frames per year).

- Consequently, something has to wear out sometime.

- The Smithsonian must make major overhauls (basically replacing everything that moves) about once or twice a year.

SOFTWARE PRODUCTION COST

- The production costs of a 16mm film will vary greatly because of such factors as: amount of research required; the writer used; length of script; studio photography vs location photography; how much location photography; lighting; studio recording; location recording; optical effects; size of crew; amount of film shot; number

of days shooting; type of equipment; lenses and cameras used; union
or non-union crews; announcer or announcers used; sound effects;
amount and source of music; editing; number of dissolves; visual
effects, etc.; colour or black and white; synchronized sound with
photographic shooting as opposed to voice over; type of film;
processing; and the form of the film and/or sound necessary for
duplication; to name just a few.

- The easiest way to establish a price for 16mm film production is
  by the cost per minute of edited mixed film ready for duplication.

- In checking prices from independent one-man producers to large
  established companies, the costs varied from approximately $1,000
  to $2,000 per minute. Thus at $1,000 per minute a 30 minute film
  on one subject or seven sequences of 4¼ minutes would cost about the
  same (for example, $1,000 x 30 minutes = $30,000). The highest
  price would be $60,000.

- The above prices are what National Film Board would pay if it used
  a totally outside production company for a film that it would want
  to show an audience and that an audience would actually stay in their
  seats and see.

- These costs could possibly be reduced by simplifying the film, by
  using some staff people if they have motion picture experience and
  fit in with the professionals making the film, and by shopping around.

- Also, some films are made completely in a studio using 35mm slide,
  8" x 10" transparencies, etc. with voice over at fairly reasonable
  costs (as long as you are not just making a 16mm motion picture out
  of a perfectly good 35mm slide presentation).

- As with the other media techniques, a lot more research should be
  done before choosing a method to present a story, or part of one.

SOFTWARE DUPLICATION COST

- If the software production has resulted in a 16mm internegative and a 16mm magnetic track, the price of duplicating the 30 minute film (remembering that it could be made up of one 30 minute film, or seven 4¼ minute subjects) would be calculated as follows:

  - Make an optical track print from the 16mm magnetic audio track at 9¢ per foot. (A 30 minute film is 1,050 feet long.)

    Thus, 1,050 feet x $0.09 = $94.50

  - Marry the optical and visual rolls.

    Cost for this is $3

  - Produce an answer print (lab is responsible for colour balance, synchronization, etc. to the client's satisfaction) at 28¢ per foot.

    Thus, 1,050 feet x $0.28 = $294

  - The second copy of this film will cost 13.5¢ per foot.

    Thus, 1,050 feet x $0.135 = $141.75

  - For three to ten more copies, the cost is 11¢ per foot.

    Thus, next eight copies will cost - 8 copies x 1,050 feet x $0.11 = $924

  - If you estimate you need twelve copies per year (one per month), the next two copies will cost 10¢ per foot.

    Thus, 2 copies x 1,050 feet x $0.10 = $210

- Thus, the cost of twelve copies of a 30 minute film will be:

Optical work	$ 94.50
Optical and visual marriage	3.00
Answer print	294.00
Second print	141.75
Next eight prints	924.00
Next two prints	210.00
Thus, twelve prints cost	$1,667.25 per year

   Or $1,667.25 divided by 365 days = $4.56 per day

- This is a system which is heavily dependent on maintenance, dust, humidity, film coating and lubrication, the mechanical reliability of the projector, the mechanical reliability of the film loop device, number of film runs, etc. (For example, 25,200 feet of film will run through a projector a day, or 766,500 feet per month, or 9,198,000 per year.) If through experience you need a few more copies, for example, another twelve per year (a conservative number as the Smithsonian uses one copy of film per week), the cost of the 24 copies of film will cost:

First 12 copies	$1,667.25
Next 12 copies (12 months x 1,050 feet x 10¢ per foot)	1,260.00
Thus, 24 copies cost	$2,927.25 per year

   Or $2,927.25 divided by 365 days = $8.02 per day

BULB COST

- The bulb normally used in the above projector has a life of fifty hours.

- Thus, in one year's operation, that is twelve hours per day for 365 days, we would need 88 bulbs.

- The cost of a bulb is $15.97.

- Thus, cost of bulbs per year is $1,405.36 or $3.85 per day.

RADIO BROADCAST LOOPS

DESCRIPTION OF SYSTEM

- System consists of light-weight headsets or wands which pick-up and audio program broadcast from a loop antenna mounted on the floor.

- Each loop antenna is adjacent to an exhibit for which a program has been written and recorded.

- Each program is played continuously on the same loop and listener can move freely between loops and programs.

- Size of broadcast area can be as large or small as required.

- Up to four different channels can be broadcase from each loop.

- Loop antennae are installed at same time as installation of carpet or flooring.

APPLICATION

- A gallery can be designed in such a way as to have a series of programs relating to specific exhibits located throughout a gallery.

- Each program broadcast by a localized loop antenna in the floor could explain the significance of the exhibit to the viewer.

- As the viewer is listening through a headset or ear-speaker in a wand, he does not disturb other visitors to that gallery.

- If the programs are written to be heard sequentially, the listener can be guided along on a tour.

- If the programs are written as separate stories, the listener can choose where he wants to go, what he wants to see and what he wants to listen to.

- As up to four channels can be broadcast through each loop, four different programs of different levels or subjects can be selected according to the frequency of that particular receiver.

- Each channel could also be used for different languages and coded by colour of each headset or wand.

OPERATION

- Audio programs are recorded on continuous loop cartridges which are played in continuous playing cartridge machines.

- Cartridge machines feed an audio signal to a transmitter which transmits the signal at 115 kilohertz through a loop antenna located in the area discussed by the program.

- The loop antenna controls very precisely the reception zone so that there is no interference between programs.

- The headset or wand receiver picks up the transmitted signal in each area when the person walks up to a loop-equipped display.

- The volume depends directly on the distance from the receiver to the floor and so is relatively constant in each listening zone.

- As four different channels can be broadcasted on each loop at different frequencies, four different frequency receivers can be used, possibly colour coded, to pick up four different programs.

- The receivers contain rechargeable batteries and are recharged when places in their storage-display-recharge cabinets.

MAINTENANCE

- The headset or wand rechargeable batteries must be charged daily.

- Someone must be at a booth to rent out the devices (get identification, etc.), collect the devices (give back deposits), check the units, sterilize the ear pieces, plug them into the rechargers, monitor the cartridge tape plays, monitor the transmitters, etc.

- The cartridge player maintenance is covered in the section on "Audio Playback Units".

- More research based on actual use of these systems is needed to determine maintenance procedures.

SOFTWARE COST

- Software production has been described in the "Audio Playback System" section.

EVALUATION

- **One** problem may be that as the programs are running continuously, a listener may have to wait for the beginning of each program if he has entered an area when it is half-way through.

<u>CASSETTE TOURS</u>

<u>DESCRIPTION OF SYSTEM</u>

- Portable cassette player in a carrying case with shoulder strap equipped with an earphone.

- Some machines have optional tape cue stop which stops the tape with a beep on the tape after an explanation or question. Viewer then starts the tape when he is ready to move on.

- If above units not yet available, an audible tone could tell the listener when to stop the tape and what to look at or do before proceeding.

- Could have rechargeable batteries with built-in charger.

- Cassettes available in sizes of up to 60 minutes per side.

<u>APPLICATION</u>

- Tours can be developed for any subject and any length of time. If the visitor had only one hour, he could choose from the selection of hour long tours, a subject that he was interested in.

- The tours could be developed for a specific gallery, a group of related galleries (e.g., Greek and Roman) or a subject that ties together unrelated galleries (e.g., plant and animal survival against the environment).

- Tours could be produced professionally using a professional announcer or written and announced by a curator or director.

- If works of art or objects are brought into a special exhibit, then the individual artists could each in turn explain their work.

- Programs could be developed to assist the viewer in looking at objects or dioramas to then pose a question and stop. The viewer could try to answer the question, then restart the cassette machine and verify the answer in the next portion of the program.

- If the tour is on musical instruments, a selection of music of each instrument discussed is programmed to give the viewer a sample of the sound.

- Cassette tour could be used to give visitor a sequenced tour rather than a random walk.

OPERATION

- The cassette playback unit would shut itself off when a stop-pulse was played through the heads, usually after a question or important point of interest.

- Viewer would carry the cassette with a strap over his shoulder listening through an earphone and not disturbing anyone else.

- Viewer can go at his own pace through the galleries.

- Rechargeable battery pack can be quickly replaced and recharged while the cassette playback unit remains available to go out.

- Each program can be produced in different languages.

- If automatic stop not available, the audible tone could inform viewer when to stop program.

- Booth and personnel would have to be available to distribute and collect machines and cassettes and to change and charge batteries.

MAINTENANCE

- Periodic cleaning of tape heads is required.

- Continuous changing and charging of batteries.

- Earphones are of light construction and easily damaged.

- Tape heads would have to be checked and cleaned.

- Cassettes would have to be checked and rewound.

SOFTWARE PRODUCTION COST

- A writer may have to be hired to work with curator to develop each tour script.

- Education department could greatly assist in subject matter and intent of each program.

- Announcer would be chosen.

- Recording and mixing.

- If auto stop units, programming has to be done.

- ¼" master then duplicated onto cassettes.

- Labelling.

35mm SLIDE PROJECTOR SYSTEMS

DESCRIPTION OF SYSTEMS

- Discussion will include a number of different 35mm projection systems from the single projector system to the multi-projector multi-screen system.

- The single 35mm slide projector makes use of a circular slide tray which holds 81 slides. It can be set by the internal timer to change the slide every 5, 8 or 15 seconds continuously all day. Each slide change requires approximately two seconds during which the screen is black. Every slide, whether it is a simple visual or a complex diagram stays on the screen for a uniform amount of time, that is the amount set by the timer.

- The single 35mm slide projector can be used with a continuous audio cartridge playback unit which will change the slides according to a programmed audio tape. The voice track will tell the viewer about a subject and a cue track on the same tape will change the slide when necessary. Thus, there can be variation in the time each slide is on the screen according to what is being said on the voice track and the content of the visual. The slide change will still result in a two second dark screen and the system will run continuously all day whether someone is watching or not.

- The dual 35mm slide projector dissolve system with the continuous audio cartridge system will greatly improve the visual presentation as the screen will not flash from light to dark but instead one visual will dissolve smoothly into another. This will allow for a more professional presentation. A refinement on this, is to have a dissolve unit with three speeds of dissolve, slow dissolve, medium dissolve and fast cut.

- A resynchronization kit can be added to Kodak Ektagraphic projectors used above which consist of steel rings which clamp onto the trays are ready to start another program in relation to the audio tape.

- The German Kodak S-AV projector should now be used for the more complex systems that follow because of its design and reliability.

- Note: The above systems usually are turned on in the morning and turned off at night with their projectors and lights running continuously and the audio cartridge machines running only when activated by a viewer. A better system based on the German Kodak S-AV projector allows the system to turn completely on only when activated by a viewer then automatically turns itself off.

- Thus a dual 35mm slide projector dissolve system with a continuous loop audio cartridge system based on a German Kodak S-AV projector and an automatic start-stop unit has the following features:

  - A projector designed and built for heavy duty continuous exhibition use with built-in program synchronization.

  - The automatic start-stop unit automates the show so that when activated by the viewer, it turns on the projectors, dissolve units, audio tape player, amplifiers, checks the trays to make sure they are at the start of the program (if not, recycles them to the start), then turns on the projector lights, then starts the audio tape, runs the program using three programmable types of visual effects, snap change, medium dissolve and slow dissolve, stops the tape at the end of the program, turns the projector light off (leaving fans on), recycles the slide trays to the beginning of the next program, waits a prescribed time (in case another viewer shows up and wants to see the program), then turns the whole system completely off and waits for the next viewer.

- A variation of the two German S-AV projector system is to have two separate programs in the same two projection trays and two audio programs giving the visitor the option of choosing either of the two programs to watch.

- The above systems are based on a digital audio signal which can be expandable to 120 functions. This could control any number of dissolve projector systems, 16mm projectors, spotlights and houselights automatically.

- Another type of system is based on an eight level punch tape system in which various combinations of holes in the tape would control 40 and even 80 functions. The punch tape itself would advance in response to an audio signal on the cue track of a magnetic tape on which is also recorded a second track containing the audio portion of the program.

APPLICATION

- The single 35mm slide system can be used to present a series of background shots, for example, to show variations in colour and design in African life in an exhibit featuring African art. The 81 slides would operate on a timer set at five second intervals and project on a large wall screen suspended above the low lit display area. If enough slides were available, several such projection units could be set up around the room to create an interesting montage of bright, colourful African patterns.

- The single 35mm slide system synchronized to a continuous loop audio cartridge system can provide a sound track geared to change with the slides. Thus, for example, as an African drum beat rhythmically to singing, the visuals would also change.

- The dual 35mm slide projector dissolve system with a continuous audio cartridge system, could present illustrative stories or descriptions of processes with a sequence of visuals and a sychronized audio commentary, e.g., the life of a young boy in a Mexican village or the spawning habits of fish. The projectors would remain on a title slide indicating that, when started, the program would deal with a particular subject matter.

- The dual German S-AV 35mm slide projector dissolve system with continuous loop audio cartridge and automatic start-stop unit is useful in gallery situations where the attendance is not constant throughout the day. Thus, as in the Dinosaur Gallery at the ROM, the equipment stays off, saving power, wear on the equipment, bulb life and slide life until a viewer wants to see the program. This system, because of its automatic start, resynchronization and shut-off, is relatively maintenance-free aside from bulb changes and tape head cleaning.

- A multi-speed dissolve unit can produce a wide range of visual effects. For instance, it can simulate motion. Another effect is the fast snap-cut; for example, when the announcer mentions a group of animals such as "bears....wolves....foxes....and moose", the illustrating slides flash on the screen. A series of slow dissolves can be used to show a bone being buried in sand. If the positions of camera and bone are constant with only the sand building up, the concept of how a bone is preserved can be dramatically illustrated. A medium dissolve can be used for the build-up of titles on a screen. A fast dissolve can be used for regular slide changes in a program.

- The viewer could be presented with the choice of watching either one of two audio visual programs, through the use of the same basic two German S-AV projector dissolve system with continuous loop cartridge player. He could press for program "A" and watch a general orientation program on the Greek gallery, or program "B" and watch a specific program about recent discoveries.

OPERATION

- The single 35mm slide projector system projecting 81 slides at five second intervals would show the complete tray of slides in approximately 9½ minutes.

- The single 35mm slide projector system coupled to a continuous loop tape unit would require that the cue pulses be recorded after the audio track is laid down. One cue pulse would activate a relay in the cartridge player which would advance the slide tray one position.

- The dual 35mm projector dissolve system with the continuous audio cartridge system would, for each pulse on the tape, immediately dissolve the light from one projector to the next, then advance the tray of the projector with the light off.

- The multi-speed dissolve unit, two projector system would require a decoder either as a separate unit or built in to tell the dissolve unit what effect is desired and when it is to occur.

- The three projector dissolve unit dissolves the lights from one projector to the other, and as there are three projectors, could change every second to produce an animated effect. (A projector requires two seconds to physically change a slide before the light can come on.) Also, you would increase the slide capacity of the show to 240 slides.

- The discussion of a multi-projector 120 channel system will not be dealt with as each variation of the system might take many pages to describe properly.

- The system having the choice of two programs "A" or "B" in the same two trays, uses an extra tape player and a little electronic switching. Program "A" is lined up in the tray as usual, and program "B" is lined up from the tray zero position in the opposite direction. One tape runs the trays forward for program "A" and the other tape runs the tapes backward for program "B".

MAINTENANCE

-    The single 35mm slide projector, if run continuously on the five
     second timer for twelve hours per day for two months, will change
     approximately 370,080 times and will probably need the timing switch
     replaced.

-    The above Kodak projector is designed to run for 3,000 hours
     (manufacturer's expected life) or 250 twelve hour days, at which
     time the projector will definitely require a major overhaul.

-    The Kodak 35mm projector AF-2 with the timer also has the automatic
     focus feature which is not recommended for use in continuous operation
     as the device sometimes malfunctions and extends the lens out so far
     that it drops out.

-    The German 35mm S-AV projector is a much heavier and better designed
     projector for continuous running (some projectors bought for use for
     the six month period at Expo 67 are still being used in continuously
     operating audio visual shows today).

-    The maintenance of the cartridge systems has been discussed in
     "Audio Playback Units."

-    The electronic control systems are basically quite reliable and do
     not require any maintenance.

EQUIPMENT COST

-    The 35mm Kodak projector model B-2 costs approximately $200.

-    The German S-AV 2000 costs approximately $500.

-    A single 35mm slide projector controlled by an endless loop cartridge
     tape player with audio amplifier, speaker and remote start button would
     cost about $400. In this system the tape player would shut off at
     the end of each program but the projector would keep on running
     (fan running and bulb burning on a blank slide).

- A single German S-AV projector with an endless loop cartridge tape player that normally remains off, is turned on by a remote button activated by the visitor. It then turns on the tape player, turns on the light, runs the show, turns off the light, turns off the tape at the end of the program, recycles the tray to zero then turns everything off. Cost of this system would be about $1,200.

- The cost of a dual German S-AV version of the above system with a three speed dissolve would cost approximately $3,000.

- A system that gives the choice of two different audio visual programs on dissolve using the same two projectors and trays, would cost an extra $400 approximately, i.e., $3,400.

- The cost of the multi-screen systems varies greatly as to number of screens, number of functions required, type of dissolve units, etc. and will not be discussed here.

EQUIPMENT MAINTENANCE COST

- Replacing a timing switch in a Kodak 35mm slide projector may be necessary after running two or three months.

- A complete overhaul may be necessary after six months of continuous use.

- The German S-AV, because it is built for heavy duty continuous use, may not require any service at all for two years, as has been the experience with the ones in the Dinosaur Gallery at the Royal Ontario Museum.

- Regular maintenance of the playback cartridge machine may require only weekly cleaning of the tape heads and capstan.

- The programmers themselves usually are trouble-free as they are completely electronic.

SOFTWARE PRODUCTION COST

- Programs produced for slide systems vary with length of script, wirter, amount of research, number and kinds of studio and location, photography, artwork, announcer, programming, studio time, sound effects, etc., but a very general price for a slide program based on 160 slides would be about $4,000 to $6,000 or about $25 to $35 per slide.

SOFTWARE DUPLICATION COST

- Slides can be duplicated, glass mounted and collated for about $1.75 per slide. A two tray program would cost $283.50.

- The life of these slides running twelve hours per day, seven days per week would be about three months, requiring four sets of slides per year.

  Thus, the cost of slides per year would be -

    4 sets times $283.50 = $1,134 per year
    Or $1,134 divided by 365 days = $3.10 per day

- The audio cartridges would last about two months at $25 each.

  Thus, the cost for six would be $300 per week
  Or $300 divided by 365 days = $0.82 per twelve hour day.

BULB COST

- In the projectors in the Dinosaur Gallery, four bulbs are required every month for the two projectors for a total of 48 bulbs per year.

  Thus, the cost of bulbs per year is -

    48 bulbs times $6.10 each = $292.80 per year
    Or $0.80 per day

VIDEO PLAYBACK SYSTEMS

This section will have to be completed some time in the future as a proper survey of present users of continuous duty playback units is not available.

- Also, the life of the video cassette has been reported by different sources as being from 100 plays to over 3,000. Further research is therefore required.

- The life of the cassette players is also questionable, particularly in regards to the tape heads, tape transport mechanism and tape guides.

COLOUR TRANSPARENCIES

DESCRIPTION OF SYSTEM

- The use of colour transparencies in galleries and exhibits range from and 8" x 10" size built into a railing, to a 6' x 12' high size to show a life size scene.

- Colour transparencies are thin films approximately 40" wide by any length which have to be sandwiched between a clear plastic outside surface and a white translucent plastic surface.

- They are rear lit by an array of florescent bulbs.

- They are sometimes built in a rigid frame, usually metal, which is hinged for easy access to the bulbs.

APPLICATION

- To show large horizontal panoramas of the terrain in Africa in a gallery on Africa.

- To show a vertical view of a rain forest, life size, with a picture 6' wide and 12' high.

  To show blow-ups of minute objects on display.

- To show the actual unearthing process while digging up a particular dinosaur on display.

- To be used in a children's area where 8" x 10" transparencies would remain unlit until the child pressed a button to get the answer to a question next to that switch.

MAINTENANCE

- Some large cibachrome transparencies such as the one used in the ROM's Dinosaur Gallery have lasted for over two years with no noticeable fading.

<u>COST</u> (using cibachrome fade-resistant material)

- An 8" x 10" produced from a colour slide would cost $16

-   16" x 20"   - $ 45
    20" x 24"   - $ 65
    24" x 30"   - $ 95
    30" x 40"   - $140
    40" x 50"   - $200
    40" x 60"   - $250
    40" x 6'   - $300
    40" x 7'   - $350
    40" x 12'   - $500

- <u>Note</u>: The larger transparencies would be made from an 8" x 10" transparency.

- Thus, for a 6' wide x 12' high transparency, the cost would be $1,000.

- This does not include plastic, door and light box manufacturing costs, design costs, bulb and fixture costs, etc.

ANIMATED DISPLAYS

TYPE OF DISPLAYS

- This type of display can show, through simple motion, the action of something which may be extremely hard to be described verbally.

- An example of this may be, the movement of moons around a planet which circles a sun and how eclipses result.

- Another may show the effects of radiation by exposing a sample, normally housed in a lead shielded box, to a monitoring device placed behind a disc containing different materials. By rotating the disc, different materials can be tested by the viewer.

- How a piano key works as compared to that of a harpsichord.

OPERATION, MAINTENANCE, COST, ETC.

- These will have to be examined when a specific display is planned.

TACTILE SAMPLES

DESCRIPTION OF SYSTEM

- The use of tactile objects placed where the viewer can touch, lift, feel, smell, shake, hit, or otherwise discover things about an object.

- This has been used in areas called "discovery rooms" where bones, wood objects, rocks, and similar items are available for children to play with.

- Another example would be to hang a recent bone section on a chain next to a million year old bone section of equal size, similarly mounted, so that their weights, cell structure, and hardness could be compared.

- This can also be done with the two types of dinosaur teeth, those used for biting and those used for grinding.

- Another example can be the availability of a section of fur and hair of different animals to compare characteristics such as coarseness, length, and thickness.

- Although these objects would probably deteriorate from the constant handling by visitors, such small exhibits provide visitors with the opportunity to satisfy their curiosity through touching.

SCREENS

TYPES OF SCREENS

- Two basic types of screen systems: front screen and rear screen.

- A rear screen is basically a translucent film or glass screen through which an audio visual device on one side projects an image which passes through to where the audience is located.

- A front screen is basically an opaque material on which an audio visual device on one side projects an image which reflects back to the audience.

- Types of front screen materials are:

  - Matte screen - such as painted plaster, wallboard, plastic

  - Glass bead - made up of white surface material on which small, clear glass beads have been embedded or attached.

  - Metallic lenticular screens - having a metallic coated surface with a raised pattern that acts as small lenses.

  - Specially treated aluminum - having a highly reflective metallic surface.

APPLICATION OF SCREENS

Front screens

- Use in areas where the ambient light is fairly low.

- Where equipment may be in a projection booth.

- Where projection throw is not obstructed by audience.

Rear screens

- Is especially useful in galleries where the audience is to see the screen without interfering with or being bothered by the projection beam, the equipment or the equipment noice.

- It is used with small self-contained projection units for use in high ambient light conditions.

- Where there is space available behind the exhibit.

ADVANTAGES OF FRONT SCREENS

Light reflective characteristics

- Matte screen - Reflects light evenly in all directions.

    - Good for situations where viewing angles may be extreme.

- Metallic grey lenticular

    - Brightness in viewing area is twice that of the matte screen.

    - Viewing angle is 45° on either side of centre axis.

- Glass bead - More than four times the brightness of the matte screen in viewing angle.

    - Viewing angle 25° on either side of centre axis.

- Polished aluminum

    - More than 16 times the brightness of the matte screen in viewing angle.

    - Viewing angle 30° on either side of centre axis.

ADVANTAGES OF REAR SCREENS

- Rear projection allows the audience area to be free.

- Projection equipment is separated and hidden from audience.

- Projection equipment area can be kept air conditioned and dust-free, permitting a longer and maintenance-free life for both hardware and software.

- If room behind the screen is too short for the required picture throw for designed screen width, first surface mirrors can be used to fold the projection beam into a small size.

- Noise of projection equipment is kept in the projection room.

- Rear screen projection allows for a better and brighter picture than front screen projection in high ambient light conditions.

DISADVANTAGES OF REAR SCREENS

- Using a long focal length lens, the screen image will be bright directly in front of the screen but dim on the sides.

- Using a short focal length lens, the screen image will be less bright directly in front of the screen but less dim on the sides.

- In order to reduce the space requirements, a short focal length lens and/or a set of first surface mirrors are used. Either of these is likely to reduce image brightness and quality.

- A rear screen is less superior than a front screen with regards to image sharpness.

- Using a short focal length lens rather than a long length lens will produce hot spot in the middle of the screen.

- A short focal length lens will give 60% more light on a front or rear screen than a long focal length lens.

SCREEN MATERIAL COST

- Does not include mounting or mounting hardware.

Front screen materials

- Matte white plastic at $1.75 per sq. foot

  Thus, 4' x 6' screen costs $42.00

- Metallic grey lenticular at $1.99 per sq. foot

  Thus, 4' x 6' screen costs $47.76

- Glass bead at $1.75 per sq. foot

  Thus, 4' x 6' screen costs $42.00

- Polished aluminum, one size only

  Thus, 40" x 40" screen costs $111.00

Rear screen materials

- Flexible thin plastic - available in 12' widths and any lenghts
  - lace and grommets at $5.95 per sq. foot

  Thus, 4' x 6' screen costs $142.80

- Rigid plastic - ¼" at $24.25 per sq. foot

  Thus, 4' x 6' screen costs $582.00

- Glass - ¼" at $21.95 per sq. foot

  Thus, 4' x 6' screen costs $526.80

SUMMARY OF SOFTWARE PRODUCTION, SOFTWARE DUPLICATION, BULBS AND EQUIPMENT MAINTENANCE COSTS

	16mm film strip	Super 8mm	Audio cartridge	16mm film	35mm slide	Video tape
Software production costs based on a ten minute program	$350-$500 per minute (80 frames)	$1,000-2,000 per minute	Total cost $25-$500	$1,000-2,000 per minute	$400-$600 per minute (160 slides)	$460-2,000
No. of copies/year	6	12	-	12	4	*
Total cost of copies/year	$210	$1,581	-	$1,667.25	$1,134	*
Software cost/day	$0.58	$4.33	-	$4.56	$3.10	*
Audio tape	Included in above	-	6 carts/yr $300/year $0.82/day	-	6 carts/yr $300/year $0.82/day	*
Bulbs	12/year $114/year $0.31/day	22/year $264/year $0.72/day	-	88/year $1,405.36/yr $3.85/day	48/year $292.80/yr $0.80/day	*
Equipt maintenance	*	*	-	*	*	*
Total software duplication plus bulbs	$0.89/day $324/year	$5.05/day $1,845/yr	$0.82/day $300/year	$8.41/day $3,072.61/yr	$4.73/day $1,726.45/yr	*

* Not available at this time

APPENDIX I
MUSEUM LIGHTING

Compiled by Paul Ellard (Ellard-Willson Ltd., Toronto) and based
upon his Background Paper "Lighting in Relation to Museum
Functions."

TABLE OF CONTENTS

PHYSICS OF LIGHT

Light cannot be properly used in illumination applications without knowing its physical characteristics, and its effect on different materials. The basic phenomena concerning the use of light can be defined as follows:-

Reflection is the process by which a part of the light falling on a medium at a given angle leaves that medium from the incident side without going through the medium. This involves two equal angles, the angle of incidence and the angle of reflection.

Diffusion is a phenomenon similar to reflection, except that when light falls on an uneven surface or a surface composed of minute crystals each single ray reflects the light at a different angle; this appears as a total spread of the incident light and is visible in all directions.

Transmission of light is a property of many materials such as glass and plastics which allows light to go through them without appreciable loss of energy and without change in direction.

Refraction is the change in velocity of light when a ray leaves one material and enters one that has lesser or greater optical density. This phenomenon causes bending of the light rays, with the degree of bending depending on the relative densities of the materials, on the wavelength of the light and on the angle of incidence, being greater for large differences in density. Refraction is a phenomenon very widely used to guide light rays in a given direction; in addition because the degree of refraction through the same medium depends on the wavelength of the incident light, it can split white light in its component colours according to their frequencies.

Absorption is the property of certain materials to let only some wavelengths pass through, while retaining the others and transforming them into heat.

Polarization is the property of some materials to eliminate one of the directions in which light propagation vibrates, while allowing the other to pass.

Surface Brightness and Glare

Glare is the result of unwanted reflection and could be defined as a condition of vision, in which there is discomfort and a reduction in the ability to see objects clearly; this is due to an unsuitable distribution or range of brightness or to extreme contrasts simultaneously or successively present in the field of view. An incident ray falling on a specular surface will be reflected in the same direction and with the same angle to the perpendicular. If the eye of the observer is within the light cone created by this reflection, it will see the light source through reflection as in a mirror.   Because the surface brightness of the source is much higher than the surface brightness of the object it illuminates, the object will appear very dull and more or less invisible. In addition, as the eye with its adaptation ability will reduce its acuity because of the reflected light from the brighter source, the observer will be somehow blinded.   The combination of these two conditions veils the object as with a gauze and makes it impossible for the observer to see any of its detail.

Glare is encountered in two basic forms:

1. <u>Discomfort glare</u> which becomes apparent when luminances and their relationships in the field of view cause visual discomfort but do not interfere with the seeing task. Its cause is usually due to inadequately shielded light sources.

2. <u>Reflected glare</u> which is caused by reflection of bright areas in specular surfaces.   A typical condition is the reflection of a filament of an incandescent lamp on a polished surface. This type of glare in its worst form produces <u>veiling reflections</u> which completely impair the visual performance. Veiling reflections are usually caused by large luminous areas such as skylights or luminous panels, reflected on a dull or matte surface containing glossy details.

The brightness level of a surface can be calculated in a manner similar to the calculation of lighting levels and is also dependent on room size and type of luminaire or source.   The table below gives a number of brightness values that we are all familiar with as a basis of comparison for other sources.

APPROXIMATE BRIGHTNESS VALUES

Source	Candles per Square Inch	Foot-lamberts
Inside Frosted Lamp (300-Watt)	30	13,560
Clear Lamp (300-Watt)	6000	2,712,000
Fluorescent Lamps	2.0 to 7.5	904 to 2,938
Opal Glass Enclosing Globes	1.5 to 5.5	678 to 2,486
White Ceiling Above Direct-Indirect Fluorescent Luminaire	0.5	226
Clear Blue Sky	2 to 3	904 to 1,356

Control of Light

Lighting materials used to control the light pattern and brightness of light sources can be grouped as follows:-

Diffusing: At small viewing angles (looking nearly straight down at the task) this material has the minimum luminance exposed to be reflected in the task. At large viewing angles it tends to have the highest luminance.   This helps reduce veiling reflections but tends to reduce visual comfort per unit area.

Prismatic: A wide range of materials comes under this category, but generally they tend to expose greater flux toward the work for small viewing angles.   Many of them have good light control at large viewing angles. Prismatic materials have been designed to produce special flux distributions referred to below.

Louvers: These materials expose the maximum luminance to the work at small viewing angles.   They generally have lower luminance at large viewing angles. Translucent louvers have the least control; opaque louvers next; and specular parabolic wedge louvers have the maximum.

Polarizing: Available materials of the flake or layer type have a degree of diffusion that exposes less luminance to the work than prismatic or louver materials. They have less luminance at large angles than diffusing, about the same as prismatic, and more than opaque louvers.

Polarization can reduce veiling reflections. The effect is greatest at large viewing angles and least at small viewing angles. For any single ray of light, polarization in a plane perpendicular to the task always tends to reduce veiling reflections. These have been termed "radial" polarizers because in azimuth they produce the same degree of polarization in all directions. "Linear" and "dichroic" polarizers can also be useful - particularly for specialized application.

Special: New optical designs of luminaires and materials have been produced with candlepower distributions that reduce the flux coming from the offending zone and minimize the luminance directed to the eye of the worker. While there are distinct variations in effective illumination and visual comfort for various orientations and positions of the worker, very significant improvements are provided in controlling veiling reflections.

DEFINITIONS

In all lighting studies certain terms are commonly used to denote specific qualitative and quantitative properties of light. These will be reviewed briefly here, so that they can be referred to in the subsequent text without further re-definition.

Luminous flux is the amount of luminous energy that flows from a light source in the unit of time. The measure of luminous flux is the lumen.

<u>Luminous intensity</u> is the amount of luminous flux per unit solid angle, in a specific direction.   It is measured in candelas.

<u>Illumination</u> is the density of luminous flux per unit of uniformly illuminated area.   It is measured in footcandles or lux.

<u>Luminance or photometric brightness</u> is the amount of luminous energy reflected from an illuminated surface in a given direction.   It is measured in foot lamberts or candles per square inch.
(1 C/sq. in. = 452 Ft.L).

<u>Colour temperature</u> is the colour of light produced by a blackbody at a given temperature in degrees Kelvin.   Degrees Kelvin are degrees centigrade plus 273°C.

<u>Inverse square law</u>.   The illumination of a surface from a point source is inversely proportional to the square of its perpendicular distance from the source.

LIGHT AND THE ENVIRONMENT

Colour of Light and Colour Temperature of Light Sources

There often appears to exist a confusion in terms, when referring
to colour and to colour temperature of light sources.

Although both terms express similar concepts, there are distinct
differences as to their use.

The first refers only to the quantity and quality of the
electromagnetic radiation in the spectrum of a light source, as
our eye normally senses it, while the second refers to rendering
of a colour by the incident light of a source and the feeling we
receive when viewing it; the terms of warm and cold light or
colour or faithful rendering of colour in a painting refer to
this second concept.

Colour of Light Sources and Objects.

A light source emitting radiant energy relatively balanced in all
visible wavelengths will appear white to the eye. However, if a
narrow beam of white light passes through a prism of transparent
material it will spread and separate the individual wavelengths
of visible energy so that the normal eye will see three wide bands
of blended colours - violet, green and red, with several narrower
bands - blue, yellow and orange inserted between these wider bands.
As the total colour synthesis creates a white light, colour can be
described as the inbalance of visible radiant energy reaching the
eye from light sources and objects; this inbalance is defined
as any deviation from the average amount of energy at all
wavelengths.   Nevertheless there is a difference between the
colour of a light and the colour of an object.   A coloured light
source radiates more energy at some wavelengths than at others

while a coloured object reflects or transmits some wavelengths more readily than others.   This qualitive characteristic of light is therefore determined by the wavelengths that are present in its spectrum, while the quantitative characteristic refers to the amount of energy that is present at each wavelength.   The qualitative characteristic determines colour while the quantitative characteristic determines luminance or photometric brightness of the light source.

From the above analysis it is apparent that without light there can be no colour, for colours are simply other names to describe the various mixtures of electromagnetic energy.   It should be noted that the colours of light are additive giving as a resultant white light, while the colours of pigments are subtractive and their resultant is black.   A good illustration of our colour perception is shown below.   The spectral emmission of two light sources is shown as modified by the reflectance of the object they illuminate.   The results, which are quite different indicate the object as we ultimately see it in the two cases.

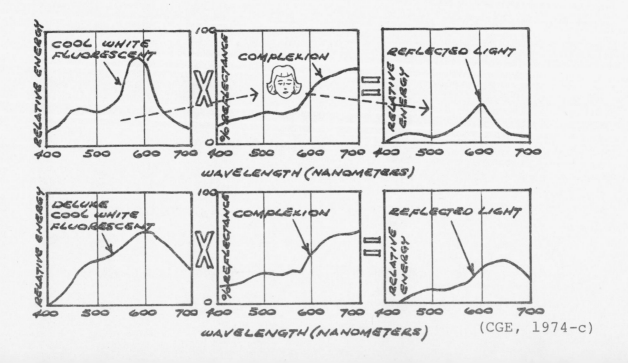

(CGE, 1974-c)

Many apparent differences in intensity between radiant energy
of various wavelengths are in reality the differences in ability
of the various receiving and sensing devices to detect them
uniformly.   The most common of
these receivers is the human eye,
the detecting ability of which
is shown on the adjacent graph.
Two elements of this graph are
of importance:

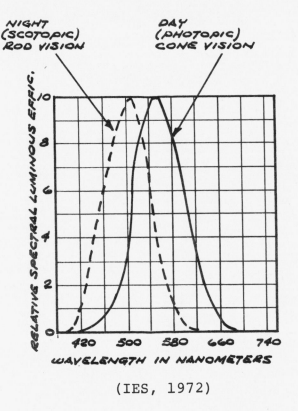

(IES, 1972)

(a)   The eye reacts to different
      frequencies in a different
      way in daytime (photopic)
      and at night (scotopic).

(b)   The eye efficiency is at
      maximum for wavelengths of
      550 nm (yellow-green) in
      daytime and 500 nm (green)
      at night.

This means that when comparing sources of light, the human eye
will consider those in the green spectrum as most efficient as
it can see more of their energy in that zone.   That is why
fluorescent or mercury lamps which have a high content in these
zones appear to the human eye as more response creating and
therefore more efficient.

At the same time although a reaction to a colour in an object
creates one impression, the same colour in the incident light
source creates the exact opposite impression.

For instance green in nature or other objects has the association
of pleasing restfulness, while in the light source it gives an
unpleasant and unnatural feeling.

It appears that certain reactions to colours are universal;
for instance reds and oranges are considered stimulating while
blues and greens are considered restful.   Similarly warm colours
give the impression of advancing at the observer while cool colours
appear to recede; as a result rooms of the same size look larger
if painted in cool colours and smaller if painted in warm colours.
Where peoples' appearance is involved, there is preference for
white light sources which are rich in reds, while for interiors
low levels of illumination appear pleasant with warm light and
dingy with cold light.   The opposite is true for high levels
of illumination, as shown in the attached amenity graph.

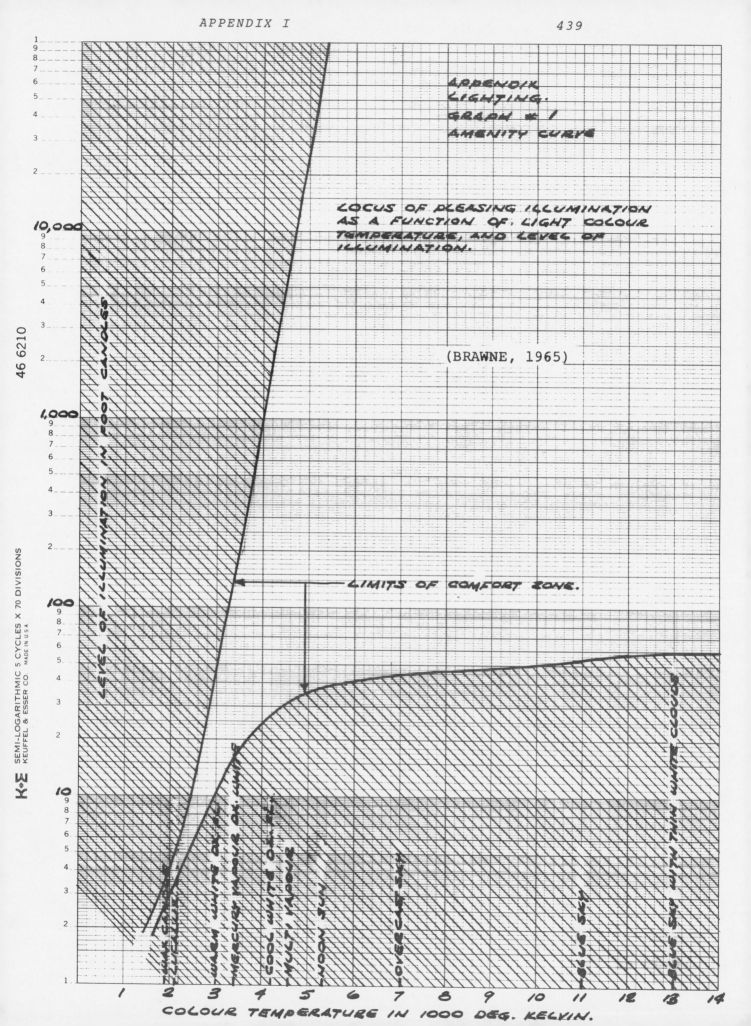

APPENDIX
LIGHTING.
GRAPH # 1
AMENITY CURVE

LOCUS OF PLEASING ILLUMINATION
AS A FUNCTION OF LIGHT COLOUR
TEMPERATURE, AND LEVEL OF
ILLUMINATION.

(BRAWNE, 1965)

LIMITS OF COMFORT ZONE.

LEVEL OF ILLUMINATION IN FOOT CANDLES

COLOUR TEMPERATURE IN 1000 DEG. KELVIN.

Colour Rendering and Colour Temperature

The colour temperature of a light source is the temperature at which the perfect energy transmitter (blackbody) must operate in order that its output in all wavelengths be as close as possible to the light source under consideration.   The higher this temperature, the whiter the visible light radiation it produces.   Colour rendering and colour reproduction of light sources is of the greatest concern to all viewing, printing or photographing processes. The requirements in each case are different as the manner in which the finished product is viewed changes with the application. The human eye adapts ideally to the spectrums produced by the blackbody radiation and by daylight, therefore two standards are used for colour evaluation or colour comparison of sources: The blackbody for colour temperature between $3,000^{\circ}$K and $5,000^{\circ}$K, and daylight for colour temperature from $7,500^{\circ}$K and higher;   both reference sources are rated as 100% in their own respective groups. Because of the inequality of energy in each wavelength band, comparison would be almost impossible.   It was therefore decided to take a number of representative standard colours which would be the points of reference;   two such systems were devised, one with 8 and one with 14 test colours, the latter being more complicated but obviously more accurate as it includes hues and tones.   Having rated the test source for each frequency band, a number is allocated to it showing the deviation from the standard.   These 8 or 14 numbers are then averaged and the resultant figure is the colour rendering index for the source under consideration.   The higher this figure the better its colour rendering.

The attached graphs of the

spectral distribution of two

Philips lamps give an

excellent colour rendition

with a very low UV content.

Cool white deluxe No. 37 gives

good flesh tones, has a colour

rendering index of 96, a

colour temperature of 4,200^{O}K.

and its lumen output is 1,700

lumens.   It is the type of

lamp that is highly recommended

for museum use.

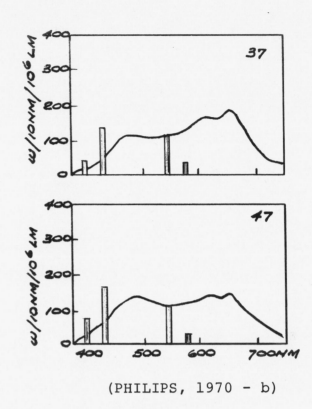

(PHILIPS, 1970 - b)

Lamp No. 47 is ideal for colour

matching, with a colour temperature of 5,000^{O}K and colour

rendering indexes of 98 for an 8 colour rating and 97 for a 14

colour rating.   It has a slightly lower UV content than No. 37 as

well as a slightly higher output of 1,830 lumens.   It is ideal

for graphic arts and is very widely used in that field for colour

matching and colour comparison.

Colour rendering by the spectral distribution of the incident

light is summarized in the following table, for a variety of the

most common types of fluorescent lamps and colours and is of great

value when determining the type of fluorescent lamps to be used

in a specific installation.

PAINT COLOR	APPROX. REFLECTANCE FACTOR	INCANDESCENT FILAMENT	WARM WHITE FLUORESCENT	STD. COOL WHITE FLUORESCENT	DAYLIGHT FLUORESCENT	WARM WHITE DELUXE FLUORESCENT	COOL WHITE DELUXE FLUORESCENT
Cherry Red	.13	Brilliant Orange Red	Pale Orange Red	Yellowish Red	Light Red	Orange Red	Good Match
Orchid	.44	Light Pink	Pale Purplish Pink	Light Pink	Good Match (Grayer)	Pale Pink	Light Pink
Plum	.04	Deep Orange Red	Dull Reddish Brown	Light Reddish Brown	Deep Bluish Purple	Reddish Purple	Darker Brown
Chestnut Brown	.19	Medium Yellow Brown	Light Yellow Brown	Light Brownish Gray	Light Gray	Dark Brown	Good Match
Peach	.58	Pinkish Yellow	Light Yellowish Pink	Very Light Pink	Fair Match (Lighter)	Light Orange	Good Match (Yellower)
Orange	.44	Bright Orange	Light Orange Yellow	Light Yellow	Gray Yellow	Yellowish Orange	Good Match
Canary Yellow	.44	Orange Yellow	Fair Match (More Vivid)	Light Yellow	Fair Match	Good Match	Good Match (Brighter)
Light Yellow	.58	Vivid Orange Yellow	Medium Yellow	Light Bright Yellow	Light Greenish Yellow	Deep Yellow	Bright Yellow
Light Blue	.46	Light Yellowish Green	Pale Grayish Blue	Blue Gray	Fair Match (Lighter)	Grayish Blue	Grayish Blue
Medium Blue	.23	Blue Green	Light Gray Blue	Light Gray Blue	Fair Match (Lighter)	Purple Blue	Reddish Blue
Silver Gray	.57	Light Yellow Gray	Light Yellowish Gray	Very Light Gray	Bluish Gray	Yellowish Gray	Light Gray

COLOUR RENDERING FOR CONVENTIONAL
FLUORESCENT LAMPS

INCANDESCENT LAMPS
(INCLUDING TUNGSTEN-HALOGEN)

(CGE, 1974 - c)

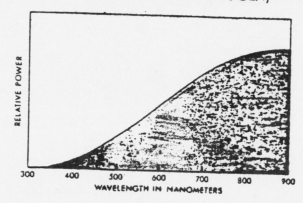

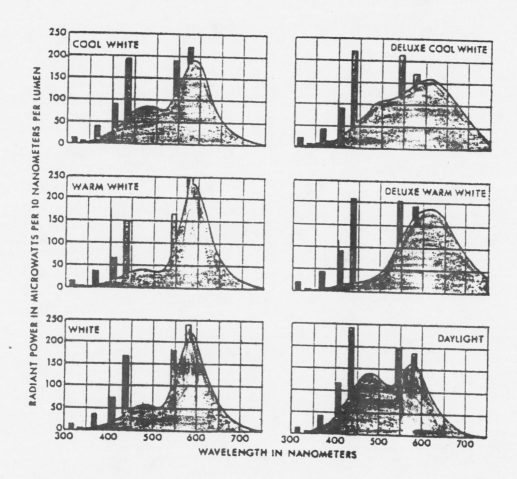

FLUORESCENT LAMPS
(CGE, 1974 - c)

SPECTRAL CHARACTERISTICS OF LAMPS

DISPLAY LIGHTING

Gallery Design Principles

The direction of a concentrated beam of light directed at an object should be at an incident angle of 60° from the horizontal and should be centered at an adult sight line height of 5'-6" as shown on the attached sketch.

The dimensions given on the sketch are based on nominal dimensions of beam and height of object.   If the object is higher than the 52" height shown, the light source should move back by 1½" for every 1" of additional height.

The basic geometry of this specific layout is represented by the following formula:

X = (H-66") X 0.577

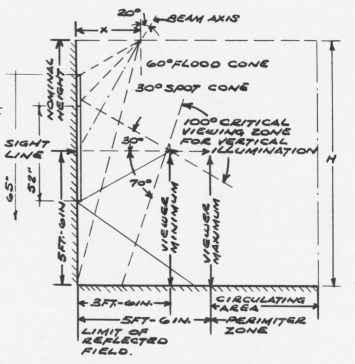

(IES, 1972)

The viewing height of 5'-6" could be adjusted by one foot maximum to compensate for short viewers in galleries of prime interest to children, in which case the angles given have to be re-adjusted. The limit of reflected field is an important dimension as it indicates that any general lighting behind the observer can be reflected on the picture and can cause glare if the floor material is reflective.

The distance "X" provides a term of reference around the gallery ceiling for the peripheral viewing zone. The control of ceiling heights on the other hand should be based on the expected height of displayed materials, the ideal utilization of the light beam of the illuminating source and the minimum effective viewing distance for the maximum permissible height of exhibits.

The illumination levels on the vertical surface for the angles given in the sketch should be adjusted for the angle of projection. Using an 80% maintenance factor and the lumen output within the 10° beam cone, the illumination level can be calculated from the following formula:

$$E = \frac{0.214 \times I}{h^2} \quad \text{where}$$

E : the illumination in footcandles.

I : the manufacturers listed initial lumens for the lamp within the 10° beam cone.

h : the ceiling distance above the sight line.

It should be kept in mind that the excessive use of concentrated light sources during recent years decreases visual efficiency, and increases photochemical damage and power costs. It is recommended that the use of accent lights be kept to a reasonable balance with the general diffuse lighting in the room, and that small wattage lamps with narrow beams be used instead of high wattage floodlamps.

The average lighting in a gallery containing non-light sensitive materials should be maintained at 30 FC, which is a good average for viewing, studying and copying.

It is also recommended that the luminance (brightness) ratios between adjacent light sources be kept to a ratio of 3:1, and if a fully luminous ceiling is used it should extend to within a foot of the gallery wall if the ceiling height is 15 ft. or less and within two feet if the gallery ceiling is in excess of 16 ft., so that 40% of the calculated diffuse horizontal illumination becomes available on the vertical plane, measured along the sight line height.

The control of the peripheral area of such a luminous ceiling should be separate from the control of the central area, with the central area having provisions for dimming.

TYPICAL DETAILS OF GALLERY ILLUMINATION -

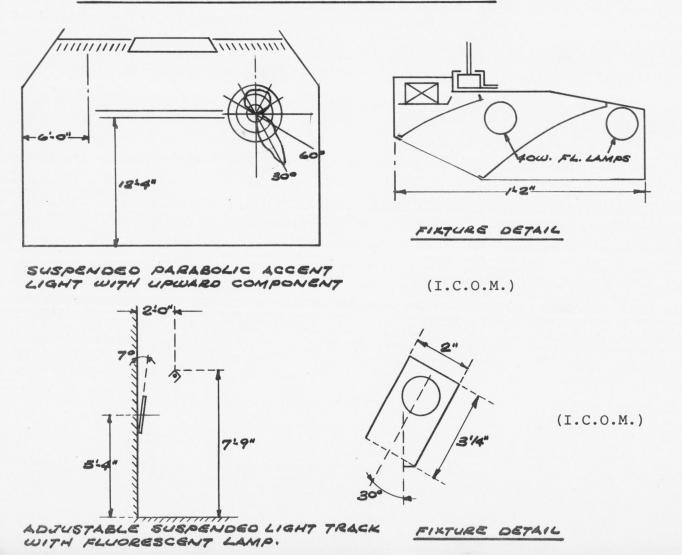

6'-0"

12'-4"

60°

30°

SUSPENDED PARABOLIC ACCENT
LIGHT WITH UPWARD COMPONENT

40w. FL. LAMPS

42"

FIXTURE DETAIL

(I.C.O.M.)

2'-0"

7°

7'-9"

5'-4"

ADJUSTABLE SUSPENDED LIGHT TRACK
WITH FLUORESCENT LAMP.

2"

3 1/4"

30°

(I.C.O.M.)

FIXTURE DETAIL

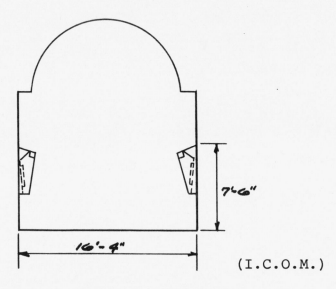

(I.C.O.M.)

SECTION TROUGH GALLERY

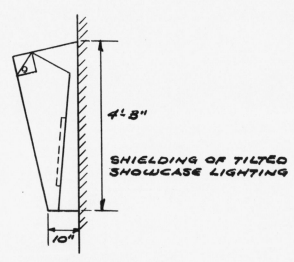

SECTION TROUGH SHOWCASE

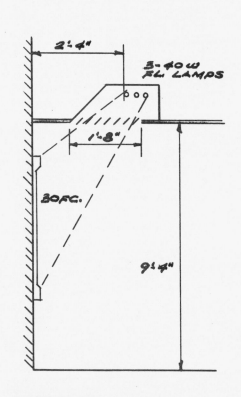

RECESSED TROFFER WITH ANGLE LOUVERS.

(I.C.O.M.)

SCULPTURE HIGHLIGHTING

(BRAWNE, 1965)

EDGE LIGHTING OF GLASSWARE SHELVING

(I.C.O.M.)

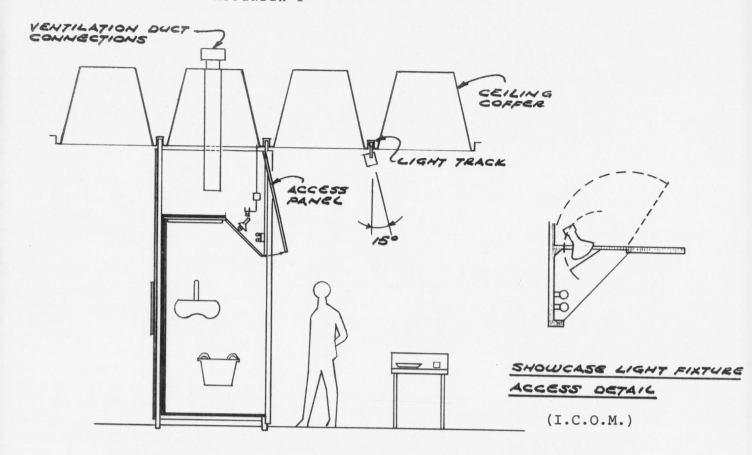

VENTILATION DUCT CONNECTIONS

CEILING COFFER

LIGHT TRACK

ACCESS PANEL

15°

LIGHTING AND AIR CONDITIONING IN INTEGRATED SHOWCASE AND CEILING DESIGN

(I.C.O.M.)

SHOWCASE LIGHT FIXTURE ACCESS DETAIL

(I.C.O.M.)

LIGHTING AND CONSERVATION

The extent of the damage caused by light depends on three factors: the illumination level, the duration of exposure and the spectral composition of the light.   The product of the first two is referred to, as a footcandle-hour.   Following many tests the theory of reciprocity was formulated which indicates that the degree of damage to material and dyes is a function of the footcandle hours the object has been exposed to; for instance, an object exposed to 100 FC for 100 hours will show the same damage as an object exposed to 10 FC's for 1,000 hours. Nevertheless, the "rate" of damage is increased by the higher footcandle exposure, with the damaged outer layers providing a "cushion" to the inner layers of the material; the ultimate damage is of course the same in both cases.   As the materials of museum objects are varied it is obvious that no prediction of the life of any single museum object can be made even if it is subjected to controlled irradiation.   It is all the more impossible to assign to a light source a rate of damage applying simultaneously to all museum objects.   The best that can be hoped for, is an evaluation of the radiation hazard associated with each light source indicating the probable rate of damage to the average museum object as affected by the density of the incident luminous flux from this source.

Although materials differ in their reaction to light, radiation of short wave length is more destructive than that of long wave length.   Consequently "warm" rather than "cool" light sources are preferred.

The recommended maintained illumination in a museum gallery for light incident on the object on its chief plane, should be selected in accordance with the following table:

OBJECT	LIGHTING TEMPERATURE	ILLUMINATION LEVEL
Insensitive to light (metal and stone)	Daylight, fluorescents of $4,200^{\circ}K$ - $6,500^{\circ}K$	30-40FC plus up to 60 FC for emphasis
Most museum objects including oil and tempera painting, leather, horn, wood, ivory and lacquer	Daylight, Tungsten, Fluorescents of $4,200^{\circ}K$	15 FC
Specially sensitive objects (textiles, costumes, water colour, books, manuscripts, stamps, tapestries, dyed leather, skins and botanical specimens	Tungsten or fluorescents of $4,200^{\circ}K$	5 FC or less

Cumulative effects of exposure to IR radiation are primarily due to the heating/cooling cycle. After this cycle is performed many times, the effect will in fact be cumulative. In the case of paper and textiles where the destruction is due to the deterioration of the polymer molecules, the effect is definitely cumulative.

Recent tests have proved that an increase of $10^{\circ}C$ will increase the _fading_ of pigments by a factor of 1.3 times.

A rule of thumb based on the Arrhenius equation was that the rate of _chemical_ reactions taking place in a room may be expected to almost double for a rise of $10^{\circ}C$.

To avoid these conditions four simple steps can be followed when allowing photographs to be taken inside the galleries or in the museum photographic studios:

1. Maintain the illumination level to the minimum compatible with proper photographic requirements.

2. Reduce radiant heat by using heat absorbing filters and heat transmitting reflectors.

3. Use portable fans to provide forced ventilation.

4. Reduce the time of exposure by switching on full lights only during filming and low intensity modelling lights during rehearsal, or by using flash.

The use of flash is very highly recommended because of its short duration; the quantity of infrared heat it can produce is less than 1/100th. of the heat produced for equivalent illumination by tungsten lamps.

Tests conducted by the National Research Council in the National Gallery of Canada indicated that an object photographed with a 1,600 watt/sec flash or an electronic flash is equivalent to 1,500 FC for three seconds, or 1.25 FC-Hrs. Using 25,000 flash exposures it was found that stable colours did not shift, while fugitive colours did, in a manner similar to exposure to U.V. radiation. The implication therefore is that objects that have fugitive colours should be photographed with as great a caution as they are illuminated in their permanent display environment, and that extensive photography is to be avoided wherever possible. The attached graphs indicate the effect of ultraviolet and infrared radiation on light sensitive objects and can be used to determine the amount and type of illumination that should be used in museums as well as conditions that could be detrimental to the exhibits.

APPENDIX
LIGHTING AND IT'S EFFECT ON CONSERVATION
GRAPH NO. 2

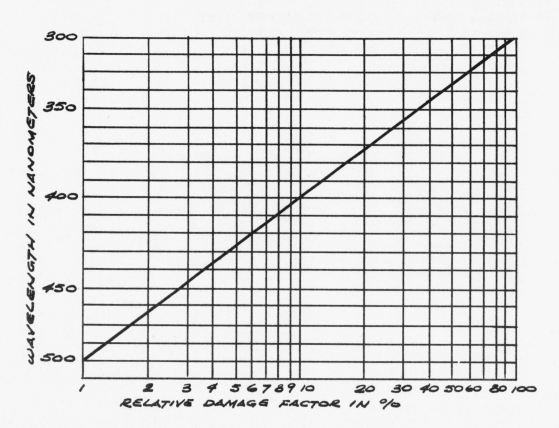

DAMAGE FACTOR OF LIGHT SENSITIVE MATERIALS AS A FUNCTION
OF SPECTRAL WAVELENGTH.

SOURCE	COL. TEMP, $^\circ$K	LUMENS	ULTRAVIOLET		VISIBLE LIGHT
			220nm-320nm	320nm-400nm	400nm-700nm
6W Inc.	2,400	44	–		0.18
60W Inc.	2,820	855	0.003	0.062	3.40
100W Inc.	2,900	1,350	0.008	0.132	6.90
150W Inc.	2,900	1,730	0.012	0.185	9.60
500W Inc.	3,000	10,500	0.067	0.994	41.30
500W Quartz	3,000	10,500	0.100	0.981	41.90
40W Fl. CWDX	3,850	2,230	0.038	0.180	7.83
40W Fl. WWDX	2,950	2,180	0.030	0.199	7.42
40W Fl. Daylight	7,000	2,660	0.050	0.431	9.06
Philips No. 37 Fl.	4,200	1,700	0.06		6.00
Philips No. 47 Fl.	5,000	1,830	0.04		6.60
250W MV WDX	3,350	12,100	10.00		30.60
250W MV WWDX	3,400	9,500	6.00		27.20
175W MV WDX	3,350	8,600	7.00		21.70
175W MV WWDX	3,400	6,500	4.00		19.30
125W MV WDX	3,350	6,320	5.00		16.00
125W MV WWDX	3,400	4,740	4.00		15.00
400W MV WDX	3,350	22,500	19.00		57.00
400W MV WWDX	3,400	20,000	13.00		50.00

SPECTRAL ENERGY DISTRIBUTION IN LIGHT SOURCES

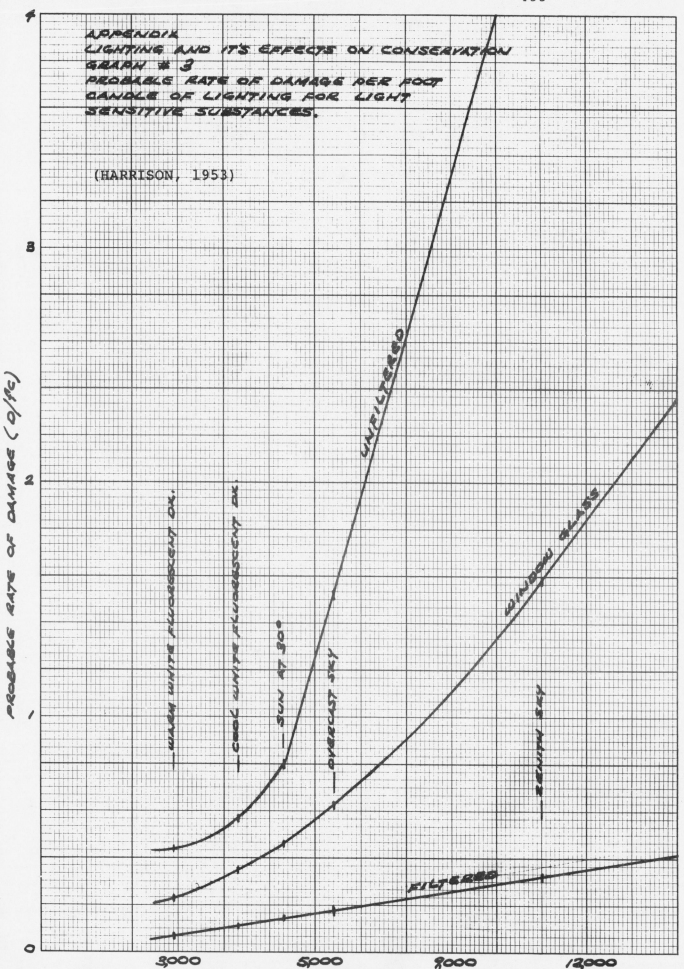

APPENDIX
LIGHTING AND IT'S EFFECTS ON CONSERVATION
GRAPH # 3
PROBABLE RATE OF DAMAGE PER FOOT
CANDLE OF LIGHTING FOR LIGHT
SENSITIVE SUBSTANCES.

(HARRISON, 1953)

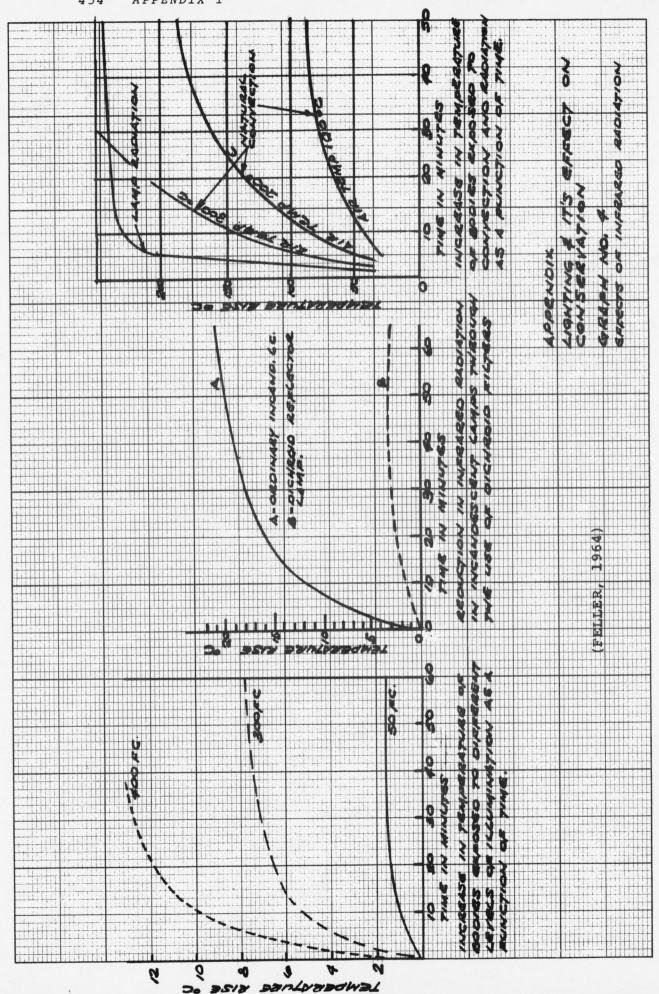

LIGHTING CALCULATIONS

Calculations of Illumination for Artificial Lighting

Artificial lighting can be designed to provide uniform
illumination in an area or to provide accent lighting on an
object.   The methods of calculation for these two functions
are completely different as the first assumes the existance of
a luminous plane above the task area, while the second is based
on a point luminous source.   In the first instance the illumination
level is inversely proportional to the distance between the source
and the task level, while in the second it is inversely
proportional to the square of the distance between object and
source.

(A)   Uniform Illumination Calculations

The average uniform horizontal illumination in a room is the total
number of lumens produced by the lamps divided by the area of the
room;   this figure is reduced by three depreciation coefficients;
the coefficient of utilization (CU) which is a function of the
room, the lamp lumen depreciation factor (LLD) and the luminaire
dirt depreciation factor (LDD).   The product of the last two
gives us the maintenance factor (MF) for a specific type of
lighting fixture and its lamps.   These quantities are related
by the following formula:

Maintained Foot Candles =

No. of luminaires X lamps per luminaire X Initial lumens per lamp X CU X MF
Area in Square Feet

These factors will be explained and their values obtained from
the graphs and tables provided in the next few pages.

So as to achieve a luminous plane above the task level, the
spacing of the luminaires must be such that the light patterns
of the individual light fixtures intersect as close as possible
to the ceiling.   It is a specific characteristic of each type
of luminaire that determines the spacing that is necessary and
which for wide distribution fixtures is usually one and one quarter
times their mounting height, while for narrow distribution fixtures
it is approximately 0.6 of their mounting height.

All factors, except for the coefficient of utilization, are
obtainable from the tables and graphs provided on the next page.
The coefficient of utilization, on the other hand, must be calculated.
The most popular method used for this calculation is the zone
cavity method which was adopted recently because of its accuracy.

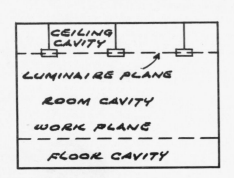

As can be seen from the typical
sketch to the left, the room space
is subdivided into three cavities:
the ceiling cavity, the floor
cavity and the room cavity.
These cavities are very important
when stem hung fixtures are used.

As this type of fixture is no longer in common use the
calculations involving floor and ceiling cavities will be ignored.
The first step in the simplified calculation is the determination
of the ceiling, wall and floor reflectances.   The next step
determines the room cavity which in this case is the cavity for
the full height of the room.   From the width, length and height
of the room (cavity depth) one obtains a figure from the Cavity
Ratios table shown on the next tables.

This entire procedure is so simple that a single example should suffice.   Assume a room size of 20 ft. X 45 ft., 12 ft. high and with a floor reflectance of 20%, a wall reflectance of 50% and a ceiling reflectance of 80%.   The room is to be illuminated with recessed fluorescent fixtures.   From the cavity ratios table we obtain a cavity ratio of 4.3.   Using this figure as the RCR (room cavity ratio) and the reflectances given, we obtain by interpolation a coefficient of utilization (CU) of 0.46.   We also notice from the next table that this fixture is a type 'V', for which the dirt depreciation factor (LDD) is 88% for a clean area. In addition we find the lumens depreciation factor (LLD) for 40 watt fluorescents is 86%.

The product of LDD X LLD is 0.88 X 0.86 which is approximately 76%. By introducing these figures in the basic formula for illumination in footcandles we can find the desired number of fixtures, or if we know the number of fixtures, we can find the footcandles.

(B)   Accent Illumination Calculations

As mentioned before the illumination level on a plane
perpendicular to a light beam is inversely proportional to the
distance between the plane and the source of light.

I = 1 CANDLE-   E = 1 FOOT-   E = ¼ FOOT- $E = \frac{1}{D^2}$
      POWER   CANDLE   CANDLE

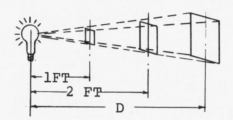

ILLUMINATION E = $\dfrac{\text{FLUX IN LUMENS (F)}}{\text{AREA IN SQ FT (A)}}$

If the beam is not perpendicular to the surface the illumination
level of the surface is reduced by the cosine of the angle of
incidence.

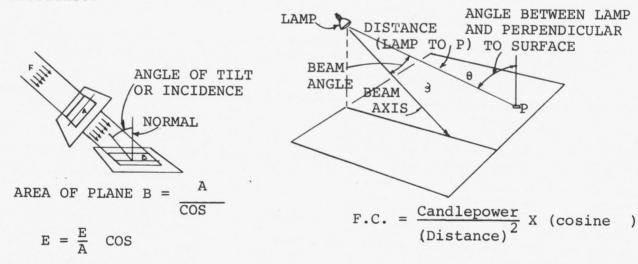

AREA OF PLANE B = $\dfrac{A}{COS}$

$E = \dfrac{E}{A}$ COS

F.C. = $\dfrac{\text{Candlepower}}{(\text{Distance})^2}$ X (cosine   )

For example the illumination delivered to point P in the diagram by
a 150 PAR/FL would be:

$\vartheta°$= 20 degrees (beam angle)   cos 75° = 0.26
$\theta°$= 75 degrees (angle of incidence)   d = 4 feet

F.C. = $\dfrac{1400 \text{ Lumens}}{(4)^2}$ X (cos 75°) = 22.8 ft. candles.

CAVITY RATIOS

ROOM DIMENSIONS		CAVITY DEPTH																		
Width	Length	1.0	1.5	2.0	2.5	3.0	3.5	4.0	5.0	6.0	7.0	8	9	10	11	12	14	16	20	25	30
8	8	1.2	1.9	2.5	3.1	3.7	4.4	5.0	6.2	7.5	8.8	10.0	11.2	12.5	—	—	—	—	—	—	—
	10	1.1	1.7	2.2	2.8	3.4	3.9	4.5	5.6	6.7	7.3	9.0	10.1	11.3	12.4	—	—	—	—	—	—
	14	1.0	1.5	2.0	2.5	3.0	3.4	3.9	4.9	5.9	6.9	7.8	8.8	9.7	10.7	11.7	—	—	—	—	—
	20	0.9	1.3	1.7	2.2	2.6	3.1	3.5	4.4	5.2	6.1	7.0	7.9	8.8	9.6	10.5	12.2	—	—	—	—
	30	0.8	1.2	1.6	2.0	2.4	2.8	3.2	4.0	4.7	5.5	6.3	7.1	7.9	8.7	9.5	11.0	—	—	—	—
	40	0.7	1.1	1.5	1.9	2.3	2.6	3.0	3.7	4.5	5.3	5.9	6.5	7.4	8.1	8.8	10.3	11.8	—	—	—
10	10	1.0	1.5	2.0	2.5	3.0	3.5	4.0	5.0	6.0	7.0	8.0	9.0	10.0	11.0	12.0	—	—	—	—	—
	14	0.9	1.3	1.7	2.1	2.6	3.0	3.4	4.3	5.1	6.0	6.9	7.8	8.6	9.5	10.4	12.0	—	—	—	—
	20	0.7	1.1	1.5	1.9	2.3	2.5	3.0	3.7	4.5	5.3	6.0	6.8	7.5	8.3	9.0	10.5	12.0	—	—	—
	30	0.7	1.0	1.3	1.7	2.0	2.3	2.7	3.3	4.0	4.7	5.3	6.0	6.6	7.3	8.0	9.4	10.6	—	—	—
	40	0.6	0.9	1.2	1.6	1.9	2.2	2.5	3.1	3.7	4.4	5.0	5.6	6.2	6.9	7.5	8.7	10.0	12.5	—	—
	60	0.6	0.9	1.2	1.5	1.7	2.0	2.3	2.9	3.5	4.1	4.7	5.3	5.9	6.5	7.1	8.2	9.4	11.7	—	—
12	12	0.8	1.2	1.7	2.1	2.5	2.9	3.3	4.2	5.0	5.8	6.7	7.5	8.4	9.2	10.0	11.7	—	—	—	—
	16	0.7	1.1	1.5	1.8	2.2	2.5	2.9	3.6	4.4	5.1	5.8	6.5	7.2	8.0	8.7	10.2	11.6	—	—	—
	24	0.6	0.9	1.2	1.6	1.9	2.2	2.5	3.1	3.7	4.4	5.0	5.6	6.2	6.9	7.5	8.7	10.0	12.5	—	—
	36	0.6	0.8	1.1	1.4	1.7	1.9	2.2	2.8	3.3	3.9	4.4	5.0	5.5	6.0	6.6	7.8	8.8	11.0	—	—
	50	0.5	0.8	1.0	1.3	1.5	1.8	2.1	2.6	3.1	3.6	4.1	4.6	5.1	5.6	6.2	7.2	8.2	10.2	—	—
	70	0.5	0.7	1.0	1.2	1.5	1.7	2.0	2.4	2.9	3.4	3.9	4.4	4.9	5.4	5.9	6.8	7.3	9.7	12.2	—
14	14	0.7	1.1	1.4	1.8	2.1	2.5	2.9	3.6	4.3	5.0	5.7	6.4	7.1	7.8	8.5	10.0	11.4	—	—	—
	20	0.6	0.9	1.2	1.5	1.8	2.1	2.4	3.0	3.6	4.2	4.9	5.5	6.1	6.7	7.3	8.6	9.8	12.3	—	—
	30	0.5	0.8	1.0	1.3	1.6	1.8	2.1	2.6	3.1	3.7	4.2	4.7	5.2	5.8	6.3	7.3	8.4	10.5	—	—
	42	0.5	0.7	1.0	1.2	1.4	1.7	1.9	2.4	2.9	3.3	3.8	4.3	4.7	5.2	5.7	6.7	7.6	9.5	11.9	—
	60	0.4	0.7	0.9	1.1	1.3	1.5	1.8	2.2	2.6	3.1	3.5	3.9	4.4	4.8	5.2	6.1	7.0	8.8	10.9	—
	90	0.4	0.6	0.8	1.0	1.2	1.4	1.6	2.0	2.5	2.9	3.3	3.7	4.1	4.5	5.0	5.8	6.6	8.3	10.3	12.4
17	17	0.6	0.9	1.2	1.5	1.8	2.1	2.3	2.9	3.5	4.1	4.7	5.3	5.9	6.5	7.0	8.2	9.4	11.7	—	—
	25	0.5	0.7	1.0	1.2	1.5	1.7	2.0	2.5	3.0	3.5	4.0	4.5	5.0	5.5	6.0	7.0	8.0	10.0	12.5	—
	35	0.4	0.7	0.9	1.1	1.3	1.5	1.7	2.2	2.6	3.1	3.5	3.9	4.4	4.8	5.2	6.1	7.0	8.7	10.9	—
	50	0.4	0.6	0.8	1.0	1.2	1.4	1.6	2.0	2.4	2.8	3.1	3.5	3.9	4.3	4.5	5.4	6.2	7.7	9.7	11.5
	80	0.4	0.5	0.7	0.9	1.1	1.2	1.4	1.8	2.1	2.5	2.9	3.3	3.5	3.9	4.3	5.1	5.8	7.2	9.0	10.9
	120	0.3	0.5	0.7	0.8	1.0	1.2	1.3	1.7	2.0	2.3	2.7	3.0	3.4	3.7	4.0	4.7	5.4	6.7	8.4	10.1
20	20	0.5	0.7	1.0	1.2	1.5	1.7	2.0	2.5	3.0	3.5	4.0	4.5	5.0	5.5	6.0	7.0	8.0	10.0	12.5	—
	30	0.4	0.6	0.8	1.0	1.2	1.5	1.7	2.1	2.5	2.9	3.3	3.7	4.1	4.5	4.9	5.8	6.6	8.2	10.3	12.4
	45	0.4	0.5	0.7	0.9	1.1	1.3	1.4	1.8	2.2	2.5	2.9	3.3	3.6	4.0	4.3	5.1	5.8	7.2	9.1	10.9
	60	0.3	0.5	0.7	0.8	1.0	1.2	1.3	1.7	2.0	2.3	2.7	3.0	3.4	3.7	4.0	4.7	5.4	6.7	8.4	10.1
	90	0.3	0.5	0.6	0.8	0.9	1.1	1.2	1.5	1.8	2.1	2.4	2.7	3.0	3.3	3.6	4.2	4.8	6.0	7.5	9.0
	150	0.3	0.4	0.6	0.7	0.8	1.0	1.1	1.4	1.7	2.0	2.3	2.6	2.9	3.2	3.4	4.0	4.6	5.7	7.2	8.5
24	24	0.4	0.6	0.8	1.0	1.2	1.5	1.7	2.1	2.5	2.9	3.3	3.7	4.1	4.5	5.0	5.8	6.7	8.2	10.3	12.4
	32	0.4	0.5	0.7	0.9	1.1	1.3	1.5	1.8	2.2	2.6	2.9	3.3	3.6	4.1	4.5	5.0	5.8	7.2	9.0	11.0
	50	0.3	0.5	0.6	0.8	0.9	1.1	1.2	1.5	1.8	2.2	2.5	2.9	3.3	3.6	4.3	5.1	5.8	7.2	9.0	11.0
	70	0.3	0.4	0.6	0.7	0.8	1.0	1.1	1.4	1.7	2.0	2.2	2.5	2.8	3.1	3.4	3.8	4.4	5.5	6.9	8.2
	100	0.3	0.4	0.5	0.6	0.8	0.9	1.0	1.3	1.6	1.8	2.0	2.2	2.5	2.8	3.0	3.8	4.4	5.5	6.9	8.2
	160	0.2	0.4	0.5	0.6	0.7	0.8	1.0	1.2	1.4	1.7	1.8	2.1	2.4	2.6	2.9	3.7	4.2	5.2	6.5	7.9
30	30	0.3	0.5	0.7	0.8	1.0	1.2	1.3	1.7	2.0	2.3	2.7	3.0	3.3	3.7	4.0	4.7	5.4	6.7	8.4	10.0
	45	0.3	0.4	0.6	0.7	0.8	1.0	1.1	1.4	1.7	1.9	2.2	2.5	2.8	3.1	3.3	3.8	4.4	5.5	6.9	8.2
	60	0.3	0.4	0.5	0.6	0.7	0.9	1.0	1.2	1.5	1.7	1.9	2.2	2.5	2.7	3.0	3.5	4.0	5.0	6.2	7.4
	90	0.2	0.3	0.4	0.6	0.7	0.8	0.9	1.1	1.3	1.6	1.8	2.0	2.2	2.5	2.7	3.1	3.6	4.4	5.6	6.7
	150	0.2	0.3	0.4	0.5	0.6	0.7	0.8	1.0	1.2	1.4	1.6	1.8	2.0	2.2	2.4	2.8	3.2	4.0	5.0	5.9
	200	0.2	0.3	0.4	0.5	0.6	0.7	0.8	1.0	1.1	1.3	1.5	1.6	1.8	2.0	2.2	2.5	3.0	3.7	4.7	5.6
36	36	0.3	0.4	0.6	0.7	0.8	1.0	1.1	1.4	1.7	1.9	2.2	2.5	2.8	3.0	3.3	3.9	4.4	5.5	6.9	8.3
	50	0.2	0.4	0.5	0.6	0.7	0.8	1.0	1.2	1.4	1.7	1.9	2.1	2.5	2.6	3.3	3.9	4.4	5.5	6.9	8.3
	75	0.2	0.3	0.4	0.5	0.6	0.7	0.8	1.0	1.2	1.4	1.6	1.8	2.0	2.2	2.5	2.9	3.3	4.3	4.7	5.7
	100	0.2	0.3	0.4	0.5	0.6	0.7	0.8	1.0	1.1	1.3	1.5	1.8	2.0	2.1	2.3	2.9	3.3	4.1	5.1	6.1
	150	0.2	0.3	0.3	0.4	0.5	0.6	0.7	0.9	1.0	1.2	1.3	1.5	1.7	1.9	2.1	2.4	2.8	3.5	4.3	5.2
	200	0.2	0.2	0.3	0.4	0.5	0.6	0.7	0.8	1.0	1.1	1.2	1.4	1.6	1.7	1.9	2.3	2.6	3.3	4.1	4.9
42	42	0.2	0.4	0.5	0.6	0.7	0.8	1.0	1.2	1.4	1.6	1.9	2.1	2.4	2.6	2.8	3.3	3.8	4.7	5.9	7.1
	60	0.2	0.3	0.4	0.5	0.6	0.7	0.8	1.0	1.2	1.4	1.6	1.8	2.0	2.2	2.4	2.8	3.2	4.7	5.9	6.0
	90	0.2	0.3	0.3	0.4	0.5	0.6	0.7	0.9	1.0	1.2	1.4	1.6	1.7	1.9	2.1	2.4	2.8	3.5	4.4	5.2
	140	0.2	0.2	0.3	0.4	0.5	0.5	0.6	0.8	0.9	1.1	1.2	1.4	1.6	1.7	2.1	2.4	2.8	3.5	4.4	5.2
	200	0.1	0.2	0.3	0.4	0.4	0.5	0.6	0.8	0.9	1.0	1.2	1.4	1.5	1.7	1.9	2.2	2.5	3.1	3.9	4.6
	300	0.1	0.2	0.3	0.3	0.4	0.5	0.5	0.7	0.8	0.9	1.0	1.1	1.3	1.4	1.6	2.0	2.3	2.9	3.6	4.3
50	50	0.2	0.3	0.4	0.5	0.6	0.7	0.8	1.0	1.2	1.4	1.6	1.8	2.0	2.2	2.4	2.8	3.2	4.0	5.0	6.0
	70	0.2	0.3	0.3	0.4	0.5	0.6	0.7	0.9	1.0	1.2	1.4	1.5	1.7	1.9	2.4	2.8	3.2	4.0	5.0	6.0
	100	0.1	0.2	0.3	0.4	0.4	0.5	0.6	0.7	0.9	1.0	1.2	1.3	1.5	1.6	2.0	2.4	2.7	3.4	4.3	5.1
	150	0.1	0.2	0.3	0.3	0.4	0.5	0.5	0.7	0.8	0.9	1.1	1.2	1.3	1.5	1.8	2.1	2.4	3.0	3.7	4.5
	300	0.1	0.2	0.2	0.3	0.3	0.4	0.5	0.6	0.7	0.8	0.9	1.0	1.2	1.3	1.6	1.9	2.1	2.7	3.3	4.0
60	60	0.2	0.2	0.3	0.4	0.5	0.6	0.7	0.8	1.0	1.2	1.3	1.5	1.7	1.8	2.0	2.3	2.7	3.3	4.2	5.0
	100	0.1	0.2	0.3	0.3	0.4	0.5	0.5	0.7	0.8	1.0	1.2	1.3	1.5	1.7	2.0	2.3	2.7	3.3	4.2	5.0
	150	0.1	0.2	0.2	0.3	0.3	0.4	0.5	0.6	0.7	0.8	0.9	1.1	1.2	1.3	1.6	1.9	2.1	2.7	3.3	3.5
	300	0.1	0.1	0.2	0.2	0.3	0.4	0.4	0.5	0.6	0.7	0.8	0.9	1.0	1.1	1.2	1.4	1.6	2.0	2.5	3.0
75	75	0.1	0.2	0.3	0.3	0.4	0.5	0.5	0.7	0.8	0.9	1.1	1.2	1.3	1.5	1.6	1.9	2.1	2.7	3.3	4.0
	120	0.1	0.2	0.2	0.3	0.3	0.4	0.4	0.5	0.6	0.8	0.9	1.0	1.1	1.2	1.3	1.6	1.9	2.1	2.7	3.3
	200	0.1	0.1	0.2	0.2	0.3	0.3	0.4	0.5	0.6	0.7	0.8	0.9	1.0	1.1	1.2	1.3	1.5	1.7	2.2	2.7
	300	0.1	0.1	0.2	0.2	0.2	0.3	0.3	0.4	0.5	0.6	0.6	0.7	0.8	0.8	0.9	1.1	1.3	1.5	1.8	2.3	2.7
100	100	0.1	0.1	0.2	0.2	0.3	0.3	0.4	0.5	0.6	0.7	0.8	0.9	1.0	1.1	1.2	1.4	1.6	2.0	2.5	3.0
	200	0.1	0.1	0.1	0.2	0.2	0.3	0.3	0.4	0.4	0.5	0.6	0.7	0.7	0.8	0.9	1.2	1.4	1.6	2.0	3.0
	300	0.1	0.1	0.1	0.2	0.2	0.3	0.3	0.4	0.4	0.5	0.6	0.7	0.7	0.8	0.9	1.0	1.2	1.5	1.9	2.2
150	150	0.1	0.1	0.1	0.2	0.2	0.2	0.3	0.3	0.4	0.5	0.5	0.6	0.7	0.7	0.8	0.9	1.1	1.3	1.7	2.0
	300	—	0.1	0.1	0.1	0.1	0.2	0.2	0.3	0.3	0.4	0.4	0.5	0.5	0.6	0.6	0.7	0.8	1.0	1.2	1.5
200	200	—	0.1	0.1	0.1	0.1	0.2	0.2	0.2	0.3	0.3	0.4	0.5	0.5	0.6	0.6	0.7	0.8	1.0	1.2	1.5
	300	—	0.1	0.1	0.1	0.1	0.1	0.2	0.2	0.2	0.3	0.3	0.4	0.4	0.5	0.5	0.6	0.7	0.8	1.0	1.2
300	300	—	—	0.1	0.1	0.1	0.1	0.1	0.2	0.2	0.2	0.3	0.3	0.3	0.4	0.4	0.5	0.5	0.6	0.7	0.8
500	500	—	—	—	—	0.1	0.1	0.1	0.1	0.1	0.1	0.2	0.2	0.2	0.2	0.2	0.3	0.3	0.4	0.5	0.6

COLOUR REFLECTANCE TABLE

Wall Finishes

Hue	Grey	Blue	Green	Yellow	Brown	Orange	Red
Very Light	82%	69%	62%	79%	70%	71%	70%
Light	65%	64%	49%	76%	51%	69%	62%
Medium	50%	50%	39%	70%	41%	60%	47%
Medium Dark	35%	40%	21%	65%	29%	53%	41%
Dark	27%	23%	14%	60%	19%	45%	29%
Very Dark	15%	8%	8%	55%	15%	36%	22%

Wood Finishes

Light Blond	58%
Medium Blond	52%
Medium Grainy	44%
Dark Grainy	27%
Very Dark Grainy	19%

Chalkboards

Dark Green	15% - 20%

Desk Tops

Light Brown Linoleum	45%
Light Green Linoleum	48%

Typical Luminaires		pcc →		80			70			50			30			10		0
		pw →	50	30	10	50	30	10	50	30	10	50	30	10	50	30	10	0
		RCR ↓	Coefficients of Utilization for 20 Per Cent Effective Floor Cavity Reflectance, ρfc															

Single row fluorescent lamp cove without reflector, mult. by 0.93 for 2 rows and by 0.85 for 3 rows.

RCR	50	30	10	50	30	10	50	30	10								
1	.42	.40	.39	.38	.35	.33	.25	.24	.23	Coves are not recommended							
2	.37	.34	.32	.32	.29	.27	.22	.20	.19	for lighting areas having							
3	.32	.29	.26	.28	.25	.23	.19	.17	.16	low reflectances.							
4	.29	.25	.22	.25	.22	.19	.17	.15	.13								
5	.25	.21	.18	.22	.19	.16	.15	.13	.11								
6	.23	.19	.16	.20	.16	.14	.14	.12	.10								
7	.20	.17	.14	.17	.14	.12	.12	.10	.09								
8	.18	.15	.12	.16	.13	.10	.11	.09	.08								
9	.17	.13	.10	.15	.11	.09	.10	.08	.07								
10	.15	.12	.09	.13	.10	.08	.09	.07	.06								

Fluorescent unit with flat prismatic lens, 4 lamp 2' wide

V   1.4/1.2

RCR	50	30	10	50	30	10	50	30	10	50	30	10	50	30	10	0
0	.71	.71	.71	.69	.69	.69	.66	.66	.66	.63	.63	.63	.61	.61	.61	.60
1	.65	.63	.61	.63	.62	.60	.61	.59	.53	.59	.57	.56	.57	.56	.55	.54
2	.59	.55	.53	.57	.55	.52	.55	.53	.51	.54	.52	.50	.52	.50	.49	.48
3	.53	.49	.46	.52	.49	.46	.50	.47	.45	.49	.46	.44	.47	.45	.43	.42
4	.48	.44	.40	.47	.43	.40	.46	.42	.40	.45	.42	.39	.43	.41	.39	.38
5	.43	.39	.35	.43	.38	.35	.42	.38	.35	.40	.37	.34	.39	.36	.34	.33
6	.39	.35	.31	.39	.34	.31	.38	.34	.31	.37	.33	.31	.36	.33	.31	.29
7	.36	.31	.28	.35	.31	.28	.34	.30	.27	.33	.30	.27	.33	.30	.27	.26
8	.32	.27	.24	.32	.27	.24	.31	.27	.24	.30	.27	.24	.30	.26	.24	.23
9	.29	.24	.21	.29	.24	.21	.28	.24	.21	.27	.24	.21	.27	.23	.21	.20
10	.26	.22	.19	.26	.22	.19	.25	.21	.19	.25	.21	.19	.24	.21	.18	.17

PARACUBE LOUVER

LIGHT SOURCE

PARACUBE LOUVER — STANDARD LOUVER

IV   0.7

RCR	50	30	10	50	30	10	50	30	10	50	30	10	50	30	10	0
0	.53	.53	.53	.52	.52	.52	.49	.49	.49	.47	.47	.47	.45	.45	.45	.44
1	.51	.50	.49	.50	.49	.48	.48	.47	.47	.46	.46	.45	.45	.44	.44	.43
2	.48	.47	.46	.48	.46	.45	.46	.45	.44	.45	.44	.44	.44	.43	.43	.42
3	.47	.45	.44	.46	.45	.43	.45	.44	.43	.44	.43	.42	.43	.42	.41	.41
4	.45	.43	.42	.44	.43	.42	.43	.42	.41	.43	.41	.41	.42	.41	.40	.40
5	.43	.41	.40	.43	.41	.40	.42	.40	.39	.41	.40	.39	.41	.40	.39	.38
6	.42	.40	.39	.41	.40	.38	.41	.39	.38	.40	.39	.38	.40	.39	.38	.37
7	.40	.38	.37	.40	.38	.37	.39	.38	.37	.39	.38	.37	.38	.37	.38	.36
8	.39	.37	.36	.38	.37	.36	.38	.37	.35	.38	.36	.35	.37	.36	.35	.35
9	.37	.36	.34	.37	.35	.34	.37	.35	.34	.36	.35	.34	.36	.35	.34	.33
10	.36	.34	.33	.36	.34	.33	.36	.34	.33	.35	.34	.33	.35	.34	.33	.32

R-40 flood with specular anodized reflector skirt; 45° cutoff

IV   0.7

RCR	50	30	10	50	30	10	50	30	10	50	30	10	50	30	10	0
0	1.00	1.00	1.00	.98	.98	.98	.94	.94	.94	.90	.90	.90	.86	.86	.86	.84
1	.96	.94	.92	.94	.92	.91	.90	.89	.88	.87	.86	.85	.84	.84	.83	.82
2	.91	.88	.86	.90	.87	.85	.87	.85	.83	.84	.83	.82	.82	.81	.80	.79
3	.87	.84	.81	.88	.84	.81	.84	.81	.79	.82	.80	.78	.80	.78	.77	.76
4	.83	.80	.77	.82	.79	.77	.81	.78	.76	.79	.77	.75	.78	.76	.74	.73
5	.79	.76	.73	.79	.75	.73	.77	.74	.72	.76	.73	.71	.75	.73	.71	.70
6	.76	.73	.70	.76	.72	.70	.75	.72	.69	.74	.71	.69	.73	.70	.68	.67
7	.73	.69	.66	.73	.69	.66	.72	.68	.66	.71	.68	.66	.70	.67	.65	.64
8	.70	.66	.63	.70	.66	.63	.69	.65	.63	.68	.65	.63	.67	.65	.63	.62
9	.67	.63	.60	.67	.63	.60	.66	.62	.60	.65	.62	.60	.65	.62	.60	.59
10	.64	.60	.58	.64	.60	.58	.63	.60	.58	.63	.60	.57	.62	.59	.57	.56

"BATWING" LENS

RCR	50	30	10	50	30	10	50	30	10	50	30	10	50	30	10	0
0	.65	.65	.65	.63	.63	.63	.60	.60	.60	.58	.58	.58	.55	.55	.55	.54
1	.58	.56	.54	.56	.54	.53	.54	.53	.51	.52	.51	.49	.50	.49	.48	.47
2	.51	.47	.44	.50	.47	.44	.48	.45	.43	.46	.44	.42	.45	.43	.41	.40
3	.45	.41	.37	.44	.40	.37	.43	.39	.36	.41	.38	.36	.40	.37	.35	.34
4	.40	.35	.32	.39	.35	.32	.38	.34	.31	.37	.33	.31	.35	.33	.30	.29
5	.35	.30	.27	.35	.30	.27	.33	.29	.26	.32	.29	.26	.31	.28	.26	.25
6	.31	.26	.23	.31	.26	.23	.30	.26	.23	.29	.25	.22	.28	.25	.22	.21
7	.28	.23	.19	.27	.23	.19	.26	.22	.19	.26	.22	.19	.25	.22	.19	.18
8	.25	.20	.16	.24	.20	.16	.23	.19	.16	.23	.19	.16	.22	.19	.16	.15
9	.22	.17	.14	.21	.17	.14	.21	.17	.14	.20	.16	.14	.19	.16	.13	.12
10	.19	.15	.12	.19	.15	.12	.19	.15	.12	.18	.14	.12	.18	.14	.12	.11

CEILING		80%				50%		
FLOOR				20%				
WALLS	70%	50%	30%	10%	50%	30%	10%	
1	.50	.49	.48	.46	.46	.45	.44	
2	.47	.45	.43	.41	.43	.41	.40	
3	.44	.41	.39	.37	.40	.38	.36	
4	.42	.38	.35	.34	.37	.35	.33	
5	.39	.35	.32	.30	.34	.32	.30	
6	.37	.33	.30	.28	.31	.29	.27	
7	.34	.30	.27	.25	.29	.26	.25	
8	.32	.27	.24	.22	.26	.24	.22	
9	.30	.25	.22	.20	.24	.21	.19	
10	.27	.22	.20	.17	.22	.19	.17	

By zonal cavity method

LUMINAIRES FOR NON-UNIFORM ILLUMINATION

LUMINAIRE	LAMP	BEAM PATTERN	TYPICAL DATA							
			FOR 9 FT. CEILING				FOR 12 FT. CEILING			
			Distance to wall	FC at 5'6" above FL	Vertical beam spread	Horizontal beam spread	Distance to wall	FC at 5'6" above FL	Vertical beam spread	Horizontal beam spread
	75W T-3 28 volt (Tungsten-Halogen)		2.7'	15	4.6' max.	3.0' max.	3.3'	6	7.8' max.	4.8' max.
	75W T-3 28 volt (Tungsten-Halogen)		3.0'	12	5.1' max.	3.3' max.	5.9'	5	8.6' max.	5.5' max.
	150 PAR-38/3SP, 200W PAR-46/3MFL, 500W R-40/SP		2.0' / 2.0' / 2.0'	450 / 400 / 500	3.2' / 2.0' / 3.7'	1.8' / 2.6' / 1.9'	3.8' / 3.8' / 5.8'	126 / 112 / 70	6.3' / 4.0' / 4.8'	3.4' / 4.9' / 4.5'
	75W R-30/FL, 150W R-40/FL		2.0' / 2.0'	35 / 125	2.9' / 2.5'	2.7' / 2.4'	3.8' / 3.2'	11 / 25	5.4' / 4.0'	5.0' / 4.6'
	150W PAR-33/3SP, 200W PAR-46/3MFL, 150W PAR-38/FL		2.0' / 2.0' / 2.5'	450 / 400 / 98	3.2' / 2.0' / 8.0'	1.8' / 2.6' / 4.0'	3.8' / 3.8' / 5.5'	124 / 112 / 21	6.3' / 4' / 10'	3.4' / 4.9' / 5.5'
	3 LT. 40W T-10		0.6'	30	2.3'	4.0'	0.6'	30	2.3'	4.0'
	2 LT. 40W T-10		0.6'	30	2.0'	3.3'	0.6'	30	2.0'	3.3'
	1 LT. 40W T-12 (Fluorescent)		1.5'	19	4.0'	5.2'	1.5'	19	4.0'	5.2'
	2 LT. 40W T-12 (Fluorescent)		Wall mounted	EOFC at 1.0' above and below unit 3.5 above and below unit		5.3'	Wall mounted	5.0 FC at 1.0' above and below unit 5.5 above and below unit		5.3'

FOOTCANDLES AND BEAM SPREAD (LIGHTOLIER)

LUMINAIRES FOR UNIFORM WALL ILLUMINATION

Lamp	8 ft ceiling — Distance to Wall	8 ft — C. to C. Distance	8 ft — F.C. at 5'-6" above floor	8 ft — Evenness Rating	12 ft ceiling — Distance to Wall	12 ft — C. to C. Distance	12 ft — F.C. at 5'-6" above floor	12 ft — Evenness Rating
200W PAR-40/3 NSP	12"	12"	85	E	12"	12"	70	E
150W PSR-38/3 SP	12"	12"	67	E	12"	12"	39	V.G.
150W R-40/SP	10½"	12"	102	G	10½"	12"	45	F
75W R-30/SP	I	10"	25	G	I	I	I	I
300W R-40/SP	36"	36"	36	E	36"	36"	22	E
Q250W PAR-38/FL	I	I	I	I	36"	36"	38	E
500W PAR-56/MFL	36"	36"	56	E	36"	36"	45	E
300W R-40/FL	36"	36"	29	E	36"	36"	25	V.G.
150W R-40/FL	30"	30"	24	V.G.	32"	36"	10	F
300W R-40/FL	36"	36"	50	E	36"	36"	42	V.G.
100W A-19	13"	13"	18	F	I	I	I	I
150W A-21	24"	24"	36	V.G.	24"	24"	18	G
150W R-40/FL	24"	24"	30	V.G.	24"	24"	17	G
150W R-40/FL	36"	36"	43	V.G.	36"	36"	13	V.G.
200W R-40/FL	36"	36"	31	V.G.	36"	36"	47	V.G.
1 LT.-40W T-12 (Fluorescent)	Flush to wall	Continuous run	18	V.G.	Flush to wall	Continuous run	I	I
2 LT.-40W T-12 (Fluorescent)	36"	36"	32	G			19	F

FOOTCANDLES AND SPACING. (LIGHTOLIER)

TYPE	LAMP LUMEN DEPRECIATION	INITIAL LUMENS
FILAMENT LAMPS		
General Service Lamps		
150 W	0.90	2,780
300 W	0.90	4,800
500 W	0.88	9,070
1000 W	0.84	23,740
Reflector Lamps		
150 W R40	0.87	1,870
300 W R40	0.87	3,600
Fluorescent Lamps		
4 ft. RS Cool White	0.86	3,150
8 ft. SL Cool White	0.88	5,800
8 ft. HO Cool White	0.85	9,200
Mercury Vapour Lamps		
400 W Deluxe White	0.67	22,500
1000 W Deluxe White	0.59	63,000

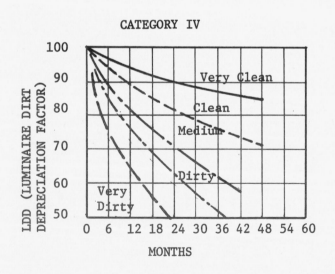

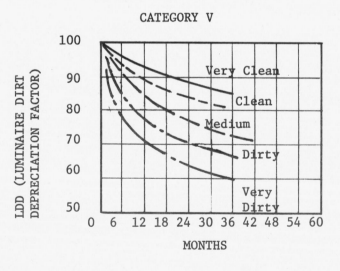

CANDLEPOWER DISTRIBUTION CURVES

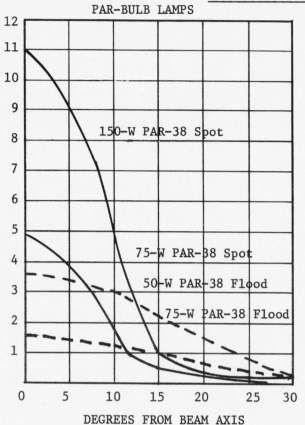

PAR-BULB LAMPS

150-W PAR-38 Spot

75-W PAR-38 Spot

50-W PAR-38 Flood

75-W PAR-38 Flood

CANDLEPOWER – THOUSANDS

DEGREES FROM BEAM AXIS

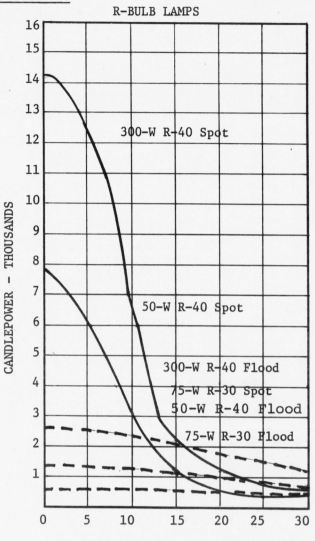

R-BULB LAMPS

300-W R-40 Spot

50-W R-40 Spot

300-W R-40 Flood

75-W R-30 Spot

50-W R-40 Flood

75-W R-30 Flood

CANDLEPOWER – THOUSANDS

DEGREES FROM BEAM AXIS

The table below gives the beam angles and candlepower for 12 volt reflector PAR lamps.   The 10% candlepower angle represents the spill outside the main beam.

LAMP ORDERING CODE	WATTS	BEAM DESCRIPTION (2)	APPROX. BEAM SPREAD		INITIAL CANDLEPOWER
			to 50% Max. Candlepower	to 10% Max. Candlepower	
25 PAR 36 NSP		Narrow Spot	8° x 10°	17° x 19°	3250
25 PAR 36 WFL	25	Wide Flood	23° x 36°	36° x 48°	480
25 PAR 36 VWFL		Very Wide Flood	30° x 40°	74° x 82°	230
50 PAR 36 NSP		Narrow Spot	10° x 12°	20° x 22°	4700
50 PAR 36 WFL	50	Wide Flood	23° x 35°	34° x 47°	950
50 PAR 36 VWFL		Very Wide Flood	35° x 42°	76° x 84°	430
120 PAR 56 VNSP		Very Narrow Spot	4° x 6°	7° x 12°	85,000
120 PAR 56 MFL	120	Medium Flood	8° x 17°	14° x 27°	15,000
120 PAR 56 WFL		Wide Flood	18° x 35°	25° x 50°	5,100
240 PAR 56 VNSP		Very Narrow Spot	6° x 8°	10° x 16°	110,000
240 PAR 56 MFL	240	Medium Flood	8° x 19°	16° x 28°	32,000
240 PAR 56 WFL		Wide Flood	18° x 35°	27° x 50°	13,000

HORIZONTAL PLANE ILLUMINATION IN F.C.

Mounting Height (Feet)	DISTANCE FROM CENTER OF BEAM (FEET)																			
	0	1	2	4	6	0	1	2	4	6	0	1	2	4	6	0	1	2	4	6
	75-Watt PAR-38 Spot					75-Watt R-30 Spot					150-Watt PAR-38 Spot					150-Watt R-40 Spot				
5	194	54	9	2	1	76	42	9	3	1	420	145	13	7	2	300	96	19	6	3
7½	86	48	8	1	1	34	25	9	2	1	190	118	17	4	3	130	75	23	6	3
10	49	37	13	1	1	19	17	8	2	1	105	87	34	3	2	75	56	25	5	2
15	22	19	12	2	1	8	8	5	2	1	47	43	29	4	1	33	30	17	5	2
	75-Watt PAR-38 Flood					75-Watt R-30 Flood					150-Watt PAR-38 Flood					150-Watt R-40 Flood				
5	60	46	17	2	1	16	15	11	2	1	138	107	37	4	1	51	44	30	8	2
7½	27	22	16	2	1	7	7	6	3	1	61	55	37	6	2	23	21	18	9	4
10	15	13	12	4	1	4	4	4	3	1	35	32	27	9	2	13	12	11	8	4
15	7	6	6	4	2	2	2	2	2	1	15	15	14	9	4	6	6	5	4	3

MINIMUM LAMP-TO-WALL DISTANCE FOR SATISFACTORY UNIFORMITY OF UPPER-WALL BRIGHTNESS Cove with Single Row of Bare 40-Watt Fluorescent Lamps in Standard Lampholders Mounted Back-to-Back			
Location of Lamps	Distance of Cove from Ceiling		
	12"	18"	24"
In Front of Channel	2½"	3½"	4½"
On Top of Channel	5"	6"	7"

BRIGHTNESS UNIFORMITY OF UPPER WALL
COVE WITH LAMPS MOUNTED IN
TWO DIFFERENT POSITIONS

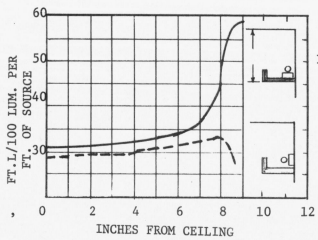

TWO FLUORESCENT LAMPS
IN STANDARD LAMPHOLDERS
BACK-TO-BACK

FT.L/100 LUM. PER FT. OF SOURCE

INCHES FROM CEILING

DAYLIGHTING

The brightness of the sky even when cloudy is extremely high, and the
light colour temperature near 10,000°K, therefore even a small
opening provides a tremendous amount of illumination with white cool
light, excellent for good vision and colour evaluation.   The
solar altitude has a great influence on the amount of available
reflected light from the sky with slightly higher values in the
summer.

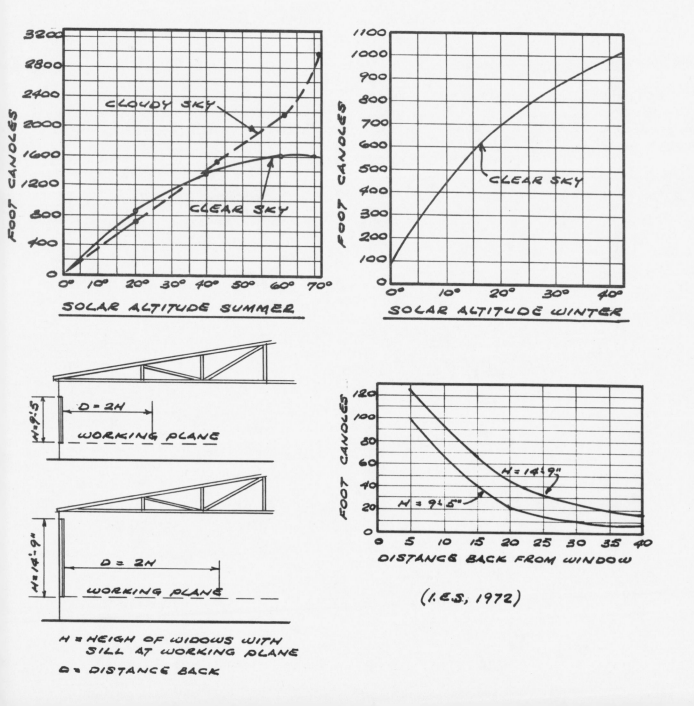

(I.E.S, 1972)

H = HEIGH OF WIDOWS WITH
    SILL AT WORKING PLANE
D = DISTANCE BACK

A satisfactory pattern of brightness requires that the sun
and sky should be shielded from view either directly or by
reflection, at all normal angles and that the brightness and
brightness contrasts in the surroundings be brought to acceptable
levels by a judicious distribution of light within the interior
and a choice of suitable surface colours and textures.

In general, depending on the daylight factors relating to the
position of the skylights, one can obtain the recommended 15 FC
illumination 330 days out of a year; the problem is that the
higher limit is not set, therefore a considerable number of days
will have much higher illumination levels; for instance for an
average of 315 days in a year we will have 20 FC, etc.

Having therefore admitted the natural light into the space and
having established the maximum and minimum values that are
acceptable, an automatic system of louvers and artificual lights
with photoelectric controls must be provided to reduce the
illumination when excessive, while turning "on" the artificial
lighting for the few days without sufficient diffuse natural
light, and at night.

Lighting from side windows at low levels if properly used,
by placing the windows away from exhibits can have very pleasing
and relaxing effects.

To make them acceptable they must be screened to prevent view
of the sky from all normal positions and must be of a size that
would allow viewing downwards but not upwards.   In addition one
can reduce, without detriment, the external brightness by using
grey glass with a light transmittance factor of 0.5 in lieu of
clear glass

Recent work on the subject of natural lighting conducted
by the BRS of England, have developed simpler calculation
procedures for establishing illumination levels.   Basically
the procedure is split into the externally and internally
reflected components as shown in the attached sketch.
Further information as to the calculation required can be
obtained from the IES Handbook and BRS Digests No. 41 and 42.
Their scope exceeds the purpose of this summary.

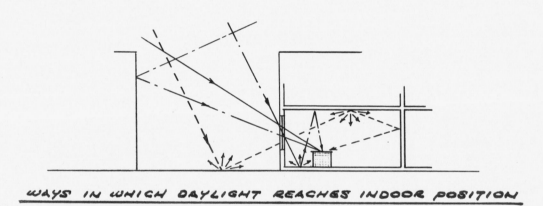

WAYS IN WHICH DAYLIGHT REACHES INDOOR POSITION

LIGHTING ECONOMICS

The economics of lighting are affected by power consumption and lighting maintenance. The first requires the use of a minimum number of highly efficient fixtures while the second requires that these be maintained so as to develop the same quantity of lighting during the life of the installation.

A.   Power Cost Economics

Over the past few years with the introduction of very efficient light sources, there has been a tendency towards higher and higher illumination levels which necessitated higher air conditioning capacities, so that as a whole, electric consumption per square foot of space increased considerably.

This was encouraged by Utilities and lamp manufacturers until recently, when the cost of power made people aware of the fact that they did not require such high illumination levels to perform tasks successfully.   The adjacent graph shows the watts/sq. ft. required for different illumination levels with incandescent and fluorescent lamps.   Lines A to F are for incandescent lamps and the balance for fluorescents of different types.

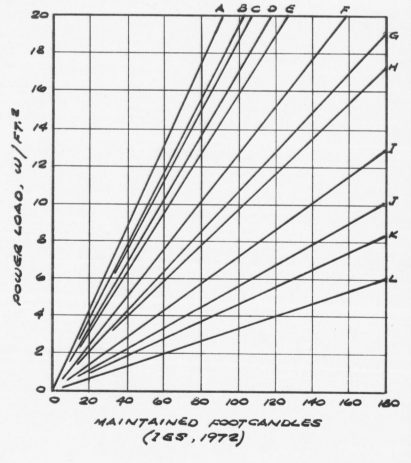

MAINTAINED FOOTCANDLES
(IES, 1972)

It has been proved conclusively through many studies, that the
ease of task performance is not necessarily a function of the
lighting level alone, but of the eveness of light distribution
and the elimination of glare.   The results of these studies
indicate that with a suitable type of vaulted ceiling
construction a power load of 2.5 watts/sq. ft. can give a nominal
level of illumination of 75 FC with an extremely high task
performance capability.

B.   Lighting Maintenance

A good lighting system is designed to provide adequate visibility
and comfortable seeing conditions.   A well maintained lighting
system continues to produce the illumination level it was
originally designed to produce as anything less will reduce
visibility and make seeing more difficult.   Dirt accumulation
plus lamp burnouts can also hurt the general appearance of the
lighting installation considerably.

Power consumption is the same whether the lamps and luminaires
are clean or dirty, therefore the cost per footcandle of lighting
becomes extremely high as the effective installation output is
reduced through lumen depreciation of lamps and reduction of
efficiency of the luminaire.

The causes of light loss can be analysed as follows:-

1.   Dirt on lamps and fixtures.

The greatest loss of light is usually due to dirt accumulation;
typical light output loss is shown on the attached graph which
indicates the effect of dirt accumulation on reflectors and lamps,
for basic types of fixtures and ambiences.

The ventilation in a room effects
dust deposit on all room surfaces
including the lighting fixtures;
conversely the ventilation of
the lighting fixture itself
affects the movement of the dust
through the fixture with the dual
beneficial effect of letting the
dirt go through the fixture
instead of being deposited on
it and by keeping the temperatures
of the fixture lower so as to
reduce convection currents.

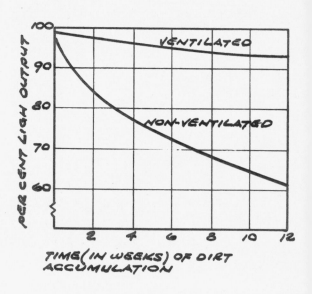

2.   Dirt on Room Surfaces.

All lighting calculations for general illumination are
based on the reflectivity of the room surfaces.   Collection of dust
and dirt on these surfaces reduces their reflectivity, therefore
reducing the effective use of light on which the original
calculations were based.   This is of great importance where indirect
and cove lighting is used, as all light produced by the lamps is
redirected by the cove and ceiling surfaces to the floor.   Coves
should be thoroughly cleaned with every re-lamping operation as
they are the natural depository of dirt within the room.

3.   Lamp Lumen Depreciation.

Light output of lamps decreases with the length of time of
operation.   This reduction in light output is called lumen
depreciation and is an inherent characteristic of all lamps.
Because of this condition the concept of group relamping was
introduced.

Group Relamping

Lamps in a lighting system can be replaced individually as they burn out, or the entire lighting installation can be replaced at one time. Individual replacement is called spot relamping while mass replacement is called group relamping. There are two reasons for changing lamps ahead of their rated life:

(a) loss of output   and

(b) increased mortality.

With increasing labour costs the set-up time for spot relamping has become very expensive. This was the reason that group relamping was devised, which changes all lamps when 70% of life has been reached with one or two variants on the exact timing or re-use of some of the surviving lamps. The economics on the use of group or spot lamp replacement can be determined from the graphs given below, for a 70% relamping cycle for fluorescents and a 75% cycle for incandescents.

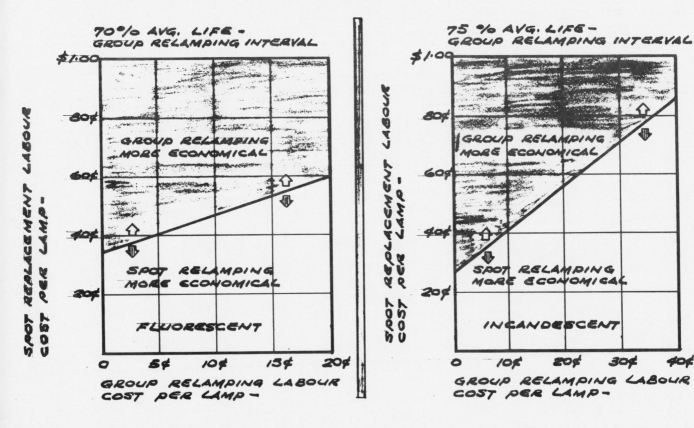

Assuming that efficient light sources are provided in all contemporary installations, the relamping system should be determined when the specifics of the installation are known. As labour and power costs vary constantly any prediction based on small differentials could be most misleading. Museum lighting installations, where showcase relamping is carried out by preparators staff require special consideration.   It is possible that certain areas would be handled by a group relamping program while in other areas spot relamping would be more satisfactory.

SELECTED BIBLIOGRAPHY

NOTE: * indicates references used in the text.

Abbey, David S. Now See Hear! Applying Communications
        to Teaching. Profiles in Practical Education,
        No. 9. Toronto: Ontario Institute for Studies
        in Education, 1973.

_____, and Cameron, Duncan F. The Museum Visitor:
        I - Survey Design. Toronto: Royal Ontario Museum,
        1959.

*   _____. The Museum Visitor: II - Survey Results.
        Toronto: Royal Ontario Museum, 1960.

        _____. The Museum Visitor: III - Supplementary Studies.
        Toronto: Royal Ontario Museum, 1961.

Abler, Thomas S. "A Study of Learning in the Museum."
        Museum Visitor, III (1968), pp. 107-119, 132, 137.

American Association of Museums. Museums: Their New Audience.
        Washington, D.C.: American Association of Museums,
        1972.

        _____, Environmental Committee. Museums and the Environ-
        ment: A Handbook for Education. Washington, D.C.:
        American Association of Museums, 1971.

Arnheim, Rudolf. Visual Thinking. Los Angeles: University
        of California Press, 1969.

Basalla, George. "Museums and Technological Utopianism."
        Curator, XVII (February, 1974), pp. 105-118.

* Bayley, W. Hewitt. "To Make the Artifact Speak." Paper
        presented at the Canadian Museums Association
        Seminar on Design, Ste. Marie Among the Hurons,
        Midland, Ontario, October, 1973.

* Bechtel, Robert B. "Hodometer Research in Museums."
        Museum News, XLIII (July, 1967), pp. 23-26.

* Bell, James A.M. Museum and Gallery Building: A Guide to
        Briefing and Design Procedure. Information Sheet,
        No. 14. London: Museums Association, 1972.

Belcher, M. Wall Coverings. Information Sheet, No. 13.
        London: Museums Association, 1972.

478   SELECTED BIBLIOGRAPHY

Bergmann, Eugene. "Exhibits that Flow." Curator, XIV
        (April, 1971), pp. 277-286.

* Bernardo, José Raul. "Museum Environments for Communi-
        cations: A Study of Environmental Parameters in
        the Design of Museum Experiences." Unpublished
        Ph.D. dissertation, Columbia University, 1972.

Bleicher, Edward. "Presentational Esthetics." Museum
        News, XLVI (October, 1967), pp. 20-23.

* Bloomberg, Marguerite. An Experiment in Museum Instruc-
        tion. New Series, No. 8. Washington, D.C.:
        American Association of Museums, 1929.

* Borhegyi, Stephan F., de. "Visual Communication in the
        Science Museum." Curator, VI (January, 1963),
        pp. 45-57.

* _____. "Space Problems and Solutions." Museum News,
        XLII (November, 1963), pp. 18-22.

* _____. "Some Thoughts on Anthropological Exhibits
        in Natural History Museums in the United States."
        Curator, VII (February, 1964), pp. 121-127.

* _____. "Testing of Audience Reaction to Museum Exhi-
        bits." Curator, VIII (January, 1965), pp. 86-93.

_____. "Test Your Knowledge." Midwest Museums Quar-
        terly, XXV, No. 4 (1965), p. 10.

_____, and Hanson, Irene A. "Chronological Bibliography
        of Museum Visitor Surveys." Museums and Education.
        Edited by Eric Larrabee. Washington, D.C.:
        Smithsonian Institution Press, 1968.

Bostick, William A. "What is the State of Museum Security?"
        Museum News (January, 1968), pp. 13-19.

* Brawne, Michael. The New Museum. New York: Praeger
        Publishers, 1965.

* _____. "Museums." Architectural Design, XLIII (1973),
        pp. 644-651.

Brooks, Joyce A.M., and Vernon, P.A. "A Study of Children's
        Interests and Comprehension at a Science Museum."
        British Journal of Psychiatry, XLVII (1956),
        pp. 175-182.

Buck, Richard. "On Conservation." Museum News (September, 1973), pp. 15-16.

_____. "On Conservation." Museum News (October, 1973), pp. 15-16.

_____. "On Conservation." Museum News (November, 1973), pp. 12-13.

* Bunning, Richard L. "A Perspective on the Museum's Role in Community Adult Education." Curator, XVII (January, 1974), pp. 56-63.

Burke, Frank G. "Innovation at the Archives - The Departure of the Freedom Train." Curator, XVI (April, 1973), pp. 333-341.

* Cameron, Duncan F. "A Viewpoint: The Museum as a Communications System and Implications for Museum Education." Curator, XI (March, 1968), pp. 33-40.

_____, and Abbey, David S. "Toward Meaningful Attendance Statistics." Bulletin of the Canadian Museums Association, XII (May, 1960), pp. 6-10.

Cannon, J.F.M. "The New Botanical Exhibition Gallery at the British Museum (Natural History)." Curator, V (January, 1962), pp. 26-35.

Carmel, James H. "Exhibit Framework and Structural Framing Systems." Curator, V (March, 1962), pp. 265-301.

* Chase, Richard A. "Museums as Learning Environments." Museum News (September/October, 1975), pp. 37-43.

"Children's Museum." Architectural Forum, CXXXV (September, 1971), pp. 32-33.

* Coleman, Laurence V. Museum Buildings: A Planning Study. Vol. I. Washington, D.C.: American Association of Museums, 1950.

Conaway, Mary Ellen. "Exhibit Labeling: Another Alternative." Curator, XV (February, 1972), pp. 161-166.

Conway, Wallace X. "Increasing the Life of Graphic Materials." Museum News, L (February, 1972), pp. 29-31.

Cordingly, David. Methods of Lettering for Museums. Information Sheet, No. 15. London: Museums Association, 1972.

Dailey, Daniel, and Mandle, Roger. "Welcome to the Museum." Museum News (January/February, 1974), pp. 45-49.

* Dandridge, Frank. "The Value of Design in Visual Communication." Curator, IX (April, 1966), pp. 331-336.

* Devenish, David C. "Methods and Problems of Archeological Display in British Provincial Museums." Curator, IX (February, 1966), pp. 156-165.

* Dixon, B.; Courtney, A.; and Bailey, R. The Museum and the Canadian Public. Toronto: Culturcan Publications, 1974.

Douglas, R. Alan. "A Commonsense Approach to Environmental Control." Curator, XV (February, 1972), pp. 139-144.

Dunning, Frederick W. "The Story of the Earth: Exhibition at the Geological Museum, London."

* Eisenbeis, Manfred. "Elements for a Sociology of Museums." Museum: A Quarterly Review, XXIV (1971), pp. 110-119.

* Evans, J.W. "Some Observations, Remarks, and Suggestions Concerning Natural History Museums." Curator, V (January, 1962), pp. 77-93.

"Exhibition Design." Architectural Review, CLV (May, 1974), pp. 275-290.

Feller, Robert L. "Control of Deteriorating Effects of Light upon Museum Objects." Museum, XVII (1964), pp. 57-75.

Fikioris, Margaret A. "A Model for Textile Storage." Museum News, LII (November, 1973), pp. 34-41.

* Fine, Paul A. "The Role of Design in Educational Exhibits." Curator, VI (January, 1963), pp. 37-44.

Francis, Sir Frank. "Security." Museums Journal, LXIII,
        Nos. 1-2 (1963), pp. 28-31.

* Freed, Stanley A. "The New Eastern Woodlands Indians Hall
        in the American Museum of Natural History."
        Curator, IX (April, 1966), pp. 267-288.

Fyson, Anthony. "Living Museums." Town and Country Planning,
        XLI (Fall, 1973), pp. 141-143.

Gabianelli, Vincent J., and Munyer, Eduard A. "A Place to
        Learn." Museum News, LIII (December, 1974),
        pp. 28-33.

* Gerald, Rex E. "A Philosophy on Publicity for Museums."
        Curator, VI (February, 1963), pp. 125-130.

* Glicksman, Hal. "A Guide to Art Installations." Museum
        News, L (February, 1972), pp. 22-27.

Goldman, Katherine, ed. "Opportunities for Extending
        Museum Contributions to Pre-College Science Educa-
        tion - Bibliography." Summary Report of a confer-
        ence, 1970.

Gossin, Francis. "A Security Chief Comments on Guards."
        Museum News, L (January, 1972), pp. 30-31.

Gross, Irwin M. "Outreach in Michigan." Museum News
        (October, 1970), pp. 33-35.

Hanlan, J.F. "The Effect of Flectronic Photographic
        Lamps on the Materials of Works of Art." Museum
        News (June, 1970), pp. 33-41.

Harrison, Laurence S. Report on the Deteriorating Effects
        of Modern Light Sources. New York: Metropolitan
        Museum of Art, 1954.

Harrison, Raymond O. "Planning for Action and Growth."
        Museum News, LI (November, 1972), pp. 21-24.

Hartman, Shirley G. "New Designs for a Systematic Exhibit
        of Birds." Curator, XV (February, 1972), pp. 113-
        120.

* _____. "Designing a Hall of Indian Archeology." Curator,
        XV (March, 1972), pp. 229-237.

Hegnes, Donald C. "What's New in Glass." Museum News, LI (September, 1972), pp. 23-25.

Henriksen, Harry C. "Your Museum: A Resource for the Blind." Museum News (October, 1971), pp. 26-28.

* Hillen, John. "The Role of the Designer." Paper presented at the Canadian Museums Association Seminar on Design, Ste. Marie Among the Hurons, Midland, Ontario, October, 1973.

* _____, and Brittain, Frances. "Some Notes on the Planning and Logistics Involved in Setting up a New Gallery." Paper presented for Master's Degree Program in Museology, joint undertaking of Royal Ontario Museum and School of Graduate Studies, University of Toronto, Ontario, October, 1972.

* Howard, Richard F. Museum Security. New Series, No. 18. Washington, D.C.: American Association of Museums, 1958.

Howell, Daniel B. "A Network System for the Planning, Designing, Construction and Installation of Exhibits." Curator, XIV (February, 1971), pp. 100-108.

* Illuminating Engineering Society. Lighting of Art Galleries and Museums. Technical Report, No. 14. London: Illuminating Engineering Society, 1970.

International Council of Museums. La lumiere et la protec- tion des objets et specimens exposés dans les musées et galeries d'art. Paris: L'Association française de l'éclairage, n.d.

Jaeger, Dirk. "New Directions for Ethnographical Museums." Museum, XXVII, No. 1 (1975), pp. 29-33.

Johnson, David A. "Museum Attendance in the New York Metropolitan Region." Curator, XII (March, 1969), pp. 201-229.

Katzive, David. "Museums Enter the Video Generation." Museum News, LI (January, 1973), pp. 20-24.

* Keck, Caroline; Block, Huntington T.; Chapman, Joseph; Lawton, John B.; and Stolow, Nathan. A Primer on Museum Security. Cooperstown, N.Y.: New York State Historical Association, 1966.

* Kenney, Alice P. "Museums from a Wheelchair." Museum News, LIII (December, 1974), pp. 14-17.

Key, Archie F. Beyond Four Walls - The Origin and Development of Canadian Museums. Toronto: McClelland and Stewart, 1973.

* Kimmel, Peter S., and Maves, Mark J. "Public Reaction to Museum Interiors." Museum News, LI (September, 1972), pp. 17-19.

Kinard, John R. "The Neighbourhood Museum and the Inner City." Architecture Yearbook, XIV (1974), pp. 108-111.

_____. "To Meet the Needs of Today's Audience." Museum News, L (May, 1972), pp. 15-16.

* Kischkewitz, Hannelore. "New Techniques in Displaying Traditional Objects." Museum, XXVII, No. 1 (1975), pp. 3-9.

* Klare, George R. "Assessing Readability." Reading Research Quarterly, X, No. 1 (1974-1975), pp. 62-105.

* _____; Sinaiko, H.W.; and Stolurow, L.M. "The Cloze Procedure: A Convenient Readability Test for Training Materials and Translations." International Review of Applied Psychology, XXI, No. 2 (1972), pp. 78-106.

* Knez, Eugene I., and Wright, A. Gilbert. "The Museum as a Communications System: An Assessment of Cameron's Viewpoint." Curator, XIII (March, 1970), pp. 204-212.

Koke, Richard J. "An Exhibition: John James Audubon and the 'Birds of America'." Curator, VII (February, 1964), pp. 144-155.

* Lakota, Robert A. The Efficacy of Three Visitor Learning Support Systems in Producing Cognitive and Affective Outcomes in an Art Museum. Washington, D.C.: Smithsonian Institution, 1973.

* _____. The National Museum of Natural History as a Behavioral Environment, Part I: An Experimental Analysis of Behavioral Performance. Washington, D.C.: Office of Museum Programs, Smithsonian Institution, 1975.

*   _____. "Good Exhibits on Purpose: Techniques to Improve Exhibit Effectiveness." Unpublished paper, Washington, D.C., January, 1976.

Lehmbruck, Manfred. "Physiology: Factors Affecting the Visitor." Museum, XXVI, Nos. 3-4 (1974), pp. 179-189.

*   _____. "Psychology: Perception and Behaviour." Museum, XXVI, Nos. 3-4 (1974), pp. 191-204.

Lemon, R.R.H. "The Hall of Science - New Directions." Curator, X (April, 1967), pp. 279-283.

Libin, Laurence. "Two Sense Worth." Museum News (January/February, 1974), pp. 50-52.

Loomis, Ross J. "Please, Not Another Visitor Survey." Museum News (October, 1973), pp. 21-26.

_____. "Museums and Psychology: The Principle of Allometry and Museum Visitor Research." Speech presented at the Northeast Museums Conference, November 2, 1973.

_____. "Social Learning Potentials of Museums." Paper presented at symposium "The Museum as a Learning Environment" of the American Educational Research Association, Chicago, Ill., April 16, 1974.

* Lusk, Carroll B. "Museum Lighting I." Museum News (November, 1970), pp. 20-23.

_____. "Museum Lighting II." Museum News (December, 1970), pp. 25-29.

_____. "Museum Lighting III." Museum News (February, 1971), pp. 18-22.

Majewski, Lawrence J. "On Conservation." Museum News (December, 1972), pp. 11-12.

_____. "On Conservation." Museum News, LI (January, 1973), pp. 10-11.

_____. "On Conservation." Museum News, LI (February, 1973), pp. 8-10.

_____. "On Conservation." Museum News, LI (March, 1973), pp. 10-11.

_____. "On Conservation." Museum News, LI (May, 1973), pp. 18-19.

_____. "Every Museum Library Should Have..." Museum News (November, 1973), pp. 27-30.

Malik, M. "Principles of Automation in Museum Exhibitions." Curator, VI (March, 1963), pp. 247-268.

* McLay, Katherine. Notes taken at "Knowing Your Museum Audience Workshop", coordinated by Ross J. Loomis, Smithsonian Institution, Washington, D.C., March 17-20, 1975.

McLuhan, Marshall, and Parker, Harley. "McLuhanism in the Museum." Museum News (March, 1968), pp. 11-18.

McQuarie, Robert J. "Security." Museum News (March, 1971), pp. 25-27.

* Melton, Arthur W. Problems of Installation in Museums of Art. New Series, No. 14. Washington, D.C.: American Association of Museums, 1935.

_____. "Visitor Behavior in Museums: Some Early Research in Environmental Design." Human Factors, XIV, No. 5 (1972), pp. 393-403.

* _____; Feldman, Nita Goldberg; and Mason, Charles W. Experimental Studies of the Education of Children in a Museum of Science. New Series, No. 15. Washington, D.C.: American Association of Museums, 1936.

* Michaels, A.F. "Security and the Museum." Museum News (November, 1964), pp. 11-16.

Minnich, Richard S. "Safety - An Integral Part of Museum Operations." Unpublished speech.

* Moore, George. "Displays for the Sightless." Curator, XI (April, 1968), pp. 292-296.

* Morrill, Ralph C. "Dust Proofing Exhibits by Air Pressure." Curator, V (January, 1962), pp. 53-54.

* Mould, Vernon T. "The Storyline." Paper presented at the Canadian Museums Association Seminar on Design, Ste. Marie Among the Hurons, Midland, Ontario, October, 1973.

"Museums and Interpretive Techniques: An Interim Report." Museums Journal, LXXV, No. 2 (September, 1975), pp. 71-74.

* National Endowment for the Arts. Museums USA: A Survey Report. Washington, D.C.: U.S. Government Printing Office, 1975.

* Neal, Arminta. "Gallery and Case Exhibit Design." Curator, VI (January, 1963), pp. 77-95.

* _____. "Function of Display: Regional Museums." Curator, VIII (March, 1965), pp. 228-234.

Nelson, Elmer R. "Do We Understand Museum Air Conditioning?" Curator, XI (February, 1968), pp. 127-136.

Neustupny, Jiri. "A New Approach to an Archeological Exhibit." Curator, X (March, 1967), pp. 211-220.

New York State Education Department, and Janus Museums Consultants. The 1966 Audience of the New York State Museum: An Evaluation of the Museum's Visitors Program. Albany, N.Y.: University of the State of New York, 1968.

Niehoff, Arthur. "The Physical Needs of the Visitor." Lore, VI, No. 4 (1956), pp. 155-157.

* Noblecourt, André F. "The Protection of Museums Against Theft." Museum, XVII, No. 4 (1964), pp. 184-196, Appendix pp. 215-232.

Norgate, Martin. Linked Tape and Slide Audio-Visual Displays. Information Sheet, No. 17. London: Museums Association, 1973.

Organ, Robert M. Design for Scientific Conservation of Antiquities. Washington, D.C.: Smithsonian Institution Press, 1968.

* Parker, Harley W. "The Museum as a Communication System."
    <u>Curator</u>, VI (April, 1963), pp. 350-360.

* _____. "New Hall of Fossil Invertebrates, Royal
    Ontario Museum." <u>Curator</u>, X (April, 1967),
    pp. 284-296.

    Parr, Albert E. "A Plea for Abundance." <u>Curator</u>, II
    (March, 1959).

* _____. "Remarks on Layout, Display, and Response to
    Design." <u>Curator</u>, VII (February, 1964), pp. 131-
    142.

    _____. "Yesterday and Tomorrow in Museums of Natural
    History." <u>Studies in Museology</u>, II (1966).

    _____. "Location, Motivation, and Duration of Museum
    Attendance." <u>Curator</u>, X (March, 1967), pp. 206-
    210.

    _____. "Theatre or Playground." <u>Curator</u>, XVI
    (February, 1973), pp. 103-106.

* Parsons, Lee A. "Systematic Testing of Display Techniques
    for an Anthropological Exhibit." <u>Curator</u>, VIII
    (February, 1965), pp. 167-189.

    Pegden, Norman. "An International Meeting on Museum
    Security, May, 1973." <u>Museum</u>, XXVI (1974),
    pp. 38-41.

* Plenderleith, H.J. <u>The Conservation of Antiquities and
    Works of Art: Treatment, Repair and Restoration</u>.
    London: Oxford University Press, 1956.

* Pope-Hennessy, Sir John. "Design in Museums." <u>The Royal
    Society of Arts Journal</u>, CXXIII (October, 1975),
    pp. 717-727.

    Prague, Rochelle H. "The University Museum Visitor Survey
    Project." <u>Curator</u>, XVII (March, 1974), pp. 207-
    212.

* Probst, Thomas. "On Guard." <u>Museum News</u> (November, 1965),
    pp. 11-17.

Reimann, Irving G. "Post-Mortem on a Museum Questionnaire."
The Museologist, LXIII (1957), pp. 1-6.

* Ripley, S. Dillon. "Museums and Education." Curator, XI
(March, 1968), pp. 183-189.

* Rivière, Georges; Visser, Henri; and Herman, F.E. "Museum
Showcases." Museum, XIII, No. 1 (1960), pp. 1-55.

Rovetti, Paul F. "Supermarketing Your Exhibit." Museum
News, LI, No. 4 (December, 1972), pp. 35-36.

* Schickel, Richard. The Disney Version: The Life, Times,
Art and Commerce of Walt Disney. New York: Simon
and Schuster, 1968.

* Schuldes, W.K.F. "Basic Principles of Exhibition Design."
Curator, X (January, 1967), pp. 49-53.

Screven, Chandler G. "Learning and Exhibits: Instructional
Design." Museum News (January/February, 1974),
pp. 67-75.

* Seligman, Thomas K. "Educational Use of an Anthropology
Collection in an Art Museum." Curator, XVII
(January, 1974), pp. 27-35.

Shannon, Joseph. "The Icing is Good, But the Cake is Rotten."
Museum News (January/February, 1974), pp. 29-34.

Shaw, Evelyn. "The Exploratorium." Curator, XV (January,
1972), pp. 39-52.

Shettel, Harris H. "An Evaluation of Existing Criteria for
Judging the Quality of Science Exhibits." Curator,
XI (February, 1968), pp. 137-158.

* _____. "Exhibits: Art Form or Educational Medium?"
Museum News, LII (September, 1973), pp. 32-41.

* _____. "The Evaluation Function." Unpublished paper,
Washington, D.C., 1975.

* _____; Butcher, Margaret; Cotton, Timothy S.; Northrup,
Judi; and Slough, Doris Clapp. Strategies for
Determining Exhibit Effectiveness. Technical Report,
No. AIR-F58-11/67-FR. Pittsburgh, Pa.: American
Institutes for Research, 1968.

*   Skramstad, Harold K., Jr.   "Interpreting Material Culture:
       A View from the Other Side of the Glass."   Paper
       presented at Winterthur Museum, Wilmington, Dela-
       ware, Autumn, 1975.

    Silver, Adèle Z.   "New Education Wing: Cleveland Museum
       of Art."   Museum, XXV (1973), pp. 229-241.

*   Silver, Stuart.   "Art as Pleasure in Contemporary Life."
       The Connoisseur, CLXXII (November, 1969), pp. 182-
       188.

    Slaughter, Randolph M.   "Making the Museum Portable."
       Museum News, LI (September, 1972), pp. 29-31.

*   Stolow, Nathan.   "The Action of Environment on Museum
       Objects, Part I: Humidity, Temperature, Atmospheric
       Pollution."   Curator, IX (March, 1966), pp. 175-185.

*   _____. "The Action of Environment on Museum Objects,
       Part II: Light."   Curator, IX (April, 1966),
       pp. 298-306.

    Swauger, James L., and Morrow, Clifford J., Jr.   "Barn Door
       Cases Solve Problems of Display in a Narrow Corridor."
       Curator, VII (January, 1964), pp. 14-18.

    Taylor, Frank A.   "Research in Exhibits."   Paper presented
       at Southeastern Museums Conference, Norfolk, Virginia,
       October 23-26, 1968.

*   Thomson, Garry.   "A New Look at Colour Rendering, Level of
       Illumination, and Protection from Ultraviolet
       Radiation in Museum Lighting."   Studies in Conser-
       vation, VI (1961), pp. 49-70.

    _____. Conservation and Museum Lighting.   Information
       Sheet, No. 7.   London: Museums Association, 1970.

    Tilden, R.   Interpreting Our Heritage.   Chapel Hill, N.C.:
       University of North Carolina Press, 1957.

*   Tynan, A.M., and McLauclin, M.P.   "Popular Geology, A New
       Approach to an Old Problem."   Curator, VII (January,
       1964), pp. 39-50.

* Waddell, Gene. "Museum Storage." Museum News (January, 1971), pp. 14-20.

Wakefield, Hugh. "Travelling Exhibitions." Museum, XXIII, No. 2 (1970/1971), pp. 146-149.

* Washburn, Wilcomb E. "The Dramatization of American Museums." Curator, VI (February, 1963), pp. 109-124.

* _____. "Do Museums Educate?" Lecture given at Hagley Museum, Wilmington, Delaware, May 14, 1969.

* Washburne, Randel F., and Wagar, J. Alan. "Evaluating Visitor Response to Exhibit Content." Curator, XV (March, 1972), pp. 248-254.

* Weiner, George. "Why Johnny Can't Read Labels." Curator, VI (February, 1963), pp. 143-156.

Weiss, Robert S. "Social Research for Planning and Design." Unpublished draft of speech delivered to Canadian Planning Association, Nova Scotia Technical Institute, Halifax, Nova Scotia, January 29, 1970.

_____, and Bouterline, Serge, Jr. A Summary of Fairs, Pavilions, Exhibits, and Their Audiences. Copyright 1962.

* Weldon, Stephen. "Winterthur: Security at a Decorative Arts Museum." Museum News (January, 1972), pp. 36-37.

Wetzel, Joseph. "Three Steps to Exhibit Success." Museum News, L (February, 1972), p. 20.

* Wilson, Kenneth M. "A Philosophy of Museum Exhibition." Museum News, XLVI (October, 1967), pp. 13-19.

* Winkel, G.H.; Olsen, R.; Wheeler, F.; and Cohen, M. The Museum Visitor and Orientational Media: An Experimental Comparison of Different Approaches in the Smithsonian Institution, National Museum of History and Technology. Washington, D.C.: Smithsonian Institution, 1975.

Wittlin, Alma S. "Absolutes and Relative Absolutes in
        Exhibit Techniques - Some Thoughts About Secondary
        Schools and Museums." Museums and Education.
        Edited by Eric Larrabee. Washington, D.C.: Smith-
        sonian Institution Press, 1968.

        _____. Museums in Search of a Useable Future.
        Cambridge, Mass.: MIT Press, 1970.

*   _____. "Hazards of Communication by Exhibits." Curator,
        XIV (February, 1971), pp. 138-150.

* Zetterberg, Hans L. Museums and Adult Education.
        Paris: Evelyn, Adams and Mackay for the Inter-
        national Council of Museums, 1968.